RICHARDS'
ULTIMATE
BICYCLE
BOOK

RICHARDS'
ULTIMATE
BICYCLE
BOOK

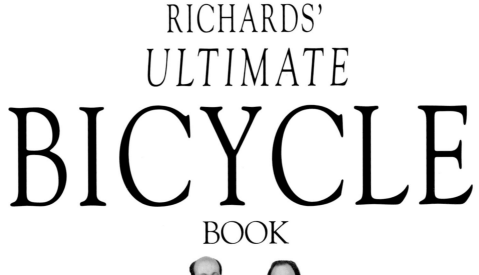

RICHARD BALLANTINE
RICHARD GRANT

~ MEMORIAL ~
5/92

PHOTOGRAPHY BY
• PHILIP GATWARD •

629.227

DORLING KINDERSLEY, INC.
NEW YORK

A DORLING KINDERSLEY BOOK

Project Editor
Phil Hunt

Art Editors
Jane Warring, Ian Callow

Editors
Terry Burrows, Susannah Steel,
Liz Wheeler

Designers
Emma Boys, Paula Burgess,
Tracy Hambleton

Managing Editor
Sean Moore

Managing Art Editor
Tina Vaughan

Production Controller
Meryl Silbert

U.S. Editors
Jeanette Mall and Laaren Brown

First American Edition, 1992

10 9 8 7 6 5 4 3 2 1

Dorling Kindersley, Inc.
232 Madison Avenue,
New York, New York 10016

Library of Congress Cataloging–in–Publication Data

Ballantine, Richard
  [Ultimate bicycle
Richards' Ultimate bicycle book / Richard Ballantine,
Richard Grant; photography by Philip Gatward – 1st
American ed.
    p. cm.
  Includes index.
  ISBN 1–56458–036–9 : $29.95
  1. Bicycles. I. Grant, Richard. II. Title.
TL410.B26 1992
629.227'2--dc20   91-31540
                                              CIP

Reproduced by Colourscan, Singapore
Printed in Italy by A. Mondadori, Verona

Contents

The ESSENTIAL BIKE

Italian bike

The bicycle was a truly exciting machine when it was first invented over a century ago – it has improved with every passing year. A bike has many advantages – it is the most energy-efficient form of transport on Earth, it is healthy, non-polluting, economical, and safe – but its most unique, outstanding, and enjoyable quality is that a bike is totally personal. You ride a bicycle. It is the ultimate intimate machine.

The Experience
Anything that you encounter while you are bicycling – swooping around corners, the wind rushing against your face and through your hair, the smells of grass, of morning bakeries and evening dew – is literally sensational, because these simple pleasures all happen to you. Moving your legs steadily and evenly, you create and experience both rhythm and pace. When you bite hard into the pedals, the power and speed you create are totally yours. You experience the stimulating synthesis that comes when mind, body, and machine all act as one. Just as the ideal of classic Greek culture was the most perfect harmony of mind and body, so a human and a bicycle are

Spanners

Brakes

Chainring

the perfect synthesis of body and machine, of art, craft, and technology; the sheer joy and vitality of life. Hand-in-hand with this enjoyment is a constant quest in bicycle design and engineering for the best possible machines.

New Developments
It is in the nature of the experience that cyclists have always wanted the best machines they could build or obtain. However, recent advances in gears, brakes, tires, and most significantly, in lightweight materials, have been huge. Compared to those of a decade ago, today's bicycles are simply amazing, and the demand for quality, lightweight machines – for bicycles that are as precise and as good as people can make them – is greater than ever before. Improvements have bred diversity in bicycle use – sport, touring, transport, a way back to nature, a fitness activity – and this book focuses on the bike as the ultimate machine: the fastest self-propelled mechanism in all its splendor and diversity.

Ornate lugwork

Toe strap

American bike

Bicycle Evolution

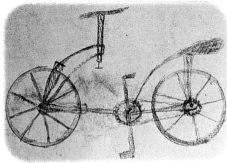
Da Vinci bicycle

In 1966, Italian monks restoring the manuscripts of Leonardo da Vinci discovered a sketch from about 1490 of a machine remarkably similar to a modern bicycle, complete with pedals and chain drive. However, as with da Vinci's aircraft and other visionary machines, his idea for a bicycle almost certainly never left the drawing board.

The practical genesis of the bicycle came 300 years later when de Sivrac, a Frenchman, invented the Celerifere: a running machine consisting of two in-line wheels connected by a beam straddled by the rider and propelled by pushing the feet against the ground. In 1817 the German Baron Karl von Drais added steering to the front wheel, and the discovery that such a machine would stay upright was a fundamental breakthrough. Hobby-Horse riding became a craze among the upper classes in France, Germany, Britain, and briefly in America. But as everyday transport the Hobby-Horse was not a success with roads too rutted to ride.

Hobby-Horse

Early Innovations and Developments

Around 1839, a Scottish blacksmith, Kirkpatrick Macmillan, built the first bicycle with pedals. His little-publicized machine was lever-driven and practical – Macmillan used it for a 140-mile (225.8 km) round trip to Glasgow in 1842, covering one 40-mile (64.5-km) stretch at an average speed of 8 mph. But the manufacture of bicycles really began in France, in 1861, when coach builder Pierre Michaux fitted **cranks** and pedals to the front wheel of a Hobby-Horse and called it a velocipede. In 1866-67 he introduced a model with a larger front wheel and other refinements. It was an immediate success and cycling began to spread. In 1869 came several crucial inventions including the ball-bearing hub, metal-spoked wheels, solid rubber tires, a freewheel, mudguards, and a lever-operated four-speed gear. A year later France's leadership in cycle development was halted with its defeat in the Franco-Prussian War, and Britain became the new focus of cycle development.

Macmillan treadle cycle

Michaux's velocipede

Because the pedals and cranks of the velocipede were attached directly to the front wheel, the larger the wheel, the faster the machine could go. By the early 1870s the velocipede had evolved into the high bicycle, an imposing machine with a front wheel that stood almost as tall as a man. For pedaling efficiency and maximum performance, the high bicycle perched the rider almost directly above the front wheel, just behind the center of

"Ordinary" bicycle

Rover Safety bicycle

gravity; if the front wheel struck a rut, the bike could cartwheel, arcing the rider head-first to the ground. This propensity to pitch forward also meant that the machine could not use effective brakes. Nonetheless, the high bicycle was internationally popular. By the early 1880s, lower bicycle prices as well as the growth of railways and the demise of horse-drawn coaches set the stage for a major development: the safety bicycle. The chain-drive rear wheel used for the Rover Safety bicycle launched by John Kemp Starley in 1885 in England enabled the use of gearing and wheels of a reasonable size. The result was a machine that could encounter obstacles without cartwheeling and could be braked. Smaller wheels meant a rougher ride, but this was offset by pneumatic tires, developed by John Boyd Dunlop in 1888. The air-filled inner tube provided shock absorption and, by reducing rolling resistance, increased speed. The high bicycle was eclipsed, and relabeled an "ordinary."

The safety bicycle, a machine that anyone could ride, spread rapidly throughout the industrialized world. In 1896 a bike might have cost an average worker three months' wages, but by 1909, it was less than a month's wages. Private transport was at last in the hands of those who needed it most. Women were liberated from the confinement of small villages. Social development was transformed and intellectual growth stimulated as people found it easier to attend meetings and classes over greater distances.

Between the World Wars in Europe the bicycle flourished. Advancements in tube technology, the development of alloy components, and the use of derailleur gears

Transformed lifestyle

(first patented in 1895) saw the emergence of high-quality, lightweight bikes. But in America the bicycle declined in popularity until it was only a toy. In 1933 Schwinn introduced wide-tire motorbike look-alikes, single-speed bikes that were heavy and impractical.

The Bicycle Boom

Sociable recumbent

In the decade after World War II, the number of cars in Europe tripled, and bike sales plunged. In America cycling underwent a gradual leisure revival with growing imports of European lightweight derailleur-gear bikes. By the 1970s the bike boom was in full swing and returning to Europe.

Then in the mid-1970s, off-road riders in Marin County, California, combined the wide tires and stable design of Schwinn's balloon-tire bomber with the lightweight technology generated by the boom in road- and BMX-bikes. The result was the mountain bike, the durable but lightweight machine that is transforming cycling worldwide. Today interest is beginning to be shown in recumbents that are setting new standards for speed, safety, and load-carrying. Just as the 1890s were the heyday of development of the safety bike, the 1990s promise to continue the evolution of the world's most important form of personal transport – the bicycle.

Swiss Twike

The Bicycle Today

The only viable means of private transport in the world today is the bicycle. The main threat to this claim is the car, which has helped industrialize the world in the twentieth century. But the car has already proved its limitations. It is running out of space and energy supplies, and is now responsible for both serious environmental pollution and 250,000 deaths and 10 million injuries worldwide each year. As the truth dawns that the automobile's liabilities outweigh its benefits, industrialized nations are beginning to seek alternatives to the car. One of the principal beneficiaries of this reawakening is the discovery of the bicycle as an ecologically clean and efficient machine. As for its technological development, the bicycle appears to be at the dawn of a golden age in the Western World: Encouraged by the upsurge of interest created by mountain bikes, manufacturers have a new impetus to make bikes as high-tech and as user-friendly as possible. Today's bikes are lighter and more durable than ever. Brakes are more reliable, gears are easier to operate and new suspension systems make riding better cushioned. Ironically, the plain, simple one-speed roadster is still the standard form of personal transportation in the Third World. With the bicycle much more affordable than a car, it continues to make a vital improvement to the quality of life there.

PEOPLE CARRIED PER METER PER HOUR

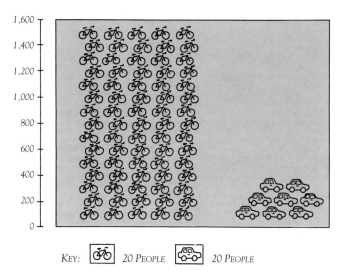

KEY: 🚲 20 PEOPLE 🚗 20 PEOPLE

CITY TRAFFIC
Surveys of traffic volume show that in one hour, a lane of highway can carry twice as many people riding bikes as those traveling by car. With traffic at a 10 mph (16 km/h) crawl in cities such as London and New York, a car has no advantage.

SPACE SAVERS
Bicycle campaigners in Montreal (above) staged this demonstration to emphasize how bikes make more economic use of road space than cars. On average, one car uses up the same space as 8 bikes.

BIKE OWNERSHIP
New road-planning initiatives in Japan, Germany, and the Netherlands (where there is almost 1 bike per person) all illustrate how some countries with high percentages of bike ownership (left) are consciously making cycling a safe and convenient alternative to the car.

BIKE OWNERSHIP AS PERCENTAGE OF POPULATION

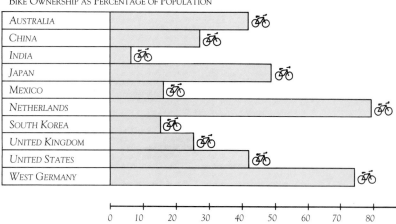

AUSTRALIA	
CHINA	
INDIA	
JAPAN	
MEXICO	
NETHERLANDS	
SOUTH KOREA	
UNITED KINGDOM	
UNITED STATES	
WEST GERMANY	

0 10 20 30 40 50 60 70 80 90

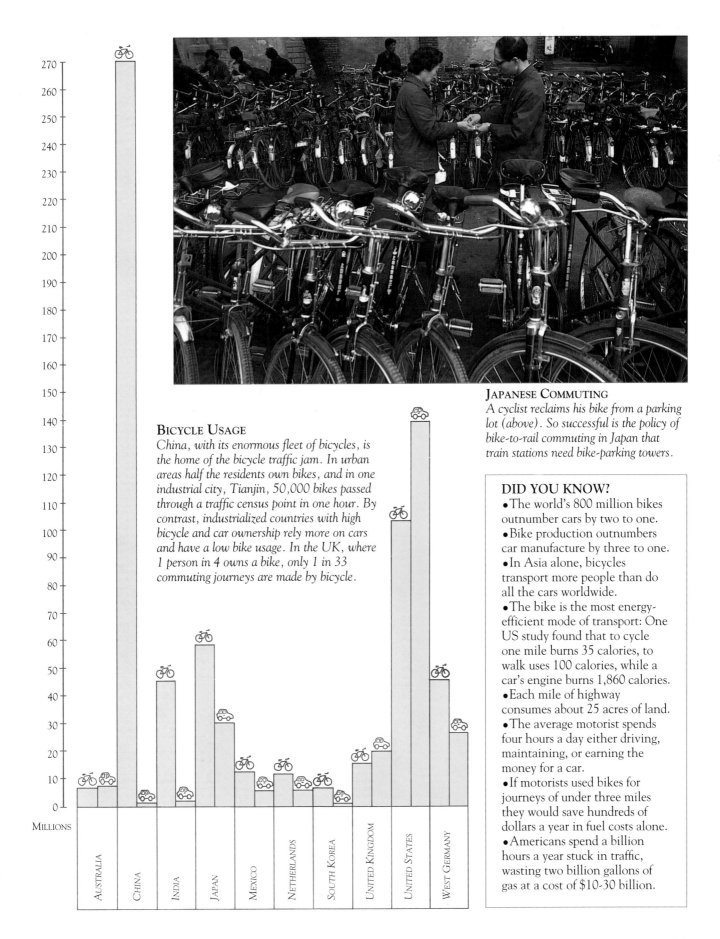

JAPANESE COMMUTING
A cyclist reclaims his bike from a parking lot (above). So successful is the policy of bike-to-rail commuting in Japan that train stations need bike-parking towers.

BICYCLE USAGE
China, with its enormous fleet of bicycles, is the home of the bicycle traffic jam. In urban areas half the residents own bikes, and in one industrial city, Tianjin, 50,000 bikes passed through a traffic census point in one hour. By contrast, industrialized countries with high bicycle and car ownership rely more on cars and have a low bike usage. In the UK, where 1 person in 4 owns a bike, only 1 in 33 commuting journeys are made by bicycle.

Chart (MILLIONS), y-axis from 0 to 270:

Country	Bicycles	Cars
AUSTRALIA	~7	~8
CHINA	~271	~2
INDIA	~45	~3
JAPAN	~58	~30
MEXICO	~12	~6
NETHERLANDS	~11	~6
SOUTH KOREA	~6	~2
UNITED KINGDOM	~15	~20
UNITED STATES	~104	~140
WEST GERMANY	~45	~27

DID YOU KNOW?
- The world's 800 million bikes outnumber cars by two to one.
- Bike production outnumbers car manufacture by three to one.
- In Asia alone, bicycles transport more people than do all the cars worldwide.
- The bike is the most energy-efficient mode of transport: One US study found that to cycle one mile burns 35 calories, to walk uses 100 calories, while a car's engine burns 1,860 calories.
- Each mile of highway consumes about 25 acres of land.
- The average motorist spends four hours a day either driving, maintaining, or earning the money for a car.
- If motorists used bikes for journeys of under three miles they would save hundreds of dollars a year in fuel costs alone.
- Americans spend a billion hours a year stuck in traffic, wasting two billion gallons of gas at a cost of $10-30 billion.

Bike Anatomy

Specialization has led to different types of bikes, but basically all bikes are the same, though components differ in quality, design, weight, and ease and method of use. In order of importance, a bicycle is made up of a frame, wheels, transmission, brakes, and finally, **stem**, handlebars, and saddle. The frame will always carry the maker's name, with the rest of the components, bought from other manufacturers, called the *specification*.

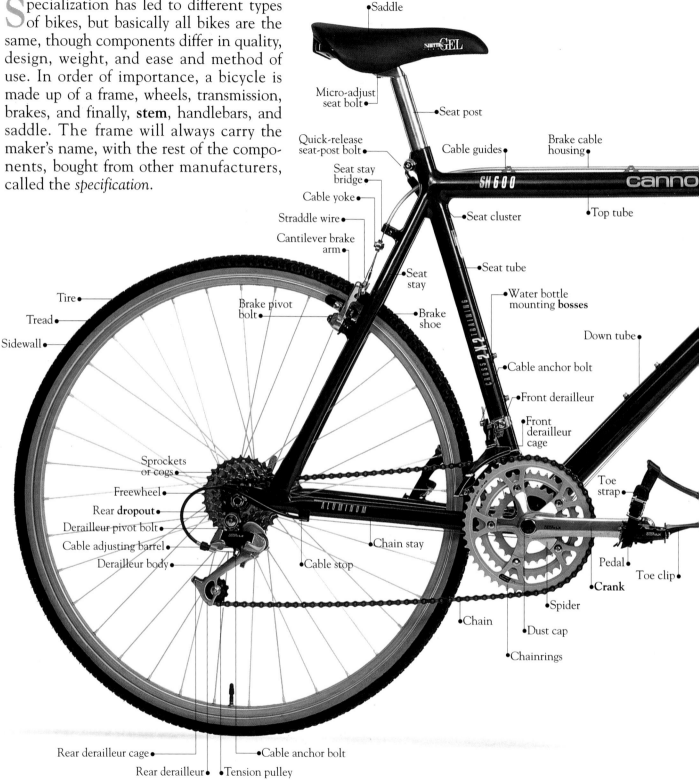

Saddle

Micro-adjust seat bolt

Seat post

Quick-release seat-post bolt

Cable guides

Brake cable housing

Seat stay bridge

SH600

canno

Cable yoke

Seat cluster

Top tube

Straddle wire

Cantilever brake arm

Seat tube

Seat stay

Water bottle mounting **bosses**

Tire

Tread

Sidewall

Brake pivot bolt

Brake shoe

Down tube

Cable anchor bolt

Front derailleur

Front derailleur cage

Sprockets or cogs

Freewheel

Rear **dropout**

Derailleur pivot bolt

Cable adjusting barrel

Derailleur body

Toe strap

Chain stay

Cable stop

Pedal

Toe clip

Crank

Spider

Chain

Dust cap

Chainrings

Rear derailleur cage

Cable anchor bolt

Rear derailleur

Tension pulley

THE HYBRID

*The Cannondale SH600 is a **hybrid** bike that blends the light weight and speed of a sport-road bike with the rugged durability and versatility of a mountain bike. It is a general-use bike, perfect for riding to the office one day and exploring a muddy track the next; it is flexible and enjoyable – the essential bike.*

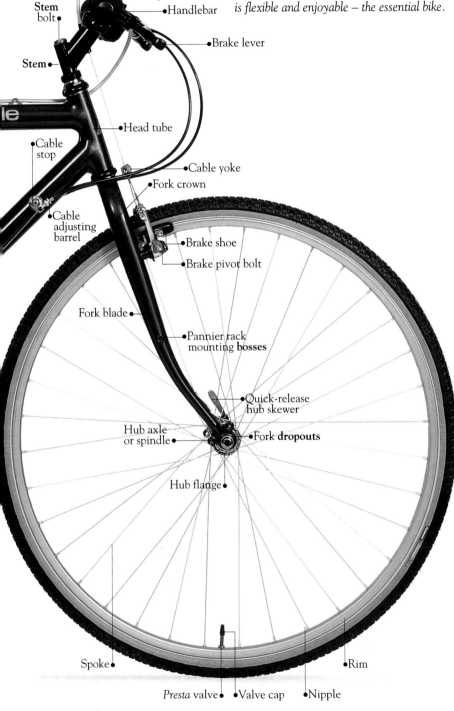

Gear lever

Stem bolt

Stem

Grips

Handlebar

Brake lever

Head tube

Cable stop

Cable yoke

Fork crown

Cable adjusting barrel

Brake shoe

Brake pivot bolt

Fork blade

Pannier rack mounting **bosses**

Quick-release hub skewer

Hub axle or spindle

Fork dropouts

Hub flange

Spoke

Rim

Presta valve

Valve cap

Nipple

TECHNICAL TERMS

Bicycles have their own terminology and language. Many bicycle parts have names that are descriptively self-evident: a seat post holds a saddle, a chainring is a circular device for moving a chain, a **crank** is a lever, and a crankset is a pair of cranks. However, other parts have names that are less self-evident: **boss**, spider, straddle wire, bearing race.

Language of bikes

Some of the terms are borrowed from engineering, others are arcane survivors from the past. But all are important to the language of bikes. To the newcomer it's a language that can require decoding. What does it mean if an enthusiastic salesperson, or magazine review, says of a bike, "It's got a tight rear end with short stays"? What is a stay, and how short is short? We've organized this book to answer these questions as they arise – and to help the reader understand the answers. This section gives the general guidelines: what bicycles are and how they are made, how your body works on a bike, and how a bike should fit you.

Words explained

These pages explain key terms in bicycle design – **wheelbase**, **trail**, **rake**, angle, and the basics of framebuilding; they introduce words that describe how you use your body to ride – **cadence**, **ankling**, and **honking**. Subsequent sections are devoted to specific types of bicycles and, with the exception of *The Everyday Bike*, include information on anatomy, frame design, construction techniques, and the sizing requirements for each style of bike. Wherever you are in the book, you should be able to find relevant information nearby. "Bicycle-speak" comes naturally enough. You don't need a lot of technical information in order to enjoy riding a bicycle – or reading this book.

Frame Works

A frame must support the rider, turn pedal force into forward motion, and steer. The contact points for the rider – pedals, saddle, and handlebar – and the space needed for the wheels are fairly constant parameters, which is why road-racing and mountain bike frames are similar in shape. Frame geometry and materials involve many elements, each strongly related to the others, so slight design variations can produce very different characteristics and performance levels. The nuances are complex and delicate, making bicycle design more an art than a science. While modern materials and technologies aid the creation of revolutionary new designs, ultimately the feel and handling of a bicycle comes about through the frame-builder's touch, instincts, and experimentation.

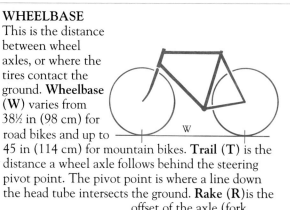

WHEELBASE
This is the distance between wheel axles, or where the tires contact the ground. **Wheelbase (W)** varies from 38½ in (98 cm) for road bikes and up to 45 in (114 cm) for mountain bikes. **Trail (T)** is the distance a wheel axle follows behind the steering pivot point. The pivot point is where a line down the head tube intersects the ground. **Rake (R)** is the offset of the axle (fork end) from the steering pivot line. Increasing rake decreases trail. Less trail means easier steering and more sensitive handling. More trail means heavier and less responsive steering, but greater stability.

MOUNTAIN BIKE FRAMES
These are designed for strength and stability over rough ground. Overall, the construction is chunky and robust, the general shape is low-slung to increase maneuverability, and the geometry is relaxed for both predictable steering and a stable ride.

•TOP TUBE: This often slopes down from the head tube to the seat tube, particularly in smaller frame sizes. This permits a longer head tube, strengthens the frame, and creates space between the frame and the rider.

•SEAT-TUBE ANGLES: These range from 68 to 74 degrees, depending on the length of top tube relative to wheelbase.

MOUNTING BOSSES: A rigid platform for cantilever brakes is provided by mounting bosses welded on.•

•SEAT TUBE: To allow more movement under the rider when on rough ground, and a low saddle on descents, the seat tube is 3 to 5 in (7.7 to 12.7 cm) lower than on a road frame.

•CHAIN STAYS: These vary from 16¾ to 18½ in (43.4 to 47.4 cm). The normal length for climbing bikes is 16¾ to 17 in (43.4 to 43.6 cm). Longer stays aid stability and provide better positioning for loads over the rear axle.

•BOTTOM BRACKET: Height varies from 11½ to 13 in (29.5 to 33.3 cm).

WHEELBASE: This can vary from 40 to 45 in (101.6 to 114.3 cm), with the fast models in regular sizes being 40 to 42 in (101.6 to 106.7 cm).

•SEAT-TUBE ANGLES: These are from 72 to 76 degrees. Steep angles are associated with fast bikes, but this dimension is primarily a function of top tube length.

•CHAIN-STAY LENGTH: On a road bike the length is from 15¾ to 16½ in (40 to 42 cm). This gives nimble handling but leaves no space for mudguards or wide tires.

•HEAD-TUBE ANGLES: These can be from 73 to 76 degrees. Steep angles move the front wheel back, shortening the **wheelbase**, and giving faster steering reaction.

•FORKS: Maximum stress from road shock is at the base of the blades, near the joint with the steerer tube. The tips do move, but vertical movement is small. Forks are **raked** for fine-tuning **trail** and steering, not suspension.

ROAD-RACING FRAMES

These are designed to be light, lean, and compact, to fit the rider like a suit of clothes. The 3Al/2.5V titanium alloy (94.5% titanium, 3% aluminum, 2.5% vanadium) in these Merlin frames is lighter than steel, extremely strong, and immune to corrosion. The tubing is produced for aircraft hydraulic systems, and, in chemical and nuclear industries, for plumbing corrosive fluids.

•BOTTOM-BRACKET: Height is 10½ to 11 in (26½ to 28 cm). The **wheelbase,** from 38½ to 39 in (98 to 99 cm), gives quicker steering, better handling and extra weight over the front wheel, improving traction and balance.

STEERING PERFORMANCE

*Trail is generous, ranging from 1¾ to 3 in (4½ to 7½ cm) or more, which helps pull the front wheel into line. On mountain bikes **rake** is from 1¾ to 2¾ in (4½ to 7 cm), allowing for the greater trail created by a shallow head tube angle of about 70 degrees. A climbing frame might steepen the head tube angle and use less rake. On racing bikes rake tends to be a shallow ⅛ to 1¾ in (⅓ to 4½ cm). Trail is 4½ to 7 in (11½ to 17¾ cm), making the bike stable at high speeds.*

•DROPOUTS : These are made from solid, ultra-hard 6Al/4V titanium, cut with a 50,000 psi water jet.

COMPUTERS

These are essential tools in modern bicycle design and construction. Stress analysis programs running on powerful computers can mimic road shock, pedaling, and other forces acting on a bicycle, enabling quick testing and measuring of a wide range of design variations. Computer-aided design (CAD) programs are used to produce blueprints. The final check is human: a handmade prototype is tested for touch and ride.

Frame Construction and Materials

Bicycle frames are made either from metals refined from ores, such as steel, aluminum, and titanium, or from composites of combined structural fibers, such as carbon, glass, aramid, or spectra, with a glue or plastic binder. Metals are isotropic – equally strong and stiff in all directions – and give the most strength for the least weight when used as tubes arranged in the classic diamond-frame pattern. Composites are anisotropic – strong and stiff along the axis of the fibers – and the fibers can be formed into almost any shape required, with the strength placed where needed. Composite materials (see p.138) are therefore uniquely suited for creating molded and one-piece **monocoque** frames .

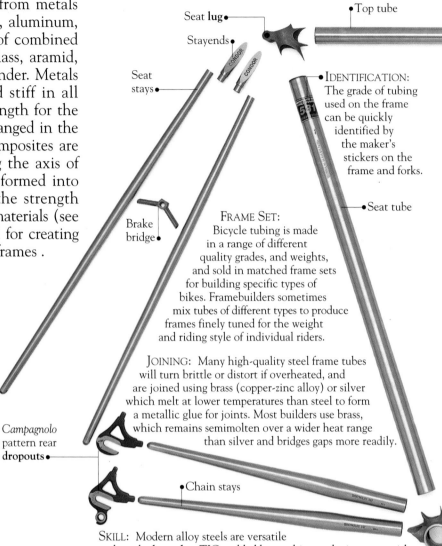

Seat lug

Stayends

Top tube

Seat stays

Brake bridge

IDENTIFICATION: The grade of tubing used on the frame can be quickly identified by the maker's stickers on the frame and forks.

Seat tube

FRAME SET: Bicycle tubing is made in a range of different quality grades, and weights, and sold in matched frame sets for building specific types of bikes. Framebuilders sometimes mix tubes of different types to produce frames finely tuned for the weight and riding style of individual riders.

JOINING: Many high-quality steel frame tubes will turn brittle or distort if overheated, and are joined using brass (copper-zinc alloy) or silver which melt at lower temperatures than steel to form a metallic glue for joints. Most builders use brass, which remains semimolten over a wider heat range than silver and bridges gaps more readily.

Campagnolo pattern rear **dropouts**

Chain stays

SKILL: Modern alloy steels are versatile and can be **brazed** or TIG-welded by machine, reducing costs with no great loss of quality. The finest, lightest tubing must be hand-joined, and top-quality frames depend upon the skill and care of the builder.

BRAZING RIG
*To keep an even temperature, gas burners are carefully positioned around the **lug** to heat it uniformly. Once at the right temperature, the puffy white flux will melt, cleaning the metal surface. The solder, a rod of alloy (brass or silver) is applied; it melts and flows around the joint by capillary action.*

WILL IT BREAK?

Metal breaks either from an impact which exceeds the strength of the metal, or from the fatigue of small, repeated stresses. Steel and titanium both have fatigue limits and will not break so long as the stresses remain under limits. Aluminum has no fatigue limit, so each and every stress causes wear and weakening, and eventual failure. Aluminum frame designers take this fatigue factor into account, overbuilding with enough strength for long-term

safety. Even if well-worn (but not abused), a steel or titanium frame will stay almost as good as new, but not aluminum frames, which are thought to have a useful life of 3 to 5 years. The life of most steel and titanium frames is measured in decades. While aluminum frames are extremely inexpensive for their weight, in the long run steel, or the very expensive titanium frames may be better value. Many professional racers claim that they exhaust steel

frames in one season or less, but it has been found that if these "dead frames" are realigned, they spring back to life in good condition. Composite frames are still too new to gauge long-term durability but, as with aluminum, the processes of internal friction may actually cause cumulative weakening, loss of vitality, and eventual failure. How eventual remains to be seen, and riders of composite frames are too excited and happy to care.

Steering tube •

THE FINISHED FRAME
*The frame (right) is tailored, **brazed**, aligned, and painted with undercoats and colored enamels; lacquer is then applied. From fitting, this frame could be produced in one week, and the bike made in a few hours.*

Head tube •

TRANSFERS: These are placed before the lacquer is applied.

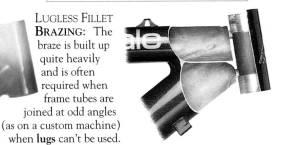

LUGS: Lugs strengthen joints by providing more surface area for **brazing** material and for absorbing load stresses. The lug points taper in thickness as they travel along the tube to distribute stress evenly and to help reduce weight. •

FORK-BLADE TUBES: One type of fork blade tube tapers in wall thickness as the tube section narrows, which is said to increase springiness and the ability to absorb road shock. Another type, the Italian or Continental blade, narrows in section toward the tip but with constant wall thickness, and is said to have greater lateral rigidity and resistance to side-to-side forces during cornering. •

Tips •

TUBE DIAMETER
Stiffness is the resistance a material has to structural change, independent of shape. Rigidity is a function of both stiffness and shape, and for a tube, can be increased by thickening the walls or widening the tube. In theory, the tube diameter should not be greater than 50 times the wall thickness. Several high-quality bicycle tubes exceed this limit by a wide margin, making them vulnerable to impact damage. To increase diameter without adding weight, a lighter, less dense material must be used so that wall thickness is sufficiently strong. Thus while aluminum and titanium are not as stiff as steel, they are lighter and can form large-diameter tubes to make rigid but light frames.

TIG-WELDED ALUMINUM: Plain, completely visible TIG-weld feathering harmonizes well with a bare metal, functional frame, that does not damage easily and hence requires minimal maintenance.

CARBON-FIBER: The tubes are glued with epoxy resins into aluminium **lugs**. The tube ends have fiber-glass sleeves to help prevent any galvanic corrosion.

LUGLESS FILLET BRAZING: The braze is built up quite heavily and is often required when frame tubes are joined at odd angles (as on a custom machine) when **lugs** can't be used.

TIG-WELDED STEEL: Techniques for TIG-welding are now very precise, and can be safely used on lightweight, heat-treated, butted **chrome molybdenum** steels.

BONDED ALUMINUM: Gluing frame joints eliminates the problem of heat damage, and the glues are usually stronger than the materials being joined.

SMOOTH TIG-WELDED ALUMINIUM: On **lug**less frames, the tubes can be cut perfectly to the precise lengths and angles required, so that each frame size is proportionally correct. Deep penetration marks (above) indicate how far the metal has been fused. After being ground smooth with abrasives, the curved welds help to distribute stress away from the joint, somewhat in the same manner as traditional lugs.

The Human Engine

The human body is similar to a combustion engine, requiring a continuous supply of oxygen and fuel to maintain its efficiency. It works most effectively when the power output and oxygen intake are balanced. Working your body too fast causes panting; running it too hard causes waste by-products to accumulate in the muscles, which leads to pain and cramps. Cycling is an excellent all-around form of exercise, particularly for the respiratory and cardiovascular systems, which are the key to good health.

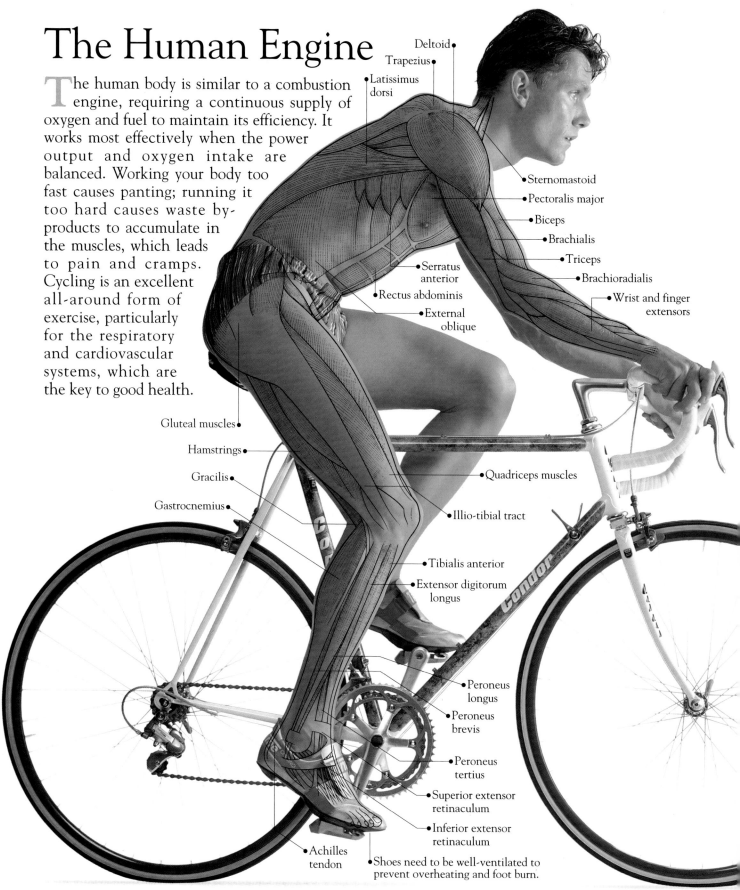

Deltoid
Trapezius
Latissimus dorsi
Sternomastoid
Pectoralis major
Biceps
Brachialis
Triceps
Brachioradialis
Wrist and finger extensors
Serratus anterior
Rectus abdominis
External oblique
Gluteal muscles
Hamstrings
Gracilis
Gastrocnemius
Quadriceps muscles
Illio-tibial tract
Tibialis anterior
Extensor digitorum longus
Peroneus longus
Peroneus brevis
Peroneus tertius
Superior extensor retinaculum
Inferior extensor retinaculum
Achilles tendon
Shoes need to be well-ventilated to prevent overheating and foot burn.

Eat often but lightly if you are cycling. Cyclists thrive on energy-rich carbohydrates such as pastas, cereals, and fruits. Proteins and fats are fine as part of a balanced diet, but they take a long time to digest, and burn too slowly.

Food and Drink

Carbohydrates, stored in the body as glycogen, can be depleted in less than 2 hours by hard riding, sometimes resulting in an overwhelming total loss of energy if care is not taken. Hence the need for frequent replenishment. Fat stores, by contrast, are almost unlimited; long, moderately intense rides burn the most fat and are the best for weight loss. Sugary foods should be avoided, for although they give a brief surge of energy, they fool the body into lowering its metabolic rate. Drinking water frequently, before you feel thirsty, is also important. By the time you feel a thirst, the body has lost enough water to impair performance, so drink often.

ARM MUSCLES
Arm muscles both help to control the bike and to move your body position back and forth over the handlebars. Avoid locking your elbows straight – bending them helps absorb any road shock.

BACK MUSCLES
Back and stomach muscles are not directly employed in pedaling, but operate in equilibrium to keep your upper body and head positioned and your chest open. Lower back muscles are not fully exercised and should be protected from the cold.

THIGH MUSCLES
Cycling utilizes the largest, most powerful muscles in the body. In the thigh, the quads and the hams work in harmony to drive the pedals around and the bike forward. As you push down with the quads at the top of your thigh and extend the leg, the hams underneath contract to bring the leg back up to complete the circular pedaling motion. Strain can occur if unnecessary force is applied by having the saddle too high and overstretching the quads, or too low and overcontracting the hams.

AVOIDING KNEE STRAIN
In the lower leg, the gastrocnemius (calf muscle), is connected to the thigh bone behind the knee and the Achilles tendon above the ankle. Upper and lower leg muscles lever and pivot through the knee. Pedaling at an aerobic cadence of 80 rpm (revolutions per minute) bends and extends the knee 4,800 times an hour. Strain occurs if a knee is pulled out of its vertical plane or if the pedal twists the foot out of its natural alignment with the knee.

VULNERABLE JOINTS

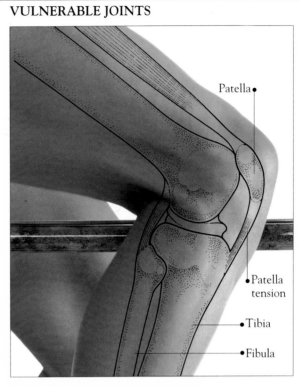

Patella
Patella tension
Tibia
Fibula

Knee Flexion
Unlike most joints, knees are held together only by muscles, tendons, and ligaments. The bones slide easily over the cartilage, lubricated by an oily fluid within the synovial capsule. The soft tissues swell when damaged.

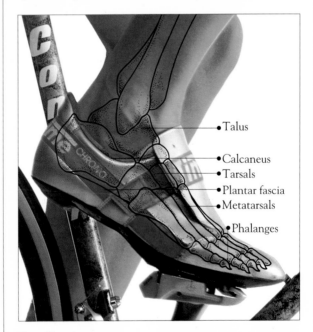

Talus
Calcaneus
Tarsals
Plantar fascia
Metatarsals
Phalanges

Foot Tension
While pedaling, the plantar fascia (the major ligament membrane in the arch of the foot), is placed under repeated tension and must be supported by a stiff-soled cycling shoe to prevent damage by overflexing.

Adjusting for Size

The most important feature of a bike is how it fits the rider. Performance, comfort, and the risk of injury can be affected by variations, sometimes as little as ¼ in (5 mm), in your riding position, so be meticulous about establishing your bike size and your cycling position. The methods for doing this are well founded, although not infallible. Physically we are each unique, so make any adjustments that will work best for your own physique and type of riding. Once you do work out your bike size and riding position, stick with it, even if initially it may feel inefficient and uncomfortable. Body muscles all need time to adjust to new patterns of movement, and your reward will be riding a bicycle that moves when you do.

FITTING THE BIKE TO THE RIDER

For mountain biking and racing, a rider should use the smallest frame that fits. Small frames save weight and are stiffer and more responsive. For touring, a larger frame provides more stability on descents and on corners. Using the fitting machine (below and right) to measure both a taller and a shorter rider illustrates that while angles will hardly change, the seat tube and top tube length will vary considerably.

SADDLE HEIGHT: Stand with your feet 4 in (10.2cm) apart with your back against a wall. Measure your inseam leg length from your crotch to the floor. Multiply this sum by 0.885, adding on 0.1181 inch (3 mm) if you have large feet for your height. This is the distance that should be set between the top of the saddle and center of the bottom bracket axle.

SEAT POST: Exposure should be 3 ½-5 in (8.9-12.7 cm) for racing, 3-4 in (7.6-10.2 cm) for touring, and 6-8 in (15.2-20.3 cm) or more for mountain bikes.

TOP TUBE LENGTH: The combined top tube and **stem** length should ideally position the handlebar so that in a normal riding position, the front **hub axle** is blocked from view by the handlebars.

CLEARANCE: You should straddle the bike with a clearance between the crotch and the top tube of 1-2 in (2.5-6 cm) on racers; 1 in (2.5 cm) on touring bikes, and 3 in (7.6 cm) or more on mountain and **hybrid** bikes.

SEAT ANGLES: These range from 68 to 75 degrees, with 72 to 74 degrees most common. Smaller bikes have steeper seat angles.

HEAD ANGLE: This results from the frame size, seat angle, top tube length, front wheel clearance, and the quickness of steering.

PEDAL POSITION: When riding a bike, make sure the widest part of your foot is over the pedal axle.

TAILORING A BIKE

Machines such as the *Elite*, the *Fit Kit*, and *Serotta Size-Cycle*, and specialized computer programs such as *ProBikeFit*, assess every aspect necessary for fitting a bike to a rider. The machines allow a custom framebuilder to adjust all the related factors in bicycle sizing in order to measure up a bike that will complement the cyclist perfectly. The *ProBikeFit* program also includes data on practically every bicycle and component currently available, and can quickly match a rider's measurements with a ready-made bicycle that will give the best fit. The vital factors in sizing are saddle height; the length of the top tube; the amount of seat post exposed when the saddle height is correct; and the clearance between your crotch and the top tube. These factors will vary, depending on whether the bike is for racing, touring, or mountain biking, and on your own physique. You should be able to ride with a straight back for easy breathing, a relaxed body, and arms slightly bent to absorb shock.

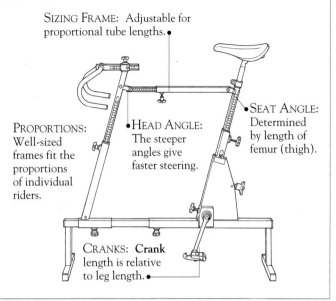

SIZING FRAME: Adjustable for proportional tube lengths.

PROPORTIONS: Well-sized frames fit the proportions of individual riders.

HEAD ANGLE: The steeper angles give faster steering.

SEAT ANGLE: Determined by length of femur (thigh).

CRANKS: **Crank** length is relative to leg length.

HANDLEBAR STEMS: Handlebar **stems** extend your reach. Most riders use 2½ to 4in (6-10 cm) extension. The longer the stem, the greater the risk of breakage. If you need longer than 4¾ in (12 cm), the top tube is too short.

HANDLEBAR HEIGHT: For normal riding, the top of the stem should be ¾ to 1½ in (2-4 cm) below the top of the saddle, and for racing, as low as 3 in (7.6 cm).

HANDLEBAR WIDTH: This should be as wide as the shoulders: 14 to 16 in (38-40 cm) for women, 15 to 17 in (40-42 cm) for men.

DROP BAR DEPTH: This is related to the size of your hands: 5½ in (14 cm) is shallow, 5½ to 6 in (14-15 cm) is medium, and 6 in (15 cm) or more is deep.

KNEES: With hands on the drop bars and forearms horizontal to the road, your knees should overlap your elbows at the top of the pedal stroke.

BIKE SIZING FOR WOMEN
Relative to height, women generally have shorter torsos and arms than do men. Sizing a woman's bike by inseam length and seat tube size can often result in too long a top tube. The best bet is to have a longer seat post and a smaller bike frame.

SADDLE POSITION: The saddle should be level: tilted up risks discomfort and nerve damage; tilted down pitches the rider forward, placing too much weight on the arms. Women have wider pelvic bones and should use broader-based saddles.

The MOUNTAIN BIKE

The mountain bike represents the most exciting development in cycling this century, a revolutionary bike that has revolutionized an industry. It gives cyclists access to places that were once thought impossible to ride, and makes cycling accessible to millions who once thought they would never enjoy riding a bike. Now the affluent world's most popular bicycle, the mountain bike, with fat

Saddle

tires, low gears, heavy-duty brakes, and beefed-up frame, has turned a century of cycling technology on its head. Like all good simple inventions, it came from somewhere least expected – not from a designer's drawing board, but from a couple of really dedicated bike bums in Marin County, California, during the mid-seventies.

Ugly Duckling

When co-inventors Charlie Kelly and Gary Fisher first paraded the mountain bike to the cycle industry it was like the debut of the ugly duckling: a fat and heavy bike in a world dominated by sleek racing machines. Instantly rejected by blinkered manufacturers, their mountain bicycle instead fostered its own grassroots industry in California. The word spread, sales began to take off, and once-reluctant manufacturers

Pedal

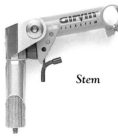

Stem

ate humble pie as the mountain bike made the USA a pioneering force in the worldwide cycle business. The mountain bike caught on because it answered a need. It appeals because it offers easy balance, certain stopping power, fewer jolts, and low gears that allow even a beginner to climb the steepest of hills; best of all, it allows you to ride off-road away from traffic.

Brake

Rapid Development

The drawbacks of the early bikes have been ironed out. The 45-lb (20.4 kg) bike Kelly and Fisher first introduced has slimmed down to 25 lb (11.4 kg) with tires that are still fat but weigh less. Cantilevers and hydraulics have replaced the heavy hub brakes, and development continues apace. Derailleur gear operations have been demystified by simple one-touch click-up, click-down levers. New suspension systems have dramatically improved comfort, performance, and ride, turning the once-ugly duckling into one of the ultimate rider-friendly bikes.

Fork

Cyclist and mountain bike

Mountain Bike Anatomy

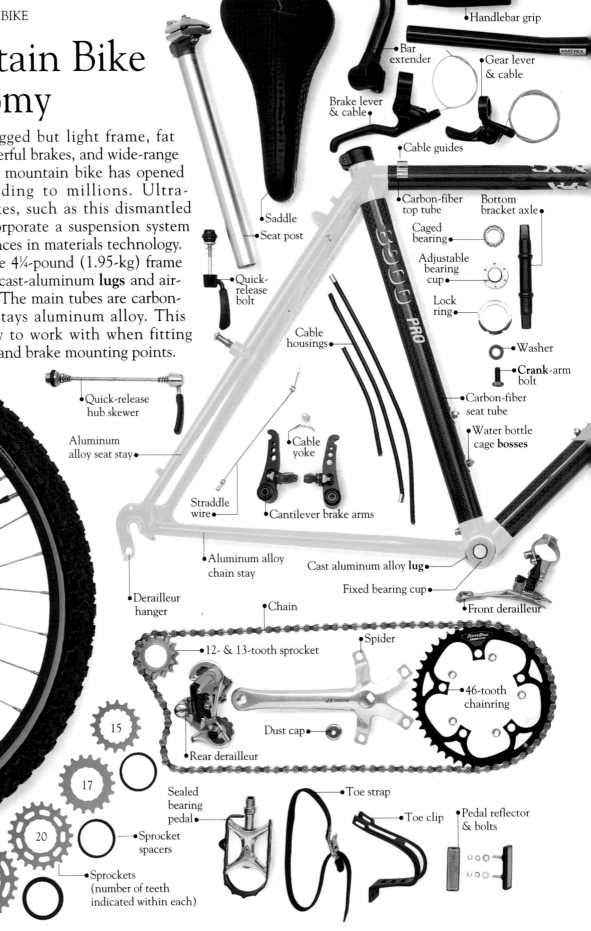

With its rugged but light frame, fat tires, powerful brakes, and wide-range **gear ratios**, the mountain bike has opened up off-road riding to millions. Ultra-lightweight bikes, such as this dismantled *Trek 8900*, incorporate a suspension system and many advances in materials technology. The tubes of the 4¼-pound (1.95-kg) frame are joined with cast-aluminum **lugs** and air-craft adhesives. The main tubes are carbon-fiber and the stays aluminum alloy. This material is easy to work with when fitting derailleur and brake mounting points.

Handlebar grip

Bar extender

Gear lever & cable

Brake lever & cable

Cable guides

Saddle

Seat post

Quick-release bolt

Carbon-fiber top tube

Bottom bracket axle

Caged bearing

Adjustable bearing cup

Lock ring

Washer

Crank-arm bolt

Carbon-fiber seat tube

Water bottle cage **bosses**

Cable housings

Cable yoke

Straddle wire

Cantilever brake arms

Quick-release hub skewer

Aluminum alloy seat stay

Aluminum alloy chain stay

Cast aluminum alloy **lug**

Fixed bearing cup

Front derailleur

Derailleur hanger

Chain

Spider

46-tooth chainring

12- & 13-tooth sprocket

15

17

20

24

28

Rear derailleur

Dust cap

Sprocket spacers

Sprockets (number of teeth indicated within each)

Sealed bearing pedal

Toe strap

Toe clip

Pedal reflector & bolts

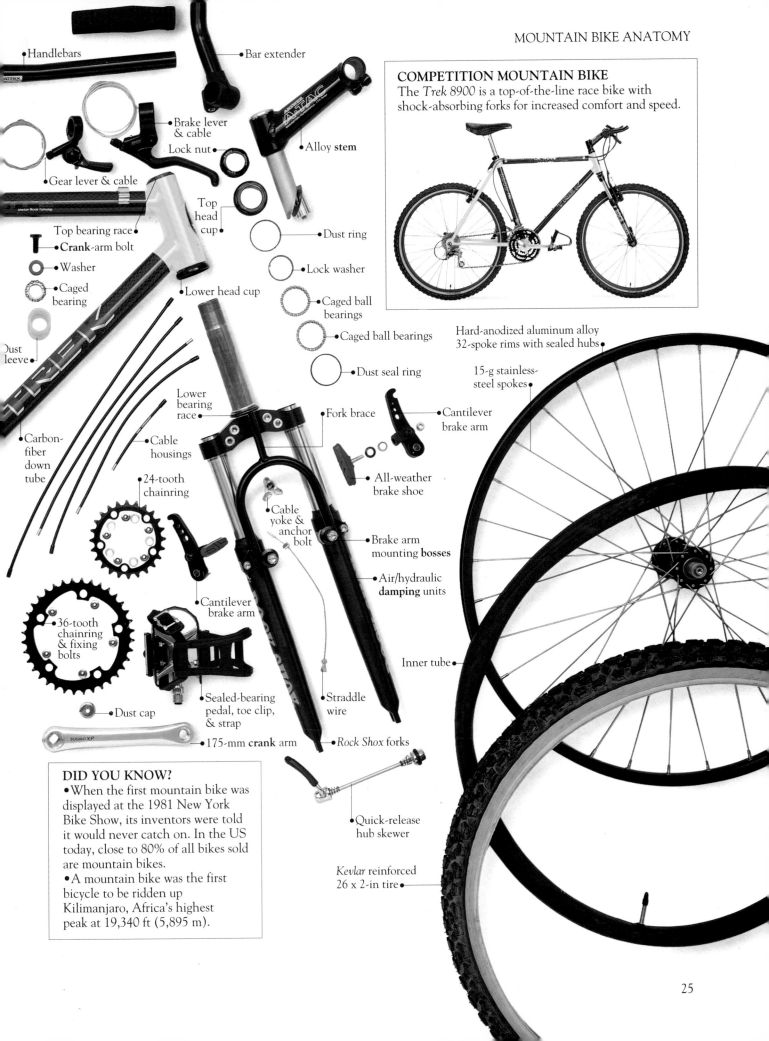

• Handlebars

• Bar extender

COMPETITION MOUNTAIN BIKE
The *Trek 8900* is a top-of-the-line race bike with shock-absorbing forks for increased comfort and speed.

• Brake lever & cable

Lock nut •

• Alloy **stem**

• Gear lever & cable

Top head cup •

Top bearing race •

•**Crank**-arm bolt

• Dust ring

• Washer

• Lock washer

• Caged bearing

• Caged ball bearings

• Lower head cup

• Caged ball bearings

Hard-anodized aluminum alloy 32-spoke rims with sealed hubs •

Dust sleeve •

• Dust seal ring

15-g stainless-steel spokes •

Lower bearing race •

• Fork brace

• Cantilever brake arm

•Carbon-fiber down tube

• Cable housings

• All-weather brake shoe

• 24-tooth chainring

• Cable yoke & anchor bolt

• Brake arm mounting **bosses**

• Air/hydraulic **damping** units

• Cantilever brake arm

•36-tooth chainring & fixing bolts

• Inner tube

• Dust cap

• Sealed-bearing pedal, toe clip, & strap

• Straddle wire

• 175-mm **crank** arm

• *Rock Shox* forks

DID YOU KNOW?
•When the first mountain bike was displayed at the 1981 New York Bike Show, its inventors were told it would never catch on. In the US today, close to 80% of all bikes sold are mountain bikes.
•A mountain bike was the first bicycle to be ridden up Kilimanjaro, Africa's highest peak at 19,340 ft (5,895 m).

•Quick-release hub skewer

Kevlar reinforced 26 x 2-in tire •

Gears and Brakes

Off-road riding is often a dynamic mixture of continuous bike handling, rapid gear changing, and frequent braking. Mountain bikes use straight handlebars for maximum bike control, and the gear and brake levers are grouped together to be operated without removing the hands from the bars. Brake levers can be adjusted to the size of your hands and positioned so that two fingers can curl over the lever and operate the brakes at any time, while the other two fingers stay curled around the handlebar to maintain bike control. The gear levers are positioned so they can be operated by a push of the thumb or by twisting the wrist. Strong, easily controlled brakes are vital for mountain bikes, and this has stimulated many variations on the simple but powerful cantilever brake design, as well as new designs in brake blocks and rims. Developments such as ultra-strong hydraulic brakes and all-weather **hub** drum **brakes** have further enhanced bike performance and control.

GEARING SYSTEM: *Rapid Fire* shifters are mechanically complex with a profusion of small parts, and reliability of the first models has been very poor. If the shifter breaks down there is no manual option, so the cyclist is truly stuck.

UPPER LEVER: One of the two front derailleur shifters, the upper lever takes you down a chainwheel at a time.

LOWER LEVER: One push shifts up a chainwheel at a time. An extended push takes you from the smallest to the largest chainwheel.

ROTARY SHIFTERS
Operated with a twist of the wrist, the Grip Shift gear changer is simple and reliable. Its key advantage is that your hands keep a firm grip on the bars. A bouncing bike can induce involuntary shifts, however, and to avoid this, devotees are hoping for a model that downshifts with a twist, but upshifts with a button.

THUMBSHIFTERS
Top-mounted Campagnolo thumbshifters are reliable, lightweight, and are the preferred gearing system for competition bikes. If the semiautomatic indexed gear-shifting system goes out of adjustment, the lever can instantly be changed to operate manually in a conventional friction mode.

HYDRAULIC BRAKES

Hydraulic brakes (left) are fluid-operated (like car brakes) and have tremendous power – enough to crush a weak rim – and yet operate easily and smoothly. They are particularly effective in wet, muddy, or icy conditions.

CANTILEVER BRAKES

Cantilever brakes (right) are light, strong, and powerful. Mounting a brake close to the rim helps to keep it rigid and prevent vibrations. Design variations such as the roller-cam brake offer even greater power and precision, but can require frequent maintenance and often clog up with mud on off-road runs.

BRAKE LEVERS: These are mounted just below, rather than horizontal with, the handlebars, for optimum reach with two-finger operation.

LEFT AND RIGHT

The international convention for gears is that the left lever operates the front changer on the chainwheel, the right lever operates the rear derailleur. With brakes, convention varies from country to country. In the US, for example, where the mountain bike originated, the left lever operates the front brake, the right lever the rear brake. In the UK, the positions are reversed. Before you ride an unfamiliar bike, always check which way the levers operate.

REAR DERAILLEUR SHIFTERS: The upper lever shifts down a cog at a time, the lower lever reverses the process.

GEARS AND GEAR RATIOS

A gear, like a lever, is a means of changing the rate at which work is done. The rate of change is called the ratio. On a bicycle the ratio is determined by relative sizes of the crankset chainrings and the freewheel sprockets or cogs. With a 52-tooth (T) chainring, one complete turn of the **cranks** will rotate a wheel with a 13T sprocket four times, a ratio of 4:1, while a 28T chainring will turn a wheel with a 28T sprocket once, a ratio of 1:1. A 52/13T gear is big, and gives speed, while a 28/28T gear is low, and gives the power to climb hills, albeit slowly.

The average cyclist produces ⅛ horsepower on a steady basis, with maximum efficiency when pedaling at **cadences** of 55 to 85 rpm. The purpose of gears is to maintain an efficient cadence, and the key to

using gears is anticipation: shift early, before a new gear is needed, so cadence remains smooth and steady. Anticipation is particularly important when downshifting to lower gears for climbing. Although modern transmissions shift quickly and positively, it helps to ease pedal pressure for just a moment – half a stroke is enough – when shifting through the gears. Never cross the chain by running it from the smallest chainring to smallest cog, or largest chainring to largest cog. These combinations will cause the chain to cut across at too severe an angle, thereby reducing efficiency and increasing wear.

With the chain on a small chainring and large sprocket, below, the bicycle moves a shorter distance for each turn of the cranks; the bicycle travels farther when the chain is on a large chainring and small sprocket.

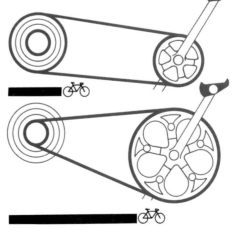

Clothing

As you cycle you generate ten times more heat than when at rest, and feel about 20°F (11°C) warmer. The key to comfort is to dress lightly, in layers that can easily be added or removed to suit conditions and pace. You're likely to need only a few well-chosen garments. It is always essential, however, even in summer, to pack extra clothes for protection in case you have to stop, or if the weather worsens. If you venture into unfamiliar territory, include a survival kit (see p.34) for any unforeseen emergency.

WINTER TOURING
Wind and rain can chill a rider far below the outside temperature. A full-length weatherproof suit (right) in Gore-Tex or another breathable material, with room underneath for additional insulating clothes, is a good defense. Ankle-length boots will also give maximum support and protection for the feet.

SUMMER TOURING
Even in warm weather, a good weatherproof jacket is a priority. Many of the lightweight models can be folded up small enough to fit into a pocket-size pouch when not being worn.

GLOVES: These insulate against shock and vibration, and protect against cuts in case of a fall.

HEAT LOSS: Prevent heat loss through the head by wearing a *Gore-Tex* helmet cover or insulated cap.

SHOES: These can be used with toe clips, or with step-in clipless pedals.

COLD-WEATHER RIDING

The rider below illustrates the protection needed in sub-zero temperatures. You need three layers of clothes: an inner layer of a quick-drying fabric, a middle layer of wool or pile fabric for warmth, and an outer windbreaker ideally made of Gore-Tex, Entrant, or Thintech. In milder weather the middle layer can be omitted, but keep it in your pack, in case you need it later. A down-filled nylon vest is one option: light and easily packed into a small bag, it quickly turns into a good insulator.

HOT-WEATHER RIDING

Lightweight shirt and shorts, as worn below, are all you need, but pack additional clothes as insurance against chill or too much sun. Add-on garments such as leg warmers, nylon vests, and long-sleeve jerseys are lightweight and can be folded into a tiny space. Be aware of exposed skin: use moisturizer and waterproof sunscreen if necessary to protect it from sun and wind. A cycling cap underneath the helmet, with the peak reversed, will shield the back of the neck from the sun.

BODY: Try wearing a thermal layer under a windbreaker to help you stay much warmer in cold weather.

HEAD: As your head loses the most heat in cold weather, protect it with a headband or cap under your cycling helmet.

LIPS: Coating your lips with a special moisturizer prevents wind chapping.

SHIRT: Wear a shirt made of a fabric that drains away perspiration, thus helping you to stay cool.

TIGHTS: Easy leg movement and warmth are gained by wearing spandex tights.

SHOES: As the **cleats** are recessed into the soles, these can also be used for walking.

SHORTS: These should be lined to prevent chafing and offer more comfort.

Sizing a Mountain Bike

Mountain bikes are made for vigorous riding. A fit that distributes the rider's weight and gives good balance is essential. With the saddle at the correct height and the **cranks** parallel with the ground, the bony protrusion just below the knee should be directly above the pedal axle. The back should have a forward lean of at least 45 degrees, so that the stronger gluteus muscles in the buttocks and lower back can be used for pedaling. Positioning in this way will shift more weight onto the arms, which should be slightly bent at the elbows to allow for shock absorption, with the wrists kept straight.

HANDLEBARS: Handlebars should be positioned 1 to 2 in below the saddle, with a width of 21 to 24 in. Wide bars offer good control at slow speeds. Narrow ones are better for speed. •

SEAT POST: The seat post should be exposed by 6 to 8 in (15 to 20 cm). For maximum pedaling efficiency, saddle height (see p.20) should be the same on and off the road. For steep descents, lower the saddle so you can hang off the back. •

• CRANKS: These are usually about 5 mm longer on mountain bikes than on standard road bikes. This extra length gives more leverage.

SIZING AND SAFETY

You need to be able to move the bike around underneath you without bruising your thighs, and to have the confidence to take a fall without any serious injury.

CROTCH CLEARANCE: For off-road riding, have at least 3 to 4 in (8 to 10cm) clearance from the crotch to the top tube.

SIZING – SOME TIPS

The standard advice on sizing a mountain bike recommends that the bike is 2 to 4 in (5 to 10 cm) smaller than your road frame size. However, mountain bikes are measured in several different ways, and many models have sloping top tubes, so try out several different bikes first to get a feel for what suits you best. Important factors are general fit and reach. In good-quality mountain bikes, each frame size is proportional; frame angles and tube lengths are adjusted so that larger sizes have more reach, smaller sizes have less reach. With the saddle at the correct height, you want plenty of seat post and distance from the top tube. Your knee should be over the forward pedal with a level **crank**, and you should have a sufficiently comfortable reach down to the handlebars to incline your back at a 45-degree angle with slightly bent arms.

Sizing for Women

Women usually have a shorter reach, and need more seat post and a shorter top tube. A rough guide to measuring the size of a frame for a woman (in inches), is as follows: FLOOR-TO-CROTCH DISTANCE X 0.52 = SIZE. This is only a rough estimate, but it should provide a basic guideline. Always test-ride several bikes for size before you finally decide to go ahead and buy one.

THINK SMALL

Many first-time mountain-bike riders feel more comfortable on a frame that is actually larger than they need. Smaller frames are much more maneuverable, lighter, and safer. Select the smallest frame that gives you a good overall fit.

TOO BIG

A high top tube is fine for town riding and smooth road touring, but you will still need at least 1 in (2.5 cm) of clearance. A top tube that fits too snugly might lead to a painful accident!

TOO SMALL

A very low top tube means that it is easier to perform stunts and tricks on the bike. However, unless you are small, the reach will be too short and the ride very uncomfortable.

Touring Mountain Bikes

In terms of sheer versatility, mountain bikes are hard to beat for touring on- and off-road. At one end of the range there are sporty, ultra-light mountain bikes with a fast and agile performance. They have short **wheelbases**, sloping top tubes, and forks that have the minimum of **rake**. Touring on these bikes usually involves carrying essentials in a backpack. A backpack is good discipline when you are trying to regulate the weight you bring – its limited capacity forces you to leave the junk behind. At the other end of the spectrum are heavy-duty, long-distance load carriers with long wheelbases, that are easily capable of carrying 66-lb (30-kg)

BACK SUPPORT: For any short distance touring off-road, carry the load on your back. This way the bike remains more maneuverable over changing terrain.

DUAL PERFORMANCE
The Klein Attitude is a racing bike, which is also excellent for lightly-laden, fast touring. The complete bike weighs 22 lb (10 kg), making it quite a featherweight among mountain bikes, and much lighter than middle-range touring and road bikes.

GEARS: A competition bike, the *Klein Attitude* has close-ratio gears. Each change of gear as you shift up or through its 21-speed transmission is small, so that you maintain maximum pedaling efficiency.

CHAIN STAYS: The lack of **bosses** for a pannier rack is deliberate. The relatively short chain stays provide speed, so there is no room for panniers.

loads – potentially all the equipment you should need for a two-week camping holiday. Stability and balance are vital, so check that front and rear panniers are evenly weighted as you load them. Place heavy items at the bottom of the panniers, keeping the bike's center of gravity low to maintain stable handling.

HEAVY-DUTY TOURER

The F.W. Evans (below) is a modern mountain bike designed for comfort, stability, and load-carrying. This bike comes with **brazed**-on **bosses** to take pannier racks both front and rear. Although no match for the Klein (opposite) in terms of speed and weight, this tourer's frame geometry is carefully calculated to minimize the effect of carrying heavy loads over very long distances. The long chain stays are typical of this standard of touring bike, allowing panniers to be used without any chance of fouling the rider's heels. Bikes like this are ideal for off-road touring vacations where you want to carry sufficient equipment to establish a base camp out in the country, then unload and use the bike as a lightweight off-road touring machine.

SPARE ELASTIC: For riding off-road in rough country, take an elasticated webbing strap. The elastic cords that secure bags to racks are seldom strong enough to withstand bumpy journeys.

WHEELBASE: The long wheelbase makes for stable handling when carrying panniers.

STEERING: The generous fork **rake** reduces the shock from bumps and potholes, and makes for an all-around smoother ride.

PANNIERS: Standard bags hook over the top of the rack and have a second hook, held by elastic, which fastens the bottom of the bag to an eyelet or **dropout**.

FRONT RACK: The low-rider front racks center the bags over the front **hub axle** for optimum steering.

CHAIN STAYS: These are long to allow the rear pannier bags to be positioned over the back axle for optimum weight distribution.

33

Expedition Planning

Riding off-road means you must be able to cope in the outdoors on your own. Any sudden change in the weather conditions, a mechanical breakdown, an injury, or simply becoming lost, can transform what may start off as a pleasurable ride, into a situation where your survival might be at stake. If you panic or give up, you could well get hurt. However, if you have a realistic plan of action, then you will almost certainly be all right. People who survive life-threatening situations tend to be decisive and adaptable. They enjoy going solo, and coping on their own in the outdoors is part of the fun. If this does not appeal then you should ride off-road with a friend. The buddy-system is common to many sports, and while it can create a misleading sense of safety, if you do crash and break your back, then having a partner to go and fetch help will make the crucial difference between life and death. A cardinal rule is always to tell someone where you are going and when you expect to return.

MINIMUM SURVIVAL KIT

On any planned off-road excursion, however brief or near the rest of civilization, take along a minimum kit. 'Be Prepared!' may sound dull, but it is a fundamental lesson of outdoor survival. Don't be caught by over-confidence and ignore basic procedures. It is unbelievably easy to become lost in a sudden whiteout, be chilled to the bone by an unexpected downpour, or do something unexpectedly foolish, such as fall into a freezing stream in bad weather. A minimum kit has three groups: clothing, map, water and food; personal survival kit; and basic bike repair kit. You should always have a jacket; trousers and a hat are a good idea. The aim is to protect your body from wet and cold or the sun, as the case may be. If the climate is mild, the clothes you wear can be lightweight; in cold conditions, have enough clothes to keep you comfortable if you have to stand around for several hours. Water is essential. You can get along without food if you wish, but carry a keep-going snack. A map of a familiar area may seem like an excessive addition, but have it as a contingency. Never ride an unfamiliar area without a map. Have your own personal survival kit and adjust it as necessary for different conditions. Ready-made survival kits can be purchased in stores, but it is much better to make up your own.

Water filter-straw

Multipurpose pocket knife

Cannondale 6-in-1 tool

Bandanna

Plasters

Foil blanket

Waterproof jacket

Map in waterproof sleeve

Mint candy bar

Hip pouch

Pump

Water bottle

Dehydrated food

Snake-bite kit

Four-in adjustable spanner

Nuts & bolts

Water-proof matches

Tire lever

Compass

Torch

Harmonica

Pouch

Tool pouch

Puncture kit

Inner tube

Whistle and cord

Saddle bag

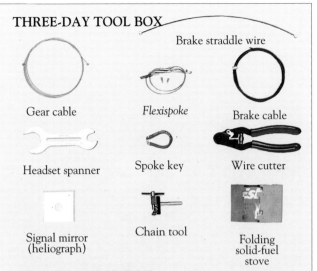

THREE-DAY TOOL BOX

Gear cable

Brake straddle wire

Flexispoke

Brake cable

Headset spanner

Spoke key

Wire cutter

Signal mirror
(heliograph)

Chain tool

Folding
solid-fuel
stove

MINIMUM TOOL BOX

You should know the function for each item in your minimum kit. The basics are: whistle and cord, water filter straw (or *Puritabs*), survival blanket (preferably two), waterproof matches, flashlight, compass, pocket knife, sticking plaster, and trail food. These should be kept in a pouch small enough to slip into your pocket. In addition, a minimum tool box should form part of your survival kit. A set of spare cables take up little room and weight. Trim the cables to size at home and glue or solder the ends to prevent fraying (see p.186); then you can leave the cable cutters behind. Add further tools and parts according to journey distance. Extra spokes, a spoke key, a chain tool, headset and bottom bracket tools – all can be important if you are far afield, but avoid excess weight whenever possible. An excellent multipurpose tool is the *Cool Tool* (see p.149). If you are riding with friends, share one set of tools among the group. The same logic can be applied to a portable stove and pot for hot drinks, and a large, comprehensive first-aid kit.

An indication of the general area where you will be riding is useful if you fail to reappear on schedule and rescue services have to search for you. A followup rule is: Look for help before you need it. If you start getting into trouble, get out of it quickly – most critical situations are the compounded effects of a cumulative series of smaller problems and errors. If help from someone else would be useful, then ask for it. If you should ever become lost and separated from your companions and then find your way back to civilization, you must report your arrival. There is nothing quite so galling as spending a rainy night looking for someone who turns out to have been home safe in bed. Panic can make

you do stupid things. Inertia often follows an accident, and the antidote is action. Review your priorities, and start on the most immediate problem. If a serious injury prevents you traveling to a safe destination and night is falling, you may well die without shelter and warmth. However, if no one knows you are there, you will probably have to travel on regardless. If you are traveling and are lost, determine the most promising direction and refer any landmarks you notice back to your map, to maintain your course. Stop and rest regularly. If you are staying overnight, organize a shelter, build a fire, and prepare signals. If you decide to travel on in the morning, leave a message with your name and destination at your camp site. There are many books and courses on first aid and survival skills, and the more you can learn, the better equipped you will be to ride off-road solo.

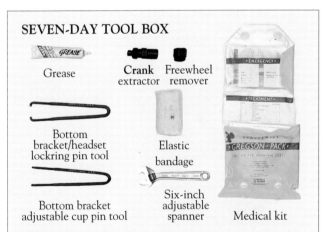

SEVEN-DAY TOOL BOX

Grease

Crank extractor

Freewheel remover

Bottom bracket/headset lockring pin tool

Elastic bandage

Bottom bracket adjustable cup pin tool

Six-inch adjustable spanner

Medical kit

SURVIVAL GUIDE

You are riding alone when a branch snags the front wheel, the bike cartwheels, and you are thrown headfirst into a tree. What do you do? Your first step after an accident is a simple mechanical check of yourself for major cuts and broken bones, because an accident can cause an adrenaline rush that snaps you into hyperdrive and makes you unaware of any injury. Equally, shock may mask pain so that you may not feel a thing. Administer first aid if necessary, and once you are okay, the next step is to check the bike. It is easy to crash, automatically jump back onto the bike, and then crash again because the bike malfunctions. If either you or the bike are damaged, there are several things to do:

1. Protect yourself immediately from panic or inertia, cold, heat, and dehydration.
2. Evaluate your resources and situation, and decide whether to stay put or travel on.
3. Organize sufficient water and food.

Open Trails

If the mountain bike has expanded the potential for off-road cycling, it has also increased the number of people making greater use of the countryside. Early on, mountain-bike riding received a hostile reception. The bikes were considered little better than motorbikes without engines, ready to plow up trails and disturb the peace. In some areas the sudden influx of riders so alarmed traditional users, such as hikers and horse riders, that mountain bikes were banned from trails. Since then, mountain-bike riding has grown enormously in popularity, and cyclists have proven that off-road riding is a valid, environmentally sound outdoor activity. Part of this about-face has occurred because mountain bikers are taking a more active rather than reactive role, and promoting a positive image of environmental consciousness. Another increasingly popular method is to set up local "Adopt-a-Trail" programs, with bikers maintaining a specific trail. Developing trail access and discovering new trails in cooperation with conservationists has become a minor industry in its own right. In wilder areas, rediscovering lost trails across public land can be as much fun as riding them.

BIKEPACKING

Taking a tent on an overnight expedition can give you the freedom to be self-sufficient, but the tent itself needs to be extremely light and compact. Specialist tents such as the one below use the bike as a support. Guy wires attached to the seatpost and handlebar **stem** mean that no poles are required, thus saving weight. (Attaching the tent to the bike gives you increased security, because you are instantly alerted to anyone trying to steal the bike.) Lightweight freestanding tents suitable for bikepacking will usually require poles. They often have a well-ventilated inner tent and a waterproof outer flysheet that keeps rain off the inner tent and reduces condensation

APPRECIATING THE COUNTRYSIDE

You can maximize your pleasure in trail riding by exploring quiet and undiscovered routes (left) that lead you away from the busier tracks. If you study a detailed large-scale map of the area you propose to ride, you can often locate routes over public land. Old maps and aerial photographs also give an indication of overgrown paths and disused rail tracks: All that may survive of an overgrown path is a gap in the trees. Single tracks may be found by exploring dried-up rivers and streams, or by following the paths worn by cattle and sheep grazing on public land. If you need to cross private land, it is imperative that you seek the owner's permission first. Respecting the countryside is always something to bear in mind – plowing up the land with violent bike maneuvers will cause harm to both the environment and to the good will of other trail users and farmers whose land you cross.

SPECTACULAR SCENERY

Reaching the most unusual and spectacular countryside and sights can involve long cross-country journeys lasting several days or weeks. Make sure that you are fit enough to enjoy a long ride and plan every aspect of your journey carefully – routes, supplies, shelter, and contingency plans. Ensure that your bike is in good condition and make sure that someone knows where you are going, what your proposed routes are, and where you expect to arrive and come back.

RULES OF THE TRAIL

Mountain bikes will finally become accepted when they cease to be an issue and can be regarded as just another legitimate means of travel. Yet because mountain bikes are still comparatively new, they are viewed with suspicion. Help to change people's minds by displaying courtesy and common sense every time you ride. Try to follow the International Mountain Bike Association's Rules of the Trail at all times. The main points of these rules are:
- Plan ahead and ride on open trails only.
- Leave no trace — take your litter home.
- Control your bicycle.
- Always yield the trail.
- Never frighten animals.

You should, in addition:
- Guard against all risk of fire.
- Help to keep all water clean.
- Protect wildlife, plants, and trees.
- Make no unnecessary noise.
- Keep to rights-of-way across farmland.
- Leave livestock, crops, and machinery alone.
- Use gates and stiles over fences, hedges, and walls.
- Leave all gates as you find them.

Kilimanjaro

The mountain bike has been aptly named – used by adventurers to climb peaks worldwide. The conquest of Africa's highest mountain, Kilimanjaro, by cousins Nick and Dick Crane was the climax of years of climbing and cycling experience. Riding at altitude made unusual demands. Approaching the 19,340-ft (5,900-m) summit, they could only ride a few yards before collapsing for lack of oxygen. But the payoff was tremendous: a descent that was the freewheel of a lifetime.

ADVENTURER'S EQUIPMENT
Nick Crane (below), equipped for the ride up Kilimanjaro. The standard production Saracen mountain bikes were used without any modifications or extras.

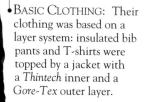

• HEADWEAR: A thermal balaclava was under the hood. It could also be folded so that its flap acted as a sun visor, or turned to protect the neck.

• EYE PROTECTION: Snow goggles were essential to protect against UV rays and reflections. Head-mounted lights were vital for night riding.

• BASIC CLOTHING: Their clothing was based on a layer system: insulated bib pants and T-shirts were topped by a jacket with a *Thintech* inner and a *Gore-Tex* outer layer.

• TIRES: These are 2.125-in (6.4-cm) standard knobbies that grip well on mud, rock, and snow. Inflated to 35 psi, they required no further attention.

WELL EQUIPPED
The Cranes (above) rode the 50-mile round trip in just over 8 days. They carried small day packs of extra clothes, tools, food, and an altitude acclimatization drug.

TEAM SUPPORT

Stoves, sleeping bags, dehydrated food, equipment, and tents (above) were carried by a support team of porters and friends, who also guaranteed that photographs and reports were sent to media sponsors for publication as the trip progressed.

CLIMBING TO THE CRATER

Some 3,000 ft (914 m) below the crater rim, the snow and ice ascent became unrideable, and the Cranes had to carry their bikes and packs (right). Later, as they approached the summit, they could ride for only 2 minutes at a time before taking 10 minutes to rest and breathe in oxygen.

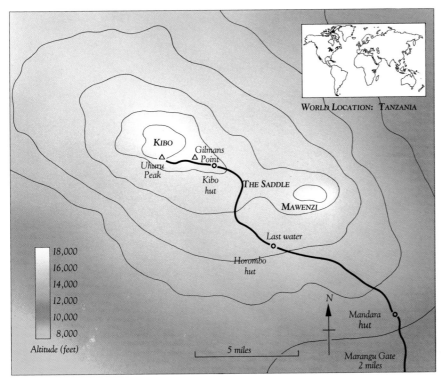

WORLD LOCATION: TANZANIA

KIBO

Gilmans Point

Uhuru Peak

Kibo hut

THE SADDLE

MAWENZI

Last water

Horombo hut

N

Mandara hut

Marangu Gate 2 miles

18,000
16,000
14,000
12,000
10,000
8,000

Altitude (feet)

5 miles

PLANNING THE TRIP

Kilimanjaro (left) was chosen because, although it is Africa's highest mountain, it is unique for the gentleness of its lower slopes. Maps indicated that the Cranes would be able to pedal through several climate zones, starting with an equatorial rain forest, before reaching 15,500 ft (4,700 m). Then they would have to carry their bikes 3,000 ft (914 m) to the rim of the volcanic crater before riding the rest of the way to the summit. One of the prices of being a pioneer is that there are insufficient accurate guidebooks. Despite consulting maps and mountaineers who had been up Kilimanjaro, the Cranes had little idea of how much of the mountain could be ridden and how frequently they would have to carry their bikes. Contour lines on a map can only reveal so much about the incline, not about the terrain. The whole event was organized to raise money for the Third World charity Intermediate Technology.

Off-Road Racer

Racing mountain bikes are built for speed and, of course, to survive rough handling. A 50-mile (80-kilometer) race, with fast descents down one-in-three rock screes, fording streams and traversing ankle-deep mud, is as wearing on the bike as on the rider. Unlike road racers, the bike that off-road competitors start on is the one they finish on. This is a big challenge for frame builders. At mass-production level, large diameter aluminum tubing is taking over from **chrome-moly** because it is light and stiff. With more expensive hand-built bikes, a skilled frame builder can make chrome-moly compete with aluminum for weight and strength.

CABLE RUNS:
Exposed runs deliver more precise braking and gear shifting by eliminating the inherent slack of long cable housings.

STEEL CRAFTSMANSHIP
The Fat Chance "Yo-Eddy" is a racing bike that is a tribute to the art of steel-frame making. The frame is TIG (tungsten inert gas) welded – a process where the tubes are actually fused together. The tubing is made from **chrome molybdenum***, a steel alloy. The combined frame and forks weight is 4¾ lb (2.15 kg) and the whole bike weighs under 26 lb (12 kg).*

CLEARANCE: The bottom-bracket height and the width of the chain stays is greater than usual, to allow for the wide tires.

CHAIN STAYS: The relatively short 17 in (43 cm) chain stays give powerful direct drive from the pedals.

GEAR SHIFTERS: For serious racing, gear-shift levers mounted on top of the bars are preferred to one-piece shifters mounted underneath. They are easier to reach when standing up, and easier to repair under race conditions.

LIGHTWEIGHT FRAME
The *Klein Attitude* has a light aluminum frame and fork, with a one-piece bar and **stem** that weighs under 1 lb (500 grams). The complete bike weighs 22 lb – a considerable advantage when climbing.

STEERING: The *Yo-Eddy*'s straight-bladed forks and vertical **dropouts** are very strong. **Rake** and **trail** are built in by slanting the forks at an angle away from the head tube.

WHEELBASE: The long, 41½-in (105-cm) wheelbase provides the bike with extra stability.

FAT TIRES: The 2½ inch-wide *Specialized* tires are among the fattest tires available and provide superb grip in all conditions.

Mountain Bike Suspension

Mountain bikes have given fresh impetus to the development of suspension systems. Shock-absorbing mechanisms may add weight, but can greatly increase comfort, performance, and control. Anyone who has experienced the hammering of a rough track or a potholed road will appreciate the benefit of a smoother ride; what is surprising is that shock absorption also gives better handling and greater speed; in fact, descents are 20 percent faster on average. Suspension gives enhanced traction, and this results in much quicker cornering as well as better climbing. Front suspension offers reduced vibration, because legs can absorb shock at the rear, but a bike with front and rear suspension will perform best of all.

A SMOOTHER RIDE
The *Girvin Offroad Flexstem* is a simple way of smoothing a ride without changing frame geometry. The *Flexstem* pivots on a bolt, which compresses an elastomer ring at the **stem**. It can only move down, so that the bars will remain rigid during climbing. If the front wheel hits a bump, the *Flexstem* deflects downward, which cushions the shock. The rings come in different sizes.

STATE-OF-THE-ART
The Fisher RS-1, with evenly balanced front and rear suspension, gives a great ride. The forks are Fisher-calibrated Rock Shox with pressure-adjustable air springs and hydraulic **damping**. *The rear unit is a floating parallelogram with four pivot points, dampened by a pair of* **durometers** *and complemented by a powerful Phil Wood* **hub brake**.

SHOCK ABSORBERS
The Cannondale EST *(Elevated Suspension Technology) (above) has a rear swing-arm attached to the bottom-bracket axle unit on the seat tube. The shock absorber has 1 in (2.5 cm) of travel and uses hydraulic fluid* **damping***. The tension is adjustable, and the spring is available in three different strengths to suit the weight of individual riders. Front suspension is an Offroad Flexstem (see left). The elevated EST chain stays are a taut 16¾ in (42.5 cm) for improved traction when climbing.*

SUSPENSION-FITTED BIKES
The Offroad Pro-Flex *(above) uses elevated, swing-arm chain stays with the pivot bolt held on a bracing tube above the bottom bracket (right). Shock absorption and* **damping** *are provided by connecting the seat stays to the base of the* **seat cluster***, via an elastomer* **bushing** *with 1 in (2.5 cm) of travel. A variety of different bushings are available to suit the full range of rider weights. This simple design is similar to the front of the Flexstem. The suspension only works when it is needed. On a smooth road, the Pro-Flex feels like a normal rigid bike; off-road, the ride is soft, yet fast. One advantage of this particular model is that because of the simple design, Pro-Flex bikes are often quite a lot cheaper than rival suspension-fitted bikes.*

Riding Techniques

Mountain-bike riding is a total experience, concentrating both your mind and your body completely. Unlike riding a sports bike, where body and bike move predominantly as a single smooth unit, riding a mountain bike requires you to use both your arms and shoulders actively and to move all your body weight around for the best control over the bike when surfaces and gradients change. Good mountain-bike riding is vigorous and dynamic. No matter how highly you rate your initial level of fitness, trail riding will soon improve your flexibility, strength, and endurance, as well as increase your bike-handling skills.

CLIMBING SLOPES: THE RIGHT AND WRONG WAY
The front rider (above) is leaning too far forward over the bars, and is about to lose back-wheel traction. The second rider has all his weight shifted back, and the front wheel is about to rear up, with a loss of steering. Both ways spell an inevitable loss of control. To climb a slope accurately, stand up for the easier sections and steep slopes, and sit down over difficult parts. Crouch jockey-style with your center of gravity over the pedals, your head over the handlebars, and keeping your arms pressed down. If an incline seems insurmountable, you may still be able to ascend by traversing the slope diagonally.

BASIC POSITIONS: SITTING AND STANDING
Check that all of your controls are correctly positioned (see pp.162-165). While you ride, make sure you stay lightly seated, with your hands resting on the bars, and your middle and index fingers covering the brake levers. Your arms should support some of your body weight. This position allows you to be ready to come out of the saddle in case of a change in terrain, or to bunnyhop over a small log. The mountain bike is at its most maneuverable at low speed with the rider standing on the pedals, and the arms forming a triangle with the bars. When you stand and pedal, try to avoid pitching your weight forward.

DESCENDING SLOPES
*The only time you may need to grip firmly on your handlebars is on bumpy downhill slopes. The slope incline and terrain can change rapidly in the space of a few yards. Don't try to steer by pushing and pulling the bars. The movement of your body weight, led by the way you incline your head and shoulders, is sufficient to steer the bike. Whatever your maneuver, you can avoid a difficult situation quite easily. Remember the basic essentials in anticipation of any change: learn to read the terrain ahead, change gear in advance, adjust your pedaling **cadence**, and be ready to move your body around the bike.*

OBSTACLES

Mountain-bike riding is about being able to deal with all the changing conditions you encounter as you travel. Approach and anticipation are everything when you are riding up and down hills. One of the trickiest problems on a downhill ride is clearing obstacles such as a log or a large rock. The most dangerous approach is to try and hit the log head-on, with your full weight behind the bike. At any speed this will damage your body as well as your bike. Anticipation, "unweighting," and most of all,

timing, will keep you on course, as the rider in the time-lapse photo above demonstrates. Although traveling downhill at high speed, he has released his front brake long enough to pull back on the bars and lift the front wheel onto the log. Natural downhill momentum carries him forward, and, by crouching jockey-style, the unweighted rear wheel rolls over the log. This will ensure that the downhill position is resumed, and only then is it safe to use the front brake again, if necessary.

CORNERING DOWNHILL

The essential elements of mountain biking are maintaining momentum and traction to keep a steady grip, while the back and front wheels stay pinned to the ground. Going downhill at speed, you must keep your body weight as far back as possible and the pedals horizontal, so that when you need to turn a corner, the bike can be steered by leaning smoothly into the curve. One advanced technique is to enter the bend with the inside pedal down and trailing. This action slopes your weight more into the curve, leaving the outside pedal cocked and ready to pedal out. Always travel at a speed that still leaves you in control, and brake to counter the inevitable acceleration as the hill becomes steeper. Squeeze both brakes gently, but remember to apply more power to the rear brake, balancing the front brake, which has more stopping power on a descent. Jamming the front brake suddenly as you corner will flip up the back wheel and tip you over the bars, or will cause the bike to jackknife.

Soft Surfaces

Part of the thrill of riding off-road is dealing with sudden changes in terrain. Loose, soft surfaces such as sand, snow, mud, loose gravel, and rocky scree are among the hardest and most challenging to ride. Climbing, braking, and descending on these surfaces requires a positive approach, a properly set-up bike, and the use of a few simple but effective techniques. Assume that everything is rideable until proven otherwise. The key to surviving any loose surface is to maintain momentum and traction by keeping the back wheel turning. If it is a long section of soft ground make sure that tire pressures are low

ROCK RIDING
On loose rocky surfaces (right) the front wheel is easily deflected and can jump disastrously if it is not controlled well. Try to avoid turning the bars to steer. Instead shift your body, especially your shoulders, to incline the bike to the direction you want to travel.

SNOW PROBLEM
Riding in snow (below) is a challenge. It is like riding in sand, except you tend to sink deeper and farther. Even keeping the bike in a straight line requires a constant series of corrections as you try to maneuver from firm spot to firm spot.

SAND RIDING: DOWNHILL
Don't always expect to be able to freewheel downhill. You will find soft sand (above) increases rolling resistance, and often it is necessary to pedal on descents to keep going. Remember to keep the tire pressure low to prevent digging in.

enough. On a soft surface fully inflated tires dig in, creating unnecessary rolling resistance. Lower tire pressures mean less digging in and more tire area in contact with the surface to generate greater traction. How far tire pressures can be lowered is a matter of degree. On a really soft surface, a lightweight rider using a wide tire can go as low as 20 to 25 psi, whereas a heavier rider on narrow rims might need 30 to 40 psi to avoid a puncture from the rim pinching. Before reaching a loose surface, shift down to a gear that will give you enough traction without spinning out. Pick the straightest line through. Shift your weight back, keep pedaling, and keep the front wheel up so that it lightly skims the surface, preventing it from its natural inclination to dig deep into sand, snow, or mud.

THE WET STUFF

Before entering a stream (below), make sure you can see the bottom. If you can't, don't try it. Before you hit the water, switch to a lower gear, shift your weight back and accelerate so that you have enough speed to carry you through.

TIRES

The differences between the bulk of mountain-bike tires is no wider than the average tread, with just a few basic types and the sizes that count. The most common size is 26 x 2.125 in, but tires are available in widths from 1.0 to 2.6 in. The three basic types of tread are slicks, knobbies, and multipurpose. The completely bald slicks bring a mountain bike as close to a road bike as possible, knobbies are for off-road riding, and multipurpose are for road and off-road.

SLICK
The Matrix Road Warrior (left) is a treadless slick tire for optimal grip on asphalt and concrete. This helps in providing a comfortable ride with minimal rolling resistance and low tire noise.

MULTIPURPOSE (1)
The Specialized Nimbus (right) is an ultra-lightweight all-around performance tire that is very stable in wet weather. If using it off-road it is suitable for hard-packed surfaces, but hates mud.

MULTIPURPOSE (2)
The Matrix Cliffhanger (left) is an all-around cross and road tire. It is satisfactory on hard-packed surfaces, but its side lugs are too closely spaced to let mud escape.

KNOBBY (1)
The Onza Racing Porcupine (right) is the quintessential soft rubber compound knobby, with well-spaced, well-beveled lugs. Traction is excellent but the rubber compound life is short.

KNOBBY (2)
A Panaracer Smoke (left) rear tire is designed to cover all off-road bets. Well-separated lugs discharge mud easily while the central horizontal bands provide traction to improve acceleration.

KNOBBY (3)
The Specialized Hardpack (right) is a popular racing tire whose tread design works well on rocky terrain. The large 2.2-in size provides a greater volume of air to ride on and consequently a more comfortable ride off-road.

Racing

From the start, mountain-bike racing has been an informal high-energy sport, unhindered by petty restrictions about bikes and clothing. The first mountain-bike races, the pioneering 1976 Repacks, were impromptu downhill time trials on a fire road that dropped 1,300 ft (396 m) in under 2 miles (3.2 km). Since then this US-invented sport has now spread worldwide, with improved organization, diverse events, and spectacular courses; but the gritty spirit of mountain-bike racing remains the same: a rider-plus-bike versus the elements and the rest of the field, without mechanical backup. Race meetings can consist of a cross-country event, a downhill, a hill-climb, a dual slalom, and observed trials (see p.50) with riders competing according to skill, age, and sex. Internationally recognized ability classes are Pro-Elite, Expert, and Sport. Age groups are Youth 12-15, Junior 16-18, Senior 19-34, Vets 35-49, Masters 50+. Courses vary accordingly. A Senior mass-start cross-country course is from 24 to 36 miles (38.8 to 58 km), the circuit is at least 4 miles (6.5 km), with 90 percent off-road and no more than 10 percent where the bike may have to be carried. Downhill races cover about 5 miles (8 km) and must descend at least 80 percent of the course.

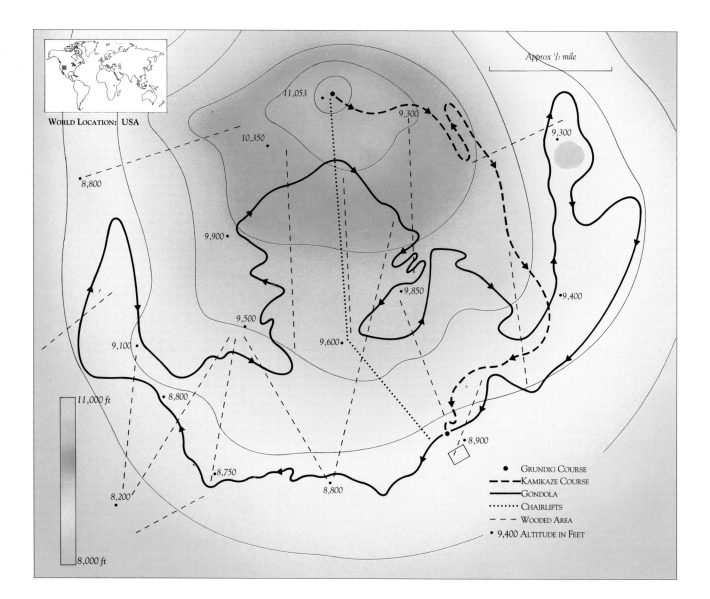

WORLD LOCATION: USA

Approx ½ mile

- 11,053
- 10,350
- 8,800
- 9,900
- 9,500
- 9,100
- 8,800
- 8,750
- 8,200
- 8,800
- 9,300
- 9,300
- 9,850
- 9,400
- 9,600
- 8,900

11,000 ft

8,000 ft

- ● GRUNDIG COURSE
- – – KAMIKAZE COURSE
- —— GONDOLA
- ⋯⋯ CHAIRLIFTS
- – – WOODED AREA
- • 9,400 ALTITUDE IN FEET

MOUNTAIN-BIKE RACING

THE CYCLO-CROSS CONNECTION

Before mountain-bike racing there was cyclo-cross (left), a grueling sport used by road racers for mid-winter training, on bikes fitted with narrow off-road tires and cantilever brakes. Cyclo-cross courses are devised with sections that are faster if the rider dismounts and carries his bike, whereas mountain bikers prefer to ride the impossible. While mountain bikers may not receive mechanical help in a race, cyclo-cross riders can switch bikes. There the differences end. Crossover between the two sports is common, with several cyclo-cross graduates becoming mountain-bike champions.

A Sport Evolved

Today, mountain-bike racing has branched out to incorporate different styles of racing. Apart from the cross-country races, there are other events. In observed trials, riders compete against the clock and incur penalty points whenever they dab (put a foot down). In dual slalom events, a field of riders compete head-to-head in pairs in sudden death races until all but the last two are eliminated. Races are over a short, downhill course of about half a mile. The hill climb event is a mass start, first-past-the-post race that climbs steeply, with competitors riding up most of the downhill course and barely managing to average 7 mph (11.3 km/h).

THE LEGENDARY RACE COURSE

Mammoth Lakes (left), in California's Sierra Nevada mountains, is at the forefront of ski resorts that have turned their facilities over to mountain-bike racing in spring and summer. Mammoth is a legend among off-road racers. The cross-country course, ridden for the 1991 World Cup series, is a long 12-mile (19.4-km) loop that the racers ride three times. Its dramatic "Kamikaze" downhill trail drops over 2,000 ft (609.6 m) in 3.88 miles (6.3 km) – the Pro record is 5 minutes, 25 seconds, an average speed of 43 mph (69.4 kmph)!

PRESTIGIOUS EVENT

The one race that determines the best overall mountain biker is the cross-country event (right). With the courses restricted to natural obstacles only, designing them has become an art. Start and finish areas have to be wide enough to allow riders to start en masse, then often narrow quickly to single track. This means that riders often sprint for position early on, only to find themselves out of breath as they hit an oxygen-sapping incline.

Observed Trials

Observed trials demand the very best in bike-handling skills. The aim is to ride through a short "section" of difficult, obstacle-rich terrain: a talented rider can climb a near-vertical cliff, see-sawing from tirehold to tirehold as if climbing a ladder. A typical course consists of 10 linked sections, with riders completing the course three times for a total of 30 stages. If a rider accidentally dabs by touching the ground, a tree, or a spectator, a maximum of five penalty points can be imposed per section ride. Crashing or riding outside the section boundaries also gains you five points. For riding the full course, the best possible score is zero, the worst as much as 150 points.

There are two distinct types of trial bikes and riders. Most top-level international riders use specially designed bikes with 20-inch wheels, bashplates, and a single low gear. It is incredibly impressive to watch these riders work their bikes, which are just about as esoteric and specialized as you can get, but are useless for ordinary riding. Most cyclists ride purely for fun and to improve their bike-handling skills. They use either stock mountain bikes or 26-in wheel trials bikes which have short chain stays, steep frame angles, and a high bottom bracket.

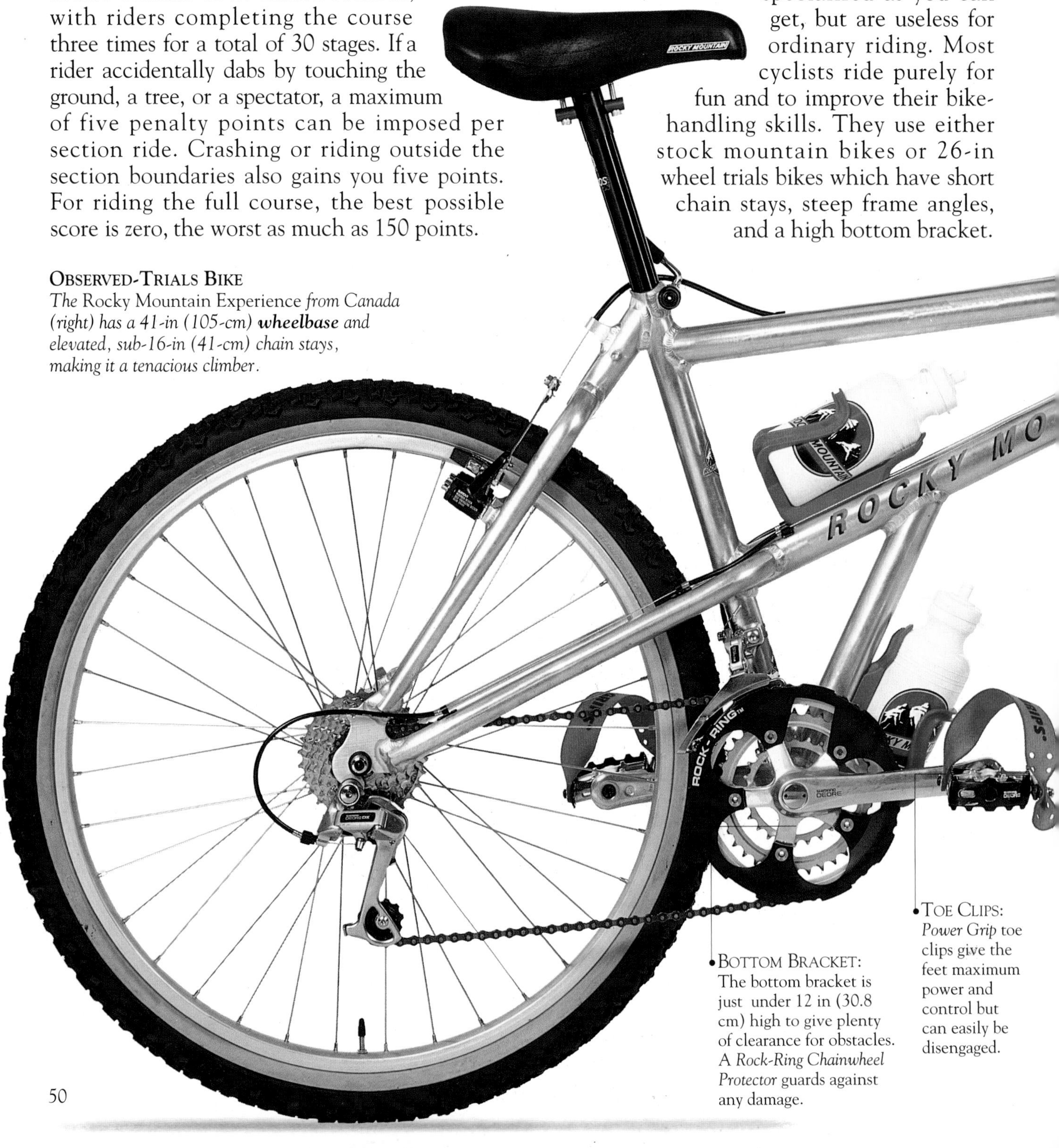

OBSERVED-TRIALS BIKE
The Rocky Mountain Experience from Canada (right) has a 41-in (105-cm) **wheelbase** *and elevated, sub-16-in (41-cm) chain stays, making it a tenacious climber.*

• TOE CLIPS: *Power Grip* toe clips give the feet maximum power and control but can easily be disengaged.

• BOTTOM BRACKET: The bottom bracket is just under 12 in (30.8 cm) high to give plenty of clearance for obstacles. A *Rock-Ring Chainwheel Protector* guards against any damage.

LOG JUMP

When you are 2 feet away from the log, pull a wheelie by pressing down on the **cranks** as you pull up on the bars (left). Accelerate slightly, sinking down on your legs to jump as you move your body weight forward, and with the cranks level place the front wheel on the log.

As you leap up over the log, push forward on the bars (below left). In this way as you crest the log the rear wheel should skim up and touch the log at the same point as the front wheel. By this time the bike should now be moving out in front of you. Go with the motion of the bike, sinking back down so that the front wheel lands lightly (below), and then rock forward so the impact of the rear wheel on the ground is also softened. The effect should be hopping the bike over the log like a pogo stick, rather than rolling on the wheels.

• BRAKES: *Suntour XC 9000* self-energizing cantilever brakes, with three-finger levers and handlebar *Grip Shift* twist gear changers, give complete control without ever needing a change in hand position.

LAYING YOUR OWN COURSE

Trials riding is one of the quickest and surest ways to improve your bike-handling skills. It is also a highly accessible sport – you can ride almost anywhere there is a tricky bit of ground or an open space to lay your own course. Find a suitable obstacle on which you can develop your skills, or learn by jumping over old tires. Tires make great obstacle jumps as they won't damage chainrings. Try and obtain the tires in various sizes and half-bury them in the ground. Alternatively, brace several tires side-by-side to simulate a log jump. If you use other obstacles, fit a chainring guard to protect your bicycle, and lower your saddle in case of unexpected bumps. Log jumping will take plenty of practice to develop the right techniques, but can be great fun.

• FORKS: The untapered, large-radius *Tange* "Big Forks" are internally butted for extra strength at points of maximum stress when riding.

Ultra-Enduros

Ultra-enduro mountain-bike events represent the extreme of what is possible on a bike. Ever since the bicycle was invented, cyclists have been using it as a tool for testing the limits of human endurance. In 1875 in Birmingham, England, bewhiskered pioneers pedaled "ordinaries" around a track nonstop for 12 hours, to see how far and how fast they could travel. These days their spandex-clad equivalents on mountain bikes keep up the tradition outdoors on an even more epic scale – such as discovering how many peaks can be ascended in 24 hours, racing snowbound over 200 miles (322 km) in Alaska in deepest winter, crossing the Sahara in the Paris-Dakar marathon, or taking on the challenge of beating a racehorse in the Welsh mountains. The off-the-wall element in these endurance events is more immediate, going back to the mid-1970s when the mountain bike was still evolving and pioneers enjoyed seeing how fast they could hurl their clunkers down the Repack, a steep hairpin track that dropped 1,300 ft (397 m) in less than 2 miles (3.2 km). Today's ultra racers have a similar thirst for crazed adventure as they apply their skills in the plethora of hair-raising races that are forever springing up, offering low prize money, considerable notoriety, and the chance to discover how long you can survive on a bike.

THE COLDEST BIKE RACE IN THE WORLD

Alaska's nonstop Iditabike contest (above) each February makes unusual demands on both competitors and machinery. One of its innovations is double-width wheels, made by lacing 2 rims to a hub. These dual tires deliver extra traction in weather conditions that can vary from 40°F above (4.4°C) and deep slush to blizzards at 40°F below (-40°C). The course, based on the Iditarod dogsled race, is 210 miles (338 km) of snow-packed trail and frozen rivers through the Alaskan tundra. Contestants need expeditionary skills to keep on course at night and have to pay an evacuation deposit in case they require airlifting out. Conditions were so bad in 1990 that the race was stopped after competitors had only been able to push for the first 52 miles (84 km).

MAN VS SNOW

In the hope of finding snow compact enough to ride, a contestant (left) in Alaska's Iditabike race tows his bike disassembled on a sled.

MAN VS HORSE VS BIKE
The world's first man-vs-horse race (left) was run in 1980 when a field of runners took on local horses in the Welsh mountains near Hay-on-Wye after a heated pub discussion over whether a man was faster than a horse. Two feet were slower than four, but in 1985 mountain bikes entered the race with pedal power running close to horsepower. In 1988 the man finally overtook the horse with Tim Gould, a mountain-bike champion, coming home ahead of the horse by 3 minutes, in 1 hour, 51 minutes.

THE COURSE
The 22-mile (35.2-km) course in the Brecon Beacons involves fording streams (below) and climbing over 4,000 ft (1,220 m). The best times for mountain bikes have been on hot days when the boggy hillsides have dried out as humans are better than horses at coping with heat.

The
RACING BIKE

Serious bike racing is one of the toughest sports in the world. If you take up racing in any of its many forms, you will face the constant desire for an improved performance and be obsessed by the relentless quest for a competitive edge. Bike racing forces you to reexamine every aspect of your bike; the way it is set up and its performance, your riding position and your pedaling **cadence**, your diet, training, and even the proportion of time you spend asleep.

Aero bars

All-consuming Obsession

Racing can easily become a total obsession: an all-consuming relationship between rider and bike, where you live to ride and ride to live, with a single objective – to optimize the harmony between your body and the bike so that together you become the ultimate machine. This urge can be experienced on the track or on the road, on short and long courses, on the flats or on hills, competing against the pack or against the clock. It's a real relationship that demands dedication and courage, and can deliver both pain and triumph, yet frequently appears to cut off the rest of the world – to whom cycle racing may seem

Brakes

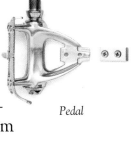

Pedal

a strange cultural ghetto, whose inhabitants worship exotic machines, observe unusual rituals of shaving their legs, wear tight-fitting clothes, and talk to each other in coded jargon.

Tri-spoke wheel

Accessible Sport

Bicycle racing is, however, primarily a very accessible sport, requiring only a bike, a body, and tons of willpower. The fascination of cycle racing endures because the sport combines the huge appeal of technology with an almost unquenchable and irresistible urge to measure the strength and endurance of a human. This mixture of technique with strength requires stamina and cunning, for which there is no known precise alchemy. For both the beginner and professional alike, the sport is varied enough to offer an ideal type of racing for everyone to pursue in their own way.

Speedometer

Water bottle

Racing cyclist

Racing Bike Anatomy

Designed and built for speed, road-racing bicycles have evolved classic frame geometry. Most modern bikes still share the same features as the machines of a decade ago: a short **wheelbase**, steep head- and seat-angles, a high bottom-bracket, and a short fork **rake**. This design allows the rider to adopt the **aero tuck**, still the most efficient way to transmit power to the pedals, and the most aerodynamic. With the frame design standardized, racing bikes optimize performance through materials and components. The carbon-fiber tubes of the *Rossin* (shown here) are 30 percent lighter than steel tubes, while its *Campagnolo* components are efficient and reliable.

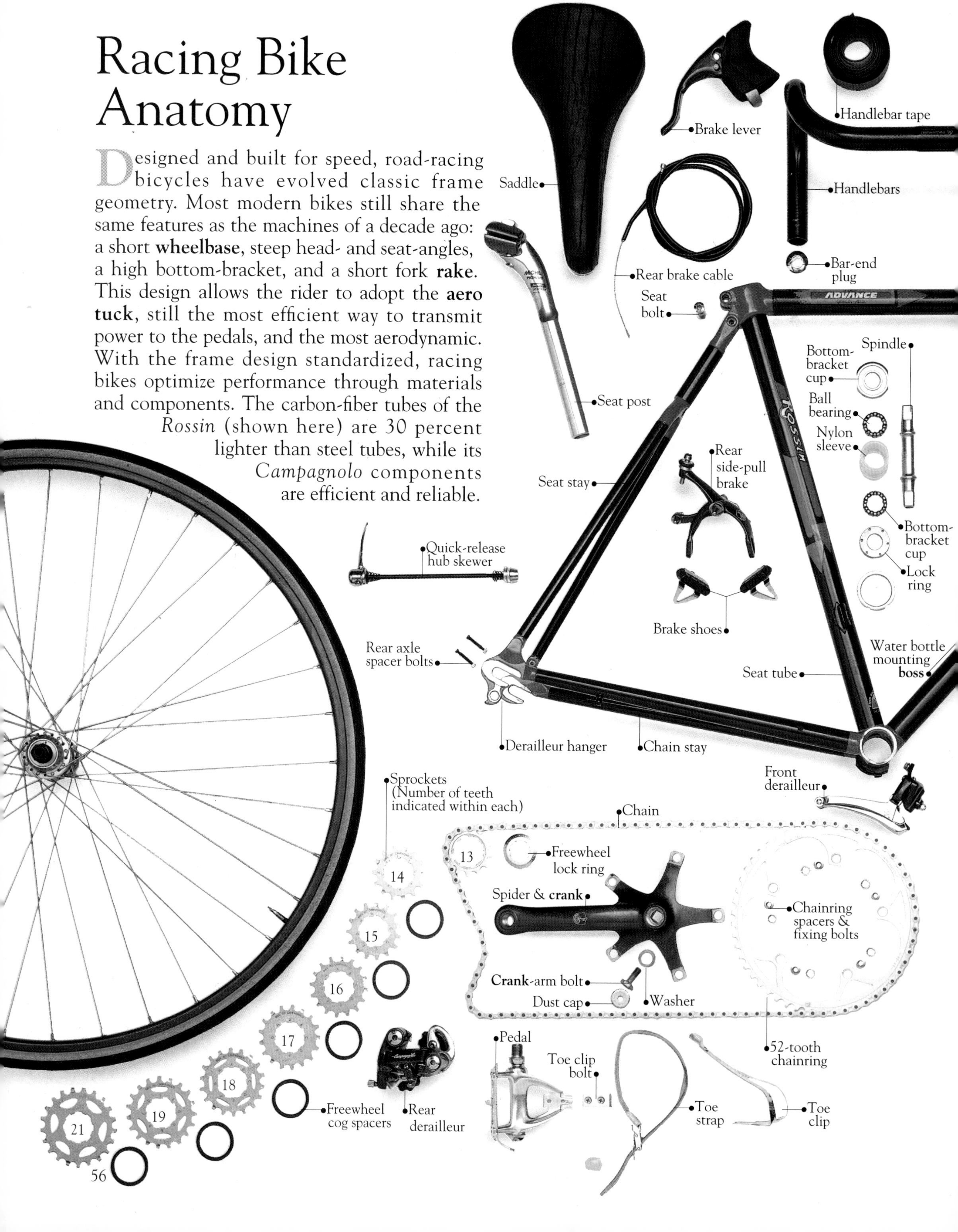

Brake lever

Handlebar tape

Saddle

Handlebars

Rear brake cable

Bar-end plug

Seat bolt

ADVANCE

Bottom-bracket cup

Spindle

Ball bearing

Nylon sleeve

Rear side-pull brake

Seat post

Seat stay

Bottom-bracket cup

Lock ring

Quick-release hub skewer

Brake shoes

Water bottle mounting **boss**

Rear axle spacer bolts

Seat tube

Derailleur hanger

Chain stay

Front derailleur

Sprockets (Number of teeth indicated within each)

Chain

13

14

Freewheel lock ring

Spider & **crank**

Chainring spacers & fixing bolts

15

16

Crank-arm bolt

17

Dust cap

Washer

18

Pedal

19

Toe clip bolt

52-tooth chainring

21

Freewheel cog spacers

Rear derailleur

Toe strap

Toe clip

Handlebar tape

Brake lever

Front brake cable & housing

Handlebar **stem**

Top tube

Bar-end plug

Head tube

Top head cup

Lock washer

Derailleur cable

Bolt

Bottom-bearing cup

Seal

Left lever

Fork tube

Ball bearings

Lever stop

Bolt

Washer

Right lever

Dust seal ring

Headset locknut

Seal

Washer

Cable housing

Right lever stop

Down tube

Derailleur cable

Aero bar arm rests

Clip-on aero bars

Front side-pull brake

42-tooth chainring

Pedal & toe clip

Fork blades

Brake shoes

Crank

Quick-release hub skewer

Crank arm bolt, washer, & dust cap

Tubular tire

Alloy rim

DEFINITIVE RACING BIKE
The *Rossin* is an Italian bike that is equipped with clip-on aero bars for time trials.

DID YOU KNOW?
Two riders can go faster than one rider by **drafting**, where the rider in front acts as a windbreak for the one behind. In a large **echelon**, no rider has to give 100 percent effort for long, and yet the echelon is much faster than a solo rider.

Frame Construction

The weight of a racing bike is crucial. The craft of building a racing machine is to make it as lean and precise as possible. The better the bike, the less there is of it. In the early days of cycling, building quality frames was a craft tradition which required skilled hand-brazing of lightweight alloy steel tubes. In the 1970s, manufacturers developed versatile alloy steels designed for machine-welding, and mass-produced, inexpensive lightweight frames became widely available. In the 1980s, the development of aluminum tubing for frames further reduced the weight and cost. In the 1990s, the choice material is now carbon-fiber, which is far stronger, stiffer, and lighter than either aluminum or steel.

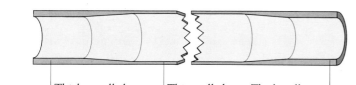

•Thicker-walled at ends •Thin-walled at center Thick wall gives• strength at joints

DECORATIVE LUGS
*The hand-finished metal **lugs** reinforcing **brazed** joints were often an ornamental design feature. In this classic lugged and brazed frame, the lugs are tapered to help distribute the stress evenly. Bike builders such as Alf Hetchins raised lugwork to a real art form, hand-sculpting designs such as the Magnum Bonum, an elaborate combination of fleur-de-lys, whorls, and swallowtails.*

STRENGTH: Lugs increase the joint strength by providing an extra surface area for the **brazing** metal.•

DOUBLE-BUTTED TUBING
*The evolution of **double-butted** tubing served to accelerate the craft tradition in frame-building. It was tricky to work with, but saved a pound in weight over plain-gauge tubing.*

STEEL FRAME
*The Reynolds 531 **double-butted** tubes in this traditional **lugged** and **brazed** frame below are heat-treated steel alloyed with manganese and other exotic elements.*

Alloy steels are light yet extremely strong. With normal use, a steel frame will last a lifetime. Many cyclists prefer the feel of steel frames despite the additional weight.

FINE TUNING: Steel frame tubes are sold in sets, but builders mix different strengths to fine-tune a frame for one rider.

SEAT STAYS: Every detail is honed and refined from many years of racing experience. The seat stays have bi-concave fluting.•

RANGE: Steel frames come in many different grades and strengths to suit specific applications such as road racing, time-trialing, or touring.

LUGWORK: Decorative details in the lugwork identify the bike maker.

FORK CROWN: The fork crown is a cast, semisloping design.•

SECTION: Oval-section fork blades have greater resistance to braking stress than do round blades.•

HAND-BRAZING
***Brazed** alloy steel frames are joined using brass or silver; metals which melt at lower temperatures than steel and serve as a metallic solder, holding the tubes together. TIG welded frames in steel, aluminum, or titanium, are joined by heating the tubes until they melt and fuse together.*

OVERBUILT: Aluminum frames fatigue but are designed with extra strength for safety reasons.

• LARGE TUBES: Aluminum is light but soft. Large-diameter tubes are used to increase rigidity and strength.

• HANGER: The derailleur gear hanger is replaceable.

• MOST STRESS: The down tube is biggest as it bears by far the greatest forces.

TIG-WELDING
The Cannondale 3.0 *aluminum TIG-welded frame is one of the lightest and stiffest frames in any material (above).* Cannondale *use the frame for its top-* line racing bike, *as well as several budget ready-to-race models. Despite a wide gap in price, the bicycles differ in component quality only: the frames are the same.*

GLUED FRAMES
With many aluminum frames, the tubes are glued together rather than welded together. Glues are simple to work with and are usually stronger than the materials they join.

MATERIAL PERFORMANCE
Steel and aluminum are both well-developed materials that are now near their performance limits. The future of lightweight frames belongs to carbon-fiber. A carbon-fiber frame can weigh at least 30 percent less than an aluminum frame, giving an overwhelming advantage in a race.

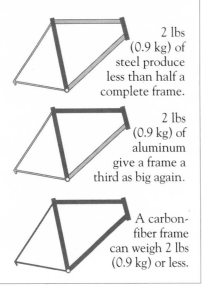

2 lbs (0.9 kg) of steel produce less than half a complete frame.

2 lbs (0.9 kg) of aluminum give a frame a third as big again.

A carbon-fiber frame can weigh 2 lbs (0.9 kg) or less.

LANDMARK FRAME
The Giant Cadex 980, (below), is an historic landmark: a carbon-fiber frame with alloy lugs, head tube, forks, and stainless steel **dropouts***, which has a comparatively low retail price.*

CARBON-FIBER
This is anistropic – strong and stiff along the axis of the fibers (right). These can be formed into any shape, with the strength placed where needed. Carbon-fiber offers the ultimate in light weight, feel and comfort. With the onset of mass production, carbon-fiber frames are becoming inexpensive – less bike and more performance than ever before.

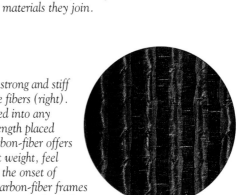

MATERIAL: Many testers feel that carbon-fiber is the best material for bike frames.

WISHBONE: The wishbone lug neatly separates the seat stays and provides a mounting point for the rear brake.

RESISTANCE: Carbon-fiber tubes are often covered with a layer of amarid or fiberglass to resist any abrasion.

SHAPE: While used for conventional tubing, carbon-fiber can also be formed into any shape required.

Wheels for Speed

After the frame, wheels are the most vital element in bike performance. Two factors in wheel design are critical: weight and shape. As the wheel spins, angular momentum creates a gyroscopic effect: the heavier the wheel and the faster it turns, the greater the momentum and the greater the amount of force you need to accelerate or brake it. To save weight, wheels are made with spokes. However, as the wheels spin, the spokes churn the air, generating aerodynamic **drag** that increases proportionately faster than ground speed. The solution is to design wheels that smooth the flow of air: even though they may be heavier than spoked wheels, these require less energy at high speeds.

COMPOSITE

The Specialized Du Pont Composite *wheel (above) is made from fibers of carbon, aramid, and glass, over a foam core, bonded to a 6061 T6 aluminum rim. An open-side area of about 50 percent reduces vulnerability to crosswinds and makes the wheel safe to use both front and rear. Each spoke acts as an airfoil that generates forward lift in a crosswind, like a sailboat tacking into the wind. Despite being almost 50 percent heavier than a standard 2 lb (1 kg) spoked wheel, at speeds over 17 mph (10.5 km/h) the Du Pont has faster acceleration. In a 25-mile (40-km) time trial, they claim to save 2 to 3 minutes.*

36-SPOKE WHEEL

Set in a "crow's foot" pattern (left) with one-third of the spokes radial and two-thirds crossed, this is an unusual combination; most wheels are either one or the other. Radial spokes traverse the shortest possible distance between hub and rim, thereby reducing weight, but they are poor for transmitting **torque** *from acceleration or braking. The crossed spokes leave the hub at a tangent, thus creating a lever that allows the spoke to transmit torque with less stress than a radial spoke. Each, arguably, has its own particular merits. However, the size and hardness of the tire, and the weight and strength of the rim, have a greater effect on wheel stiffness and on shock absorption. Radially spoked wheels have a slight aerodynamic advantage worth one second per ⅔ mile (1 km) over three-cross pattern wheels. They are often fitted to ultra-lightweight time-trial bikes.*

COMBINATION

The HED CX (right) combines 18 bladed spokes with a carbon-fiber composite rim. The spokes help reduce wheel weight to about the same as a 32-spoke wire-on wheel, giving sufficient open area for the wheels to be used both front and back in crosswinds. The spoke pattern is a mixed radial and two-cross. The carbon-fiber rim has a give similar to a hard-inflated tire. In a 25-mile (40-km) time trial, CX wheels will save around 2 minutes.

DISK WHEEL

Slicing the air, disk wheels (left) more than halve the amount of **drag** at 30 mph (48 km/h) of eggbeater spoked wheels. They are unsafe on the front: in crosswinds they produce steering **torque**, making the bike hard to handle. On the rear the aerodynamic advantage is reduced, because air flowing over the wheel has already been disturbed by the bike and rider. Disk wheels tend to be heavier than spoked, although the latest models in Kevlar are very light. Overall, however, disk wheels are much faster than spoked wheels.

TUBULAR TIRES

To save weight and maintain very high pressures, the casings of tubular tires are sewn together, and the tire is glued to the rim. The casings are made of cotton or silk fabric, and the tread vulcanized either by machine or by hand. Riders then age their tires for a period of 6 to 12 months, allowing them to dry out to exactly the right consistency: too moist and they may pick up grit and puncture; if they are too dry, the tire may slip.

Illegal Bikes

A bike with superb performance will not necessarily be the greatest racing bike. The fastest bike in the world is of limited use if it fails to comply with the rules. The prototype track bike shown here did not qualify for the 1986 World Championships because the *Union Cycliste Internationale* (UCI), cycling's governing body, ruled that its one-piece **monocoque** frame was illegal. Only five years later the bike was deemed track legal. The rules had been relaxed to catch up with technological advances. The regulations specifying exactly what a bike is are now limited mainly to the dimensions. A bike is now UCI-legal if it is "viable, marketable, and able to be used by all types of sporting cyclist." These new rules allow bike builders to use modern materials and designs in order to get the ultimate in performance from their machines.

SADDLE POST: By designing the frame so that it extends all the way to the saddle, the bike has a much more aerodynamic structure. The bike is custom-fitted to the rider and the seatpin has only 1.2 cm of up-down adjustment.

SEAT-POST ANGLE: The angle of the seat post is 75 degrees – a steep angle which moves the rider forward over the bottom bracket and allows for a riding position with the chest open.

DROPOUTS: These are solid carbon-fiber and are an integral part of the frame. Smooth-surfaced washers prevent the wheel nuts from marring the relatively soft carbon-fiber.

FIXED WHEEL: In keeping with the minimalist design of time-trial bikes, there is a single speed fixed wheel.

STREAMLINED FRAME
*Since it is molded in carbon-fiber, the Windcheetah Monocoque eliminates traditional tubes and this creates a more streamlined frame. The means to hold the wheels, **cranks**, forks, saddle, and the handlebars are all in one piece. Built by Mike Burrows as an exercise in streamlining, the frame is as stiff as a regular steel frame. The complete bike weighs 20 lb (9 kg).*

GULL-WING HANDLEBARS
*Machined from solid aluminum, the **airfoil** section of these handlebars is designed to minimize aerodynamic **drag**. Although the bars are heavier than regular round-tube handlebars, the shape is more aerodynamic, compensating for any weight disadvantages.*

• FRAME: Apart from being aerodynamic, light, and strong, **monocoque** frames can be tailored precisely to the rider and riding conditions to create the perfect bike. The number of layers of composite materials can be decided at the construction stage, depending on the strength and the amount of flex needed.

• HANDLEBARS: The head tube angle is 73 degrees to allow for fairly fast handling.

• SINGLE FORK BLADE: By substituting a single fork blade for the double forks, the weight, as well as aerodynamic **drag**, is greatly reduced. The material used originally, aluminum, had to be replaced because it flexed too easily.

• FRONT WHEEL: The small 24 in (61 cm) front wheel makes for a shorter **wheelbase** of 37 in (94 cm).

WHEEL: What the 24 in (61 cm) front wheel yields in its aerodynamic advantage tends to be offset by the increased rolling resistance that is inherent in smaller wheels. On a later model it was replaced by a 25.7 in (66 cm) wheel. •

• BRAKE: There is only one fork blade, so there is not a convenient mounting place for a cantilever or side-pull brake. A **hub brake** was the most elegant solution. The cable is routed through the fork and bars to further reduce **drag**.

Race Clothing

When choosing clothes, a racing cyclist has to take into account not only the type of race and weather conditions, but also the rules governing clothes laid down by the organization running the event. The rules are tight for road racers, less exacting for time trialists, and almost non-existent for triathletes, who jump out of the water in a quick-drying swimsuit and straight onto a bike. By contrast, road racers must wear a race jersey, cycling shoes, socks, shorts, and a helmet to meet the required safety regulations. For a stage racer who spends as much as four hours on a bike, protection and comfort are of vital importance, which explains the strict rules that are placed on their race clothing by the ruling bodies.

Ruling Body

The rules for racing cyclists are fixed by the *Union Cycliste Internationale*. The Swiss-based UCI is the cycling equivalent of the United Nations – it is no less unwieldy, but just as powerful in its field and answerable only to its 138-nation congress.

TRIATHLETE CLOTHING
Triathletes can wear what they want, according to UCI rules. The real test is whether the clothing works.

SINGLET: A running singlet is all that a triathlete needs for a 25-mile (40-km) time trial on a dry, warm day.

TRUNKS: After swimming, these trunks are comfortable for riding and running. Features include crotch padding and quick-drying material that disperses water and sweat.

The UCI has been criticized by those trying to make bicycling a popular television sport for preventing jerseys displaying individual names of riders for the benefit of the cameras. The UCI says that it refuses to let the riders look like billboards.

Shaving Legs

Professional cyclists all shave their legs because smooth skin is easier for the *soigneur*, a team masseur, to lubricate as part of the warm-up and warm-down massages. Racing as hard and as frequently as they do, cuts and knocks are very common and smooth skin is easier to clean and bandage. The notion that clean legs will make you more aerodynamic and save vital seconds is based, like all good myths, on a grain of truth: wind tunnel tests have shown that shaved legs save five seconds on a 25-mile (40-km) time trial – 0.2 seconds a mile. Despite this tiny advantage, amateurs shave their legs before a big race just to feel psychologically prepared.

ROAD-RACE CLOTHING

Despite having to meet the strict criteria laid down by the UCI, a racer can wear many types of clothing. Cycling jerseys are available in wool, wool and acrylic, and spandex. Shorts can be lined with the traditional chamois or with a more popular synthetic lining. Whatever type of jersey or shorts you choose, make sure that they are a good fit; there is no point in economizing.

SHORTS: These are long to stop thighs chafing against the saddle, and are made from a nylon/spandex material to prevent them from riding right up.

JERSEY: This allows the body to breathe and soak up sweat. It has three to five pockets at the back to carry spares or food.

RACING SHOES: Integrated shoe and pedal systems use specially designed pedals and **cleats** that lock together and keep your feet on the pedals.

Bikes for the Tour de France

To win the great Tour de France, the world's most famous bicycle race covering more than 2,000 miles (3,220 km) each July, a racer needs to win, or come close to winning, in the mountains, the time trials, and in the rest of its 23 hotly contested stages. Over the years three types of bike have been developed for the different race conditions. With as little as 8 seconds and a set of innovative aero bars being the difference between first and second place in the seventy-sixth Tour, riders are now seeking whatever technological edge they can. Apart from the $200,000 prize money, there is the potential for the winner to earn ten times that amount in sponsorship and endorsements. As a result, challengers for the yellow jersey keep their bikes under wraps until the last minute.

WHEELS: Aerodynamic resistance created by rotating wheels is reduced with a disk wheel at the rear and a radially spoked front wheel that minimizes weight.

HILL-CLIMB BIKE

The TVT is an impressive new road-racing bike that was the winning frame of the 1990 and 1991 Tours. A racing cyclist increases gear size on the way up a hill. Starting in the lowest and most comfortable gear, he climbs, moving up through the gears and increasing speed with each change. When descending a hill, the best place for a rider to be is second, about 30 ft (9 m) behind the stage leader, but still able to catch him.

WEIGHT: TVT bikes weigh just over 20.9 lb (9½ kg), which shaves 1.1 lb off the weight of an equivalent steel-tubed bike.

TIME-TRIAL BIKE

*As it's the finish time that counts, time-trial equipment, such as on this Condor, is light and aerodynamic to save vital seconds. The handlebar **stem** is lower to create a more streamlined position and the front derailleur has been removed to save weight on a flat course. There are two types of time trial in the Tour – individual and team. The individual time trials in the middle of the Tour can be crucial because a virtuoso performance can close the gap on the race leaders. In the team time trial, speed is maximized by each nine-man team riding in a tight formation in the slipstream of the lead rider, who rotates every few seconds.*

BUILT TO CLIMB

Tour de France winners are made and broken on the massive cols of the Alps and the Pyrenees that dominate its middle stages, with 1-in-4 gradients and climbs of 10,000 feet (3,000 m) in one day. The most grueling of these is the 113-mile (183-km) L'Alpe D'Huez stage where riders ascend and descend the 5,000-foot (1,525-m) Col de Madeleine before climbing the 22 hairpin bends of the 6,000-foot (1,830-m) L'Alpe D'Huez. With this formidable challenge, saving weight becomes a major priority. Improved manufacturing means carbon-fiber frames can now weigh as little as 2 lb (0.91 kg). They will probably be a dominating factor in the Tour for many more years to come.

HELMET: Since 1991 helmets have been compulsory on the Tour de France, but many riders still shun them despite incurring fines. Many claim that head-gear makes them too hot.

COMPONENTS: Racers stick to top-quality proven equipment, in preference to ultra-lightweight parts.

ROAD-RACER

*In the many road races that dominate the Tour, a rider needs endurance, power and a bike to match, such as this Rossin Carbon-fiber. The frame has to be reliable, responsive, and solid enough for the rider to remain stable while jostling and battling for a position in the **peloton**.*

Tour de France

Stage racing is a supreme test of road-racing ability, and the *Tour de France* is the ultimate stage race. To win the hardest event in cycling, a rider has to be both physically and mentally sharp, and be a disciplined strategist with a talent for time-trialing, climbing, and sprinting. Riders need to have an unswerving determination which must last them the duration of the event. Twice-winners of the Tour occur rarely and are treated like gods in the cycling world.

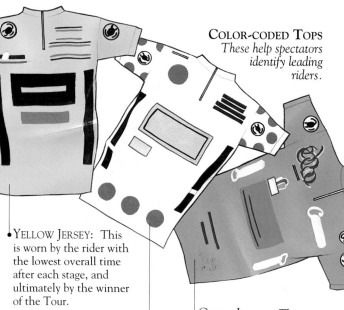

COLOR-CODED TOPS
These help spectators identify leading riders.

YELLOW JERSEY: This is worn by the rider with the lowest overall time after each stage, and ultimately by the winner of the Tour.

POLKA DOT TOP: This is won by the rider with most points from the climbing stages.

GREEN JERSEY: This signifies a cyclist with the most points from sprints.

CONTACT SPORT
The Tour is the world's third largest sporting event and one where spectators can come within an arm's reach of the competitors. The crowds in excess of 300,000 gathered early in the morning to watch the Tour leader Greg LeMond of the United States and Spain's Pedro Delgado (below) heading a break on the Alpine slopes.

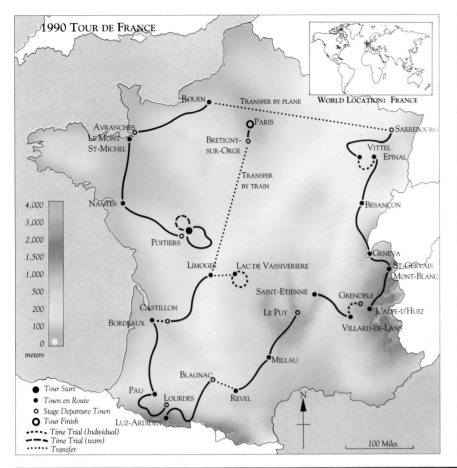

1990 TOUR DE FRANCE

ROUEN
TRANSFER BY PLANE
PARIS
AVRANCHES
LE MONT ST-MICHEL
BRETIGNY-SUR-ORGE
SARREBOURG
VITTEL
EPINAL
TRANSFER BY TRAIN
NANTES
BESANÇON
POITIERS
LIMOGES
LAC DE VASSIVERIERE
GENEVA
ST-GERVAIS MONT-BLANC
SAINT-ETIENNE
GRENOBLE
CASTILLON
LE PUY
L'ALPE-D'HUEZ
BORDEAUX
VILLARD-DE-LANS
MILLAU
BLAGNAC
PAU
LOURDES
REVEL
LUZ-ARDIDEN

WORLD LOCATION: FRANCE

4,000
3,000
2,000
1,500
1,000
500
200
100
0
meters

● Tour Start
● Town en Route
○ Stage Departure Town
◉ Tour Finish
▬ ▪ ▪ ▬ Time Trial (Individual)
▬ ▬ ▬ Time Trial (team)
▪ ▪ ▪ ▪ Transfer

N

100 Miles

THE ROUTE

Politics and business dictate the route (left) of the Tour de France. Each year the course changes: town councils and real estate developers compete for the Tour hoping that the media coverage will focus on their locality for one day, giving it a small taste of celebrity. There are no rules, no set number of time trials or hill climbs required in planning the big event. The route is seldom continuous, with the competitors flying between each stage on the rest days. The tour can even leave France and stretch over the border into neighboring countries, if the price is attractive enough to the organizers.

THE PELOTON

The pack (below) is the "motor" of any stage race and is critical for the pace and energy necessary to the Tour. Most team riders, also known as domestiques, are underpaid and over-used gofers for team leaders. The team rider's main role is a strategic one, keeping in a good position near the front of the pack to join any sudden breaks or avoid crashes. They must even be prepared to sacrifice their own water bottles and wheels to keep their leader high up in the rankings.

Criterium Racing

Criterium, or multilap "around the houses" races are fast and action-packed, with lots of prizes, and are highly popular, particularly in the US. The overall distances range from 25 to 62 miles (40 to 100 kilometers), on short courses through city center streets or parks. They are exciting for spectators because the riders pass by every 2 to 3 minutes. There can be 100 or more laps per race, and on many of these the riders compete furiously for special prizes. There are two types of criteriums: in one, the first rider over the finish line is the winner; in points races, the winner is the rider with the highest number of points for winning selected laps in the race. There are also primes: extra prizes for winning particular laps.

CRITERIUM BIKES
*Criterium frames (right) are stiff for efficiency, and tight for responsiveness and quick handling. The shorter-than-usual **cranks** allow the rider to pedal deeper into corners, and more quickly out of them – in a 100-corner race, a 4- or 6-pedal stroke-per-corner advantage can prove decisive.*

SADDLE HEIGHT: Saddle height is on the high side, for maximum power.

GEOMETRY: For fast, nimble handling, the front end geometry is sharp: with the forks **raked** at 1½ in or less, and **trail** at around 2 in.

WHEELS AND TIRES: Wheels are stiff and strong and tires as light as the smoothness of the course will safely allow – sometimes as little as 6 oz (165 g).

TIRE GLUE: Tires must be strongly glued to withstand constant cornering and sprinting.

BOTTOM BRACKET: The bottom bracket is slightly higher than on a regular road race bike, and the **cranks** should be 2.5 mm shorter than the rider would use on a road bike.

CHAIN STAYS: The chain stays can be 15¾ in (40 cm) or less, and the **wheelbase** is 38½ in (98 cm) or less.

TIRE AGE: For optimum performance, riders age their tires for 6 to 12 months and then break them in, scuffing the tread to help adhesion.

SPECTATOR SPORT

*Short courses and plenty of action
make criterium races (right) perfect for
television. As a blend of road and track
racing, there is something for everyone.
In addition to fixed cameras on the
course, a motorcycle and camera run
in a special lane alongside the riders,
capturing the excitement of sprints
and breakaways.*

● **STEM:** The stem and bars are
lower than on a road bike,
to improve aerodynamics.

● **BAR-END SHIFTERS:** *Grip Shift* or bar-
end shifters are popular; in a sudden
sprint, reaching for a down-tube mounted
shift lever would cost a rider valuable
fractions of a second.

● **HEAD TUBE:**
Depending on frame
size, head tube angles
run up to 75°.

CORNER TACTICS

Criteriums are won on corners. A short 40-km
(25-mile) race may have a hundred or more corners,
a long 100-km (62-mile) event several hundred.
Riders try to corner as fast as they possibly can. The
easiest riding position is near the front of the pack,
where the pace is smoother and faster, there is less
chance of becoming involved in a crash, and the
breakaway attempts will be made. As the main pack
funnels into corners, the riders have to slow down
and then accelerate hard to regain speed. There is a
lot of jostling and pushing as the tightly compressed
riders fight for position, and it is common enough
for a rider to fall and take down a good portion
of the pack. Tactics are very varied, depending on
the points and primes, and whether the rider is solo
or part of a team working together. Either way, the
racing is very personal, with the riders marking
and stalking each other, constantly poised for
instantaneous action. As all types of riders have
a chance for one of the prizes, the riding is
fast and furious, and you must have speed in
your legs for the final sprint to the line.

Time-Trial Bikes

Called the "race of truth," the individual time trial provides one of cycle racing's severest tests. It is a race requiring sustained all-out effort, as competitors ride as fast as possible over a fixed distance, for example 10, 25, 50 or 100 miles (16, 40, 80, or 160 km) or for a fixed time: 1, 12 or 24 hours. A time-trial (TT) rider requires a bike that is both aerodynamic and light. Aerodynamics take priority because, as wind-tunnel tests have shown, a rider's body position at speeds of 20 to 30 mph (30 to 50 km/h) is the major cause of wind resistance. The **drag** factor can be reduced by 25 percent by not riding upright, but crouched with arms resting on aero bars. This position requires its own frame geometry, and this has led to the modern "funny bike" with its short head-tube, sloping top-tube, aero handlebars, and wedge-shaped, aerodynamic tubing.

SEAT TUBE: This is steeper than on a racing bike, positioning the rider farther over the bottom bracket, increasing pedaling efficiency.

DISK WHEEL: Structurally stronger and more aerodynamic than a conventionally spoked wheel, a solid disk wheel is only suitable on the back. Here it is effectively shielded by legs and frame tubes and is therefore less likely to act like a sail in a crosswind.

NARROW TIRES: Very light silk tires with smooth treads have the lowest **drag**. Serious TT riders inflate theirs with helium, which is lighter than air and saves about ⅓ oz (10 gm) per tire.

PEDALS: Clipless pedals are preferable because they perform more efficiently than toe straps and create less **drag**.

ITALIAN TIME-TRIAL BIKE

The Rossin is a specialist bike that incorporates many features common to time-trial bikes, including disk wheels, narrow tires, and aero bars. However, aero bars have only recently been permitted in time trials run under UCI rules, and are unlikely to be accepted in mass-start stage racing. This is because they are thought to be unsafe, destabilizing the front end when a rider has to transfer weight from the bars or steer sharply.

DRAG REDUCTION
*Clip-on aero bars reduce **drag** by about 12 percent compared with riding in a racing crouch using upturned cowhorn bars.*

•HEAD TUBE: Head angle and fork **rake** are shallower than on a racing bike in order to increase steering stability.

•THREE-SPOKE WHEEL: This has less aerodynamic **drag** than a conventionally spoked wheel. It avoids the windsail effect and, depending on type, performs as well as, if not better than, a disk wheel, making it suitable for use on the front.

•WHEEL DIAMETER: A small front wheel offers less **drag** than a large one, is stiffer, weighs less, and requires less frame to mount it in, making the bike lighter. However, it has more rolling resistance, which can cancel out these advantages.

DID YOU KNOW?
The fastest one-hour time trial ever ridden was in January 1984 when the Italian Francesco Moser rode 31.78 miles (51.15 km) on a track in Mexico City.

Riding a Time Trial

There's no better way to get into cycle racing than learning to ride a time trial. Whatever your age, riding against the clock is the quickest way to gauge fitness and speed. It introduces you to the feat of maintaining constant pace and energy over a given distance. By trying to beat a personal best, you learn to endure long rides at sustained speeds. These skills are vital for mass-start races, where the self-reliant and strongest riders are best able to deal with any breaks and chases from the pack.

BODY POSITION: Your back should be flat, not hunched, to aid aerodynamics. Keep your chest open for easier breathing.

HELMET: A lightweight helmet is designed for minimum wind resistance. The tapered tail should fill the gap behind the head.

STARTING POSITION
For a stationary start, a rider needs balance. Racers start at one minute intervals – the fastest riders starting last.

GEARING: Use the highest gear you feel comfortable with. Professionals use a 55T chainring with a 12 – 18 straight block. Lighter gears for amateurs are a 52T chainring with a 13 – 19 straight block.

CLOTHING: Skinsuits or spider suits, with gloves as an integral part, have aerodynamic advantages in trial racing.

OFFICIAL: Race official provides rider with stability.

TIRE PRESSURES: Back tires are as high as 140 psi (105 psi for other races).

LEGS: Warm-up oils keep shaved legs smooth and supple.

CADENCE: On flat runs the cadence should be 86 – 92 rpm. Rest legs by easing off for five strokes on one side, then the other.

CYCLE COMPUTERS

The ability to check frequently on time, speed, and pace has added a whole new dimension to racing. Instead of merely estimating their progress, race cyclists can detect from the button-operated digital readout on their handlebars when they are under-achieving, and when they can afford to hold back.

Available Types

Stage racers and time-trial riders favour the smallest, lightest computers, such as the ½-oz *Avocet 30* (bottom, near right) or the *Cateye Vectra* (top, near right). Both give baseline readouts of current and maximum speed, trip and total distance, timer, and clock. The *Vectra* displays an average speed, as does the *Altimeter 50* (bottom, far right), which has an altimeter to record how far mountain racers have climbed in feet above sea level. The computers read the speed off a front wheel magnet and sensor wired to the computer. The exception is *Cateye Cordless* (top, far right), where data is transmitted from a sensor on the front forks.

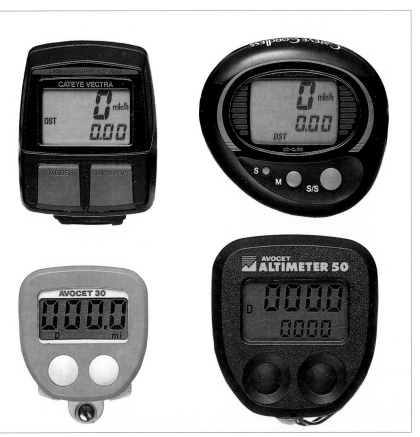

Successful time-trialing is an art, and requires serious preparation. For a club time trial you should receive course details beforehand, to check the route. Most time trials are held early in the morning, so get up early to wake your body up and eat a light breakfast.

Warming Up

Before the start of the race, warm up by riding five miles (eight km), at about 75 percent of the effort you will put in later. While you wait on the start ramp for your turn to go, pick a low gear and start to practise breathing; that way your lungs will be filled with air when you explode onto the course. Then settle into a high gear and breathe regularly. If you go full out too soon, you're likely to go into oxygen debt. This occurs when you are out of breath, using more oxygen than your body can supply. Experienced racers flirt with oxygen debt, avoiding it until the last half-mile, when they go flat out.

THE ULTIMATE CONTEST

Dedicated time-trial rider John Pritchard (right), British 50- and 25-mile champion, sees time-trialing as the ultimate contest.

Triathlete Bikes

Tri bikes are the newest breed of racing bike. Because the cycling section of a standard full triathlon is a 25-mile (40-km) time trial sandwiched between a long-distance swim and a 6-mile (10-km) run, a tri bike needs to be both fast and comfortable. Early triathletes experimented with fast-steering time-trial bikes, but quickly discovered that these were torture on arms already exhausted from the swim. In their quest for speed they adopted the forward-over-the-saddle style of track riders, but found that this shifted too much weight to the forearms. This was solved by aero bars with elbow pads, but they left the rider too far forward. The solution was to turn the seat post around so that the saddle moved forward.

RACE CLOTHING: Lightweight trunks made from quick-drying fabric avoid time-wasting changes between swimming and cycling stages.

RACE NUMBERS: These are obligatory on the front, back and sides for officials to register the triathletes as they pass through checkpoints.

SADDLE POSITION: The steep 80-degree seat angle allows the saddle to be about 4 in (10 cm) farther forward than in a conventional frame, so that the rider can rest naturally on the bars.

IRONMEN ON TRIAL
*European champion Yves Cordier (above) competes in the Hawaii Ironman, the world's longest and most prestigious triathlete event. During the 112-mile (180-km) ride across the island, riders face heat, humidity, and 40 mph (65 km/h) headwinds. The rules are the same as in a time trial: riders are penalized if they ride closer to one another than 33 ft (10 m). This prevents the unfair advantage of **drafting**, where a rider saves energy by riding in another's slipstream.*

THE UNIQUE TRIATHLON BIKE

Aero bars can save up to three minutes in a 25-mile (40-km) time trial. Riding on aeros allows a rider to sustain the optimum power position – hips forward over bottom bracket – for long periods. Power output apart, this type of pedaling extends hamstring muscles to a greater extent, making it easier for the transition to running. One of the first purpose-built bikes, the Quintana Roo Superform, is designed from its aero bars back. The forward rider position has meant radical changes in the frame geometry with a shallow head-angle to stabilize the problems aero bars can create, and a steep 80-degree seat-tube angle to place the saddle farther forward over the bottom bracket.

RIDING POSITION: By resting on his forearms, the rider's upper body weight is spread right through the skeletal system. A road racer achieves the same position in sprints when riding on drop bars, but the resulting muscular tension diverts energy away from pedaling.

GEAR-SHIFT LEVERS: The gear levers are within the reach of a thumb. This eliminates instability while changing gear in such a forward position.

AERO BARS: These allow triathletes to adopt the lower, more aerodynamic, **aero tuck** for long periods – which is vital when they are going flat out.

WHEEL SIZE: The 26-inch front wheel gives a sleeker profile for reduced wind resistance.

DID YOU KNOW?

• The first triathlon, the Hawaii Ironman, was run in 1976 to settle an argument among a group of sports-mad ex-servicemen who could not agree which sport – swimming, cycling, or running – produced the best all-around athlete. Since Hawaii already had three classic events, a 112-mile (180-km) cycle race, a 2.4-mile (3.9-km) ocean swim, and a 26.2-mile (42.3-km) marathon, it was decided to combine all three.

• Dave Scott, inventor of tri bars, has won the Hawaii Ironman six times and was also the first to complete the course in under nine hours.

• Riding the bike section, Ironman competitors average speeds of 23 mph (37 km/h) – equivalent to those of professional road racers.

• Triathlons are so popular that 10-year-olds compete in junior "Ironkids" events, swimming 109 yds (100 m), cycling 4¼ miles (7 km), and running ⁹⁄₁₀ mile (1 km).

Ultra-Marathons

In demonstrating the art of the possible, the transcontinental 3,100-mile (4,960-km) Race Across America (RAAM), the world's longest nonstop bicycle race, is without equal. Physically, it's the equivalent of running 58 marathons or even swimming the English Channel 18 times consecutively. This event is an all-out race without any stages or yellow jerseys, set against the vast panorama of America. Riders cannot **draft**, and there are no rules imposing sleep or rest: all that counts is being first across the finish line. Exhaustion and dehydration result in almost half the competitors failing to finish.

THE ROUTE

No two RAAM routes are the same. Conceived in 1978 by John Marino after riding from Los Angeles to New York in 13 days, 1 hour, 20 minutes, the fastest time has fallen steadily to Paul Solon's 1989 record 8 days, 8 hours, 45 minutes. Women's holder Susan Notorangelo took 9 days, 9 hours, and 9 minutes. The 1990 route (below) was the first to avoid the northeastern US, and included instead three 9,000-ft (2750-m) Colorado passes. Crews are issued with 60-page route plans detailing over 900 checkpoints, but riders still get lost.

GOING SOLO

After the first 30 miles (48 km) the riders begin to spread out. To retain motivation, riders obtain news of rivals by radio contact with a spy car, or from the 80 time stations at 30-50-mile (48-80-km) intervals along the vast route.

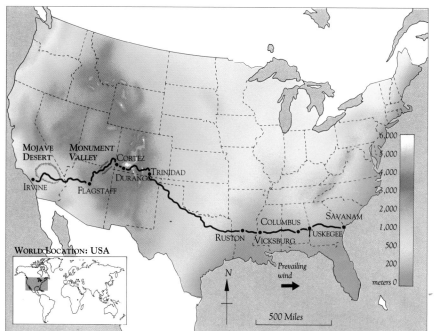

DID YOU KNOW?

- Excellent bike skills, a reliable crew, meticulous nutritional attention, and total mental and physical concentration are vital to your chances of winning a RAAM. These skills come only with experience: with one exception, every champion has been an "also-ran" in past years.
- On a flat stretch of road with no major winds, riders average 16-22 mph (26-35 km/h). With sleep/rest breaks, this drops to 13-15 mph (21-24 km/h).
- Riders use public roads, and traffic laws must be observed. Each breach results in a penalty of 15 minutes off the bike at the final time station. Six tickets result in a disqualification.

FOOD TO GO
An efficient and harmonious support crew providing food, clothing changes, and mechanical support is crucial. A minimum crew of six includes a medic, a masseur, and mechanics working in shifts.

FORERUNNER TO AERO BARS
1986 winner Pete Penseyres (below) added a homebrew platform to his handlebars. The two padded cups were custom-made, enabling him to support his body weight. A third brake lever was attached to allow braking without shifting position.

SLEEP-STARVED
Riders get about three hours sleep a night. The most dangerous time is in the chilly hours between midnight and sun-up. Each successive night of stopping gets worse (right). Hallucinations are common and riders crash falling asleep pedaling.

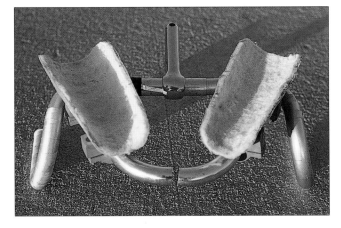

Track Racing

Track racing is bicycle racing in its fastest and most exciting form. Unlike road or mountain-bike racing, track racing is natural theater, almost gladiatorial in style. Spectators can watch the drama of a tense and tightly contested race in an enclosed amphitheater-like pit of a velodrome. The top-class track meets are a variety show, involving several different types of race: individual and team, sprint, pursuit, and time trial, in different combinations. As pure entertainment, the races vary from suspense to psychological thrillers, to marvels of endurance. The stars who please the crowd are those racers who climax a sprint by combining both nerve and strength to hurtle off the steep banking at speeds of up to 50 mph (80 km/h).

INDIVIDUAL PURSUIT
This is a physically and psychologically testing event in which two riders start at opposite ends of the track. The winner is the one who catches his opponent or records the fastest time. Distances vary from 3.1 miles (5 km) for professionals, to 1.91 miles (3 km) for women and juniors.

PURSUIT BICYCLE
A track bike (right) set up for riding pursuits is similar to a road time-trial bike (see p.74), but without brakes or gears. It is set up for sheer speed and an aerodynamic riding position. The one noticeable difference in frame geometry is that a pursuit bike has a slightly shorter wheelbase because there is less clearance between the front wheel and pedals. On road bikes this clearance prevents a foot catching as the front wheel steers into a corner. On the track there is no need to turn and, in effect, the bike follows a straight line around the velodrome bowl.

•RIDING POSITION: A relaxed crouch is the perfect riding position as it is aerodynamic and provides a comfortable stance for powerful pedaling.

NO GEARS OR BRAKES: To be track-legal, a bicycle has neither gears nor brakes, as there are no gradients to climb or obstacles to stop for.•

MATCH SPRINT RACES

These aggressive, physical contests consist of two or three riders competing over 3282 feet (1000 m) (left). They combine a game of cat-and-mouse tactics throughout the race with a final explosive burst of speed just before the finish line. Riders spend the first 2625 feet (800 m) jockeying for a decent position. This is because only the times for the last 657 feet (200 m) are ever recorded. The minimum circumference of an Olympic-class velodrome is never less than 1092 feet (333 m), though indoor tracks can be as small as 492 feet (150 m). With banking in the velodrome as steep as 50 degrees to the horizontal, sprinters can often reach speeds of up to 50 mph (80 km/h).

SPRINT BICYCLE

*Sprint bikes (below) are the greyhounds of bicycle racing, ultra-lightweight 17-20 lb (7½-9 kg) machines with short **wheelbases**, tight angles, and deeply curved drop bars for sharp handling. Bottom brackets are positioned higher than on road bikes so that the right pedal does not hit the banking during the initial slow stages of a match sprint.*

HUBS: Large flange hubs require shorter spokes. They also help to create a laterally stiffer wheel to cope with the greater forces generated by violent sprinting.

SEAT ANGLES: Track bikes have steeper seat angles 74-75 degrees than short-**wheelbase** road bikes. This allows for very fast handling since the track is a flat, vibration-free surface.

FIXED WHEEL: The hub on a track-bike rearwheel is a fixed single cog. On a fixed wheel, the **cranks** do not stop rotating until the bike stops traveling, so the rider has to keep pedaling at all times.

The Entertainers

Almost since the bicycle was first invented, promoters have been selling track racing as entertainment. Whether it's Keirin racing in Japan or Six-Day racing in Europe, these are events where sport and spectacle merge, the audience is king, and high ticket prices entice the cream of cycle racing to star in events providing thrills, spills, and glamour. Keirin stars are among Japan's highest-paid sportsmen, capable of grossing up to $300,000 a season. In Europe only proven road and track stars are invited to join the privileged Six-Day riders, whose winter earnings can easily outstrip all but those of a Tour de France winner.

Six-Day Racing

From November to March, Europe's finest earn their living riding the boards in indoor arenas. Modern Six-Day racing is not as grueling as the original races in America at the turn of the century, when riders pedaled around a circuit for six days, with only brief stops for sleep and massages. C.W. Miller set the record in 1897, riding 2,088 miles (3,361 km) and spending less than 10 hours off his bike. Injuries and exhaustion were so common that laws limited these nightmare marathons to only 12 hours per rider. Promoters evaded the law by having teams of two cycling alternately, thus still riding around the clock. Modern Sixes are more civilized, lasting only 8 hours a day. The Madison Race is a focal event in Six-Day racing, with up to 12 teams competing and as many as 24 riders on the track. Excitement is greatest during high-speed handovers between teammates, or in the tactical maneuvering that takes place before the fast sprints, which occur every 10 laps to accumulate points.

A NIGHT AT THE RACES
Spectators line the banking as riders hurtle around a 820-ft (250-m) wooden indoor track in Munich. In the center, rich spectators dine and enjoy the two-wheeled floor show.

THE ART OF KEIRIN

Every year over 25 million Japanese flock to watch Keirin racing – easily acknowledged as the toughest and most competitive track racing in the world. Unlike Six-Day racing, where there is always the occasional clown to take advantage of a lull during races, Keirin racing is deadly serious and is cycling's answer to greyhound racing. Invented in the 1950s to take advantage of gambling-madness, Keirin racing is the exception to the old rule that you should never bet on anything that can talk. More than $2.4 billion are bet every year on Keirin racing events. There are over 50 velodromes devoted to hosting Keirin races, and a whole score of magazines and newspapers available on the subject. When major races are held during the season, they are always networked on national television to a large audience.

FOLLOW THE HARE

The essence of Keirin is of a cycle sprint contested over 1.2 miles (2,000 meters), which is about five laps in a Japanese velodrome. The decisive action in the race takes place in the final 654 feet (200 meters). Each of the 9 riders, who have been kept in quarantine for 3 whole days beforehand to prevent bribery, begin the race in numbered stalls like greyhounds. About 300 feet (91 meters) ahead is the "human hare." When the starting gun goes off there is a mad dash to tuck in behind the hare's back wheel. The hare winds up the pace as the riders jockey for a decent position, before peeling off in the back straight of the penultimate lap. Then all hell breaks loose as the real race starts and the riders elbow their way forward. Shoulder pads and helmets are essential and crashes at 37 mph (60 km/h) are not uncommon.

Exercises for Cycling

If you do no other exercise to improve your cycling, you should at least stretch. Cycling exercises many muscle groups, but doesn't stretch them. It tightens them, and unless you release them you run the risk of injury. Stretching prevents this and as an added benefit, it improves posture. Try to stretch every morning and evening. Always do so before a ride to warm your muscles and after a ride to aid their recovery.

QUADRICEPS
Stand on your left leg, grasp the ankle of your right leg with your right hand, and pull up. Keep your hips forward to avoid bending your back. Hold the position for 30 seconds, then repeat with the other leg at least once.

CALF STRETCH
Start with the feet about 24 in (60 cm) from a wall. Lean forward with both hands against the wall and move one foot toward the wall so that the other leg is extended and the calf muscle stretched. Hold for 30 seconds, then repeat at least once with other leg.

BACK: As you bend forward, bend from the hips to avoid straining your back.

HAMSTRING STRETCH
Pedaling will contract hamstrings. To stretch them, stand with feet together, cross one foot over the other, and drop your head to allow the weight of your head and arms to move forward and down as far as they will comfortably go. Hold for 30 seconds, then repeat at least once with the other leg.

POSITION: Place your feet at a comfortable distance from the wall so you don't have to stretch forward.

PRESSURE: Hold your ankle so that your leg stays right in line with your thigh. Avoid pulling out sideways, as this will place unwanted pressure on your knees.

DORSAL LIFT

1 Lie flat on the floor, face down, hands cupped under your chin.

BACK EXERCISES

The exercises on this page strengthen back muscles. The dorsal lift will strengthen lower back muscles. Sit-ups counteract and complement dorsal lifts as well as strengthening abdominal muscles.

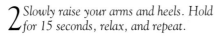

2 Slowly raise your arms and heels. Hold for 15 seconds, relax, and repeat.

SIT-UPS

1 Lie flat on your back, knees bent and arms across your chest. Slowly sit up.

2 Hold for 15 seconds, relax, and repeat 10 to 20 times.

SIDE EXTENSIONS

1 Put your hands and knees on the floor to support your back and hips. Raise your toes off the floor.

2 Bend your head and shoulders to one side, then slowly to the other side. Repeat 10 to 20 times.

BACK EXTENSIONS

1 With hands and knees on the floor allow your head to drop and your back to arch. Hold for 10 seconds.

2 Reverse the last movement, raising both your head and bottom. Repeat 10 to 20 times.

Indoor Training

Riding indoors comes into its own when the weather turns too cold, the roads become icy, darkness falls too early, or you're just too short of time to cycle out of doors. While fixed indoor machines will not improve your bike-handling skills, they can keep your training program humming along, improve strength, and tune your body for the riding season ahead. A wide choice of equipment is available, but the same results can be achieved working out on a no-frills exercise bike as on an ultimate indoor cycling simulator. The difference is price, comfort, and entertainment.

• READOUT: A nine-button, menu-driven, digital readout displays all the information about your performance, which includes heart rate, speed, **cadence**, and calories burned.

RIDING POSITION: By riding your own bike, you ride a machine that is set up for you. In contrast, exercise bikes in health clubs can only be adjusted for an approximate fit and tend to have a riding position that is far too upright.

GEARING: Indoor riding enables you to safely see and feel how your bike handles through an instant push-button gear change.

• SETTING UP: Indoor trainers using your own bike take moments to set up. Fork blade **dropouts** lock into a clamp and the rear wheel sits on a preset roller.

INDOOR TRAINER
*The Schwinn Velodyne is a top-of-the-line indoor trainer that lets you ride your own bike. Sophisticated electronics display your progress along Olympic courses, tracks, and sprints. In stage races you can ride with an imaginary **peloton** that accelerates if you get either ahead or behind, but it eases the pace somewhat when you're within the pack.*

PEDALING RATE: Advanced trainers display your **cadence** – the rate you pedal measured in revolutions per minute of one foot – with sensors attached to the bottom bracket and the **crank** arm. •

CYCLING SIMULATOR

The ultimate in both price and performance, the Precor Electronic Cycling Simulator (above) tries to overcome the major problem that confronts anyone training indoors: boredom. Simulators, favored by both health clubs and gyms, achieve this by monitoring and displaying your performance. You can compete in a group of up to seven people with a color TV wall monitor displaying your relative positions on a given course riding through digitized valleys and up electronically devised hills. Alternatively, you can ride solo on one of 10 preset courses.

The incentive to ride fast is to beat your own personal best, based upon the information displayed on a screen in front of you – speed, average speed, the distance traveled, the number of calories burned, your position in the race, how far ahead (or behind) your nearest opponent is, the course record, the gradient of the simulated road, or the gear you are in. It allows you to develop a variety of challenges to improve the amount of effort you put in, be it chasing a fictional pacemaker or trying to finish in a faster time than before.

LEVELS OF FITNESS

A heart-rate monitor is like a personal speedometer that provides reliable feedback on the amount of effort you put in. A sensor and micro-transmitter are strapped to your chest and feed the information either to a wristwatch digital display, or to the cyclo-computer's mini-screen in front of you.

The Beat of Your Heart

Monitoring your heart rate determines the amount of activity necessary to achieve fitness within safety limits. A conservative estimate of heart rate is a maximum of 220 beats per minute, minus your age. A 30-year-old should have a heart rate of 190. The *maximum* aerobic threshold is 85 percent of the maximum rate; 161 for the 30-year-old. The *minimum* aerobic threshold is 70 percent of the maximum attainable heart rate, which for a 30-year-old is 133. Maximum benefit is achieved by exercising in the 70 to 85 percent target zone for 20 to 30 minutes three times a week. Weight training is not absolutely necessary for racing, but it strengthens the upper body against backache from long hours in the saddle. Cycling is still the best way of conditioning leg muscles: spinning the wheels is effectively lifting a series of small weights very fast.

Training at Home

A folding windtrainer is a good, low-cost set up to ride regularly in a stationary position, with the back axle clamped in a mount and the back wheel on a roller. A sensor linked to a handlebar cyclo-computer (see p.75) gives the necessary information. Rollers are the hardest trainers to ride, but the only ones to improve bike skills. The back wheel rests between two rollers, the front wheel on one, linked to the first rear roller by a belt. The slightest awkward motion is instantly magnified, and rollers force you to ride smoothly with a high **cadence**.

The TOURING BIKE

Chainring

Touring by bike is a real joy. It offers variety and freedom; you can make any journey you care to make, just for its own sake. Touring can be a day spent getting quickly between two points in the countryside; or a three-month transcontinental odyssey; two weeks exploring a foreign country; or a Sunday spent gently discovering the back streets of an historic city. Touring can mean setting off on a once-in-a-lifetime adventure, with pannier racks piled high with loads that would give the average camel a hernia; or it can mean embarking on a long weekend weighed down by nothing heavier than a credit card.

You Decide

A bicycle tour can start from wherever you want: from the front drive, from an airport, a train station, a hotel, or a campsite. You can ride until you feel like stopping, and stop as many times as you like. People tour on

lightweight custom-built machines, on mountain bikes, on a broken-down wreck rescued from the junkyard. Touring can be as planned or as impromptu as you like; you can use maps, or utilize serendipity – taking pot-luck at turnings, and choosing the route as you go. Tours can be professionally organized with someone taking care of the details down

Pedal and strap

Pannier

to the bed linen; or they can demand self-reliance, self-sufficiency, and sleeping bags. Touring can be public, part of a mass ride for a charity, or it can be private. You can ride with friends, family, or plain solo: it is individual. It's like making your own private movie with the breeze on your skin, soaking up images as you coast through memorable landscapes at perfect panning speed. It is exhilarating and exhausting.

Saddle

The Unexpected

Bicycle touring can take you to the highest point on a pass, or leave you, as darkness falls, with 20 miles to go against a battering headwind. Touring exposes you to the elements; it makes you adjust to changes in wind direction and teaches you to watch the sky like a sailor. Touring stimulates and it relaxes: It utilizes the senses, alerts you to fresh smells, to the sound of birdsong, or to the changing light of evening, to the sun on your back. Bike touring is the perfect means of making unexpected, unscheduled trips: It is, in fact, real travel. Bike touring is whatever you make of it and what it makes of you. Make it fun.

Touring cyclist

Touring Bike Anatomy

Long-distance, heavy-load tour bikes are designed for comfort, a stable ride, and predictable handling. The *Cannondale ST1000* is especially stable as it is built from large-diameter aluminum tubing, which resists side-to-side sway. Stability is enhanced by the long chain stays, which keep the weight of the rear panniers centered over the rear wheel without fouling the rider's heels when pedaling. At the front, a relaxed head-tube angle and generous fork **rake** give steady and responsive handling.

Brake lever & cable

Handlebar tape

Leather saddle

Grip Shift gear shifter

Top tube

Crank-arm bolt

Washer

Bottom bracket spindle

Grease seal ring

Ball bearings

Adjustable Fixed cup

Lock ring

Water bottle cage **bosses**

Seat post

Cable housing

Cantilever brake **bosses**

Quick-release hub skewer

Straddle wire

Cable yoke & anchor bolt

Cantilever brake arms & brake shoes

Seat stay

Derailleur hanger

Chain stay

Front derailleur

Chain

Seven-speed freewheel

Spider **crank**

50-tooth chainring

Rear derailleur

Dust cap

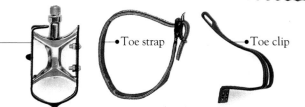

Sealed bearing pedal

Toe strap

Toe clip

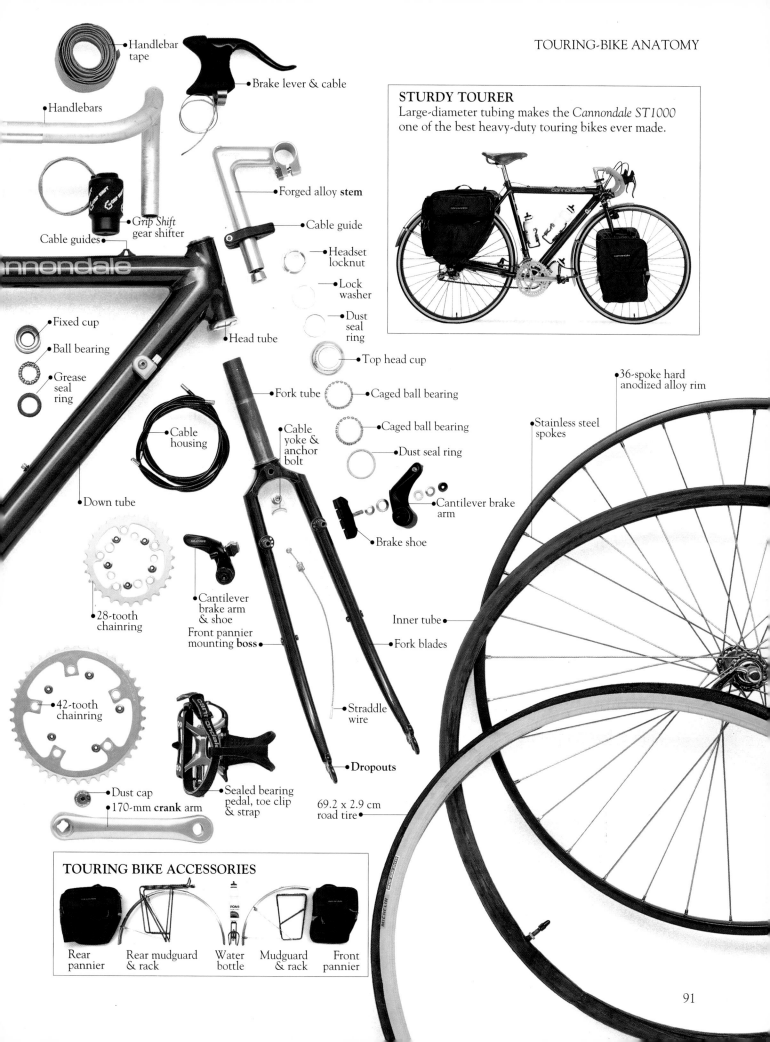

• Handlebar tape

• Brake lever & cable

• Handlebars

Grip Shift gear shifter

Cable guides •

• Forged alloy **stem**

• Cable guide

• Headset locknut

• Lock washer

• Dust seal ring

• Head tube

• Top head cup

• Fork tube

• Caged ball bearing

• Fixed cup

• Ball bearing

• Grease seal ring

• Cable housing

• Cable yoke & anchor bolt

• Caged ball bearing

• Dust seal ring

• Cantilever brake arm

• Brake shoe

• Down tube

• 28-tooth chainring

• Cantilever brake arm & shoe

Front pannier mounting **boss** •

• Fork blades

• Inner tube

• Straddle wire

• 42-tooth chainring

• Dropouts

69.2 x 2.9 cm road tire •

• Dust cap

• 170-mm **crank** arm

• Sealed bearing pedal, toe clip & strap

STURDY TOURER
Large-diameter tubing makes the *Cannondale ST1000* one of the best heavy-duty touring bikes ever made.

• 36-spoke hard anodized alloy rim

• Stainless steel spokes

TOURING BIKE ACCESSORIES

Rear pannier

Rear mudguard & rack

Water bottle

Mudguard & rack

Front pannier

91

The Open Road

Cycle touring is one of the finest ways of seeing the world. On a bike that fits you correctly you can go as fast or slow as you like: a cracking pace for the exhilaration of sheer speed and effort; a lazy meander through picturesque lanes; or a stop, to savor the moment, relax, and take in the view. Some people ride lightweight racing bikes like this *Trek 1200*, and carry no more than a small tool kit and a credit card. Others prefer to be self-contained, and carry tent, sleeping bag, and cooking gear. Some seek remote places, while others explore cities. Touring is about freedom, variety, and fun, riding where and how you like.

ROAD BIKE
The Trek 1200 is a high-performance aluminum-alloy road bike that is used for touring. Only a few years ago it would have been considered a flat-out racing machine.

HAND POSITION: Riding with the hands high on the bars eases the back, stomach, arms, and hands. Riding low does the opposite, but helps on climbs.

HANDLEBARS: These should be at least as wide as your shoulders. Extra width helps keep your chest open for easier breathing.

STEM: A slightly shorter stem than usual gives a more upright riding position and can compensate for riding a larger than normal frame.

FRAMES: Within the guidelines for correct bike sizes (see pp.20-21), a larger rather than a smaller frame is much the best for touring. This gives more stability on descents and on corners.

TIRES: These vary from the very light ⅞-in-wide "speed" models to the 1⅛ in expedition tires.

TOURING SHOES: Reinforced soles give extra support for the foot.

To get the most enjoyment out of touring, set your pace by the efficiency of your heart and lungs, rather than by muscle strength. Pace too fast and you will experience fatigue and sore muscles. Pace too slow and you will be sluggish and lethargic.

Heart and Breath

Your heartbeat and breathing should pick up tempo when riding, and on all but hard climbs, you should be able to converse or sing. A good pedaling rate or **cadence** is essential. Try to spin the **cranks** at about 55-65 rpm. Below 55 rpm, the legs push the cranks through each stroke, building up lactic acid in the muscles and giving great pain. Over 85 rpm may cause an excess use of oxygen, and heavy breathing.

• SADDLE HEIGHT: Unless you are on a racing bike, saddle height should be slightly on the low side, to ease the knees. Shifting back in the saddle will increase height and power for climbing.

• SEAT POST: Three to 4 in (7.5-10 cm) will be exposed when the saddle is at the right height for you.

GEARING: In order to sustain an efficient minimum **cadence** of 55 rpm on climbs, an average rider requires a gear of 24 in (see p.27) for unloaded climbing, and a 19-in gear for loaded climbing.

SADDLES

This is a true story: two cyclists on a 6,000-mile (10,000-km) bike ride to India stopped after the first 100 miles (160 km) because their saddles, one a leather *Brooks Pro*, the other a modern anatomic design, were causing each terrible pain. After swapping saddles, the rest of the journey proceeded without a twinge. Of the available saddles, some are lean and light to reduce weight and friction to the minimum; other anatomic models are shaped to reduce pressure where the pelvic bones meet the saddle; and gel-filled saddles shape to the rider's anatomy. You must find which kind suits you best. Don't judge the saddle just by bouncing on it. As the miles go by, your bottom becomes tougher, and the comfort of a light, slim saddle increases.

WOMEN'S SADDLE
The Madison L22 Anatomic has a contoured base and extra padding at contact points. It is wider than a man's saddle as women have wider pelvic bones.

LEATHER SADDLE
The Brooks B17 saddle has a wide touring design. It needs 500 miles (800 km) of riding before it is broken in, but fit and comfort can be superb.

GEL SADDLE
This Specialized women's saddle filled with elastopolymer gel molds to the shape of the rider. Some swear by the comfort of gel-filled saddles, others swear at them.

STANDARD
A typical saddle found on women's mass production bikes. If it is uncomfortable, a new saddle is an inexpensive way to upgrade.

MOUNTAIN SADDLE
A Brooks Coil-Spring saddle has additional suspension for mountain bikes. This leather Brooks harks back to the days when riding on rough roads was cushioned by saddles with massive coil springs.

Helmets and Touring Clothing

If you value your skull, wear a helmet. Over half of all of the critical injuries and deaths in cycling accidents result from damage to the head. A good helmet dramatically reduces the risk of head injury by cushioning your head from the impact of a fall. Recognition of this has now led to Sweden and a number of US and Australian states making the wearing of helmets compulsory for cyclists.

Safety standards for helmets are international and a helmet should conform to either the **ANSI**, **BSI**, **Snell**, or **AS** standards. These ensure that a helmet fits, stays on in a fall, and that the layer of crushable polystyrene, which absorbs impact, offers sufficient protection. A helmet should fit so that it moves when you wrinkle your brow and doesn't cover the ears or impede your peripheral or front vision in any way.

AIR VENT: The *Bell* logo-plate slides up to reveal an air vent.

PADS: These can be inserted to give a comfortable fit.

LAYERED PROTECTION
The Bell V-1 Pro *has an inner layer of polystyrene to absorb shock and an outer shell that resists penetration.*

QUICK-RELEASE STRAP: If properly adjusted, this should fit snugly under the chin.

TRACK HELMET
The aerodynamic Cinelli "Aero" *is a hard helmet for track racing.*

POLYSTYRENE SHELL
The Specialized "Air Force" *has a polystyrene shell with a mesh cover.*

BANANA HELMET
This Brancale *helmet, made of foam strips, offers very little protection.*

SOFT SHELL
The Bell "Quest" *has a ventilated soft shell with internal reinforcement.*

RACING HELMET
The Giro "Air Attack" *has a hard outer shell on a polystyrene inner.*

HEAD: In winter, wear a warm hat under your helmet. At 40°F (4°C) an uncovered head loses up to 50 percent body heat, and as much as 75 percent at 5°F (–15°C).

BODY: In cold weather, line the inside of a jacket with newspaper, to insulate against any wind chill.

Clothes for touring have to be light, comfortable, and functional. Cycle clothes are best, because they are tailored for riding and have useful features such as conveniently located pockets. What you wear depends on climate and season; but in general, cycling is warm work. You need to prevent overheating on ascents, yet also avoid hypothermia from wind chill on descents. The key is to dress in layers that can be added or peeled off one by one as the conditions change.

SUNGLASSES: These filter UV light and keep grit out of your eyes. Lenses to improve night vision are also available.

CYCLING SHORTS: These stretch to prevent them riding up, and have an absorbent, seamless, chamois-type crotch insert, which gives you greater freedom of movement.

SHOES: Stiff soles and cleats that slot into the pedals are best for riding, but hard to walk in. Most tourists prefer dual-purpose shoes, with soles reinforced for cycling, yet flexible enough for walking.

SEASONAL TOURING CLOTHING

In winter and fall, wear at least two layers of clothing. The inner layer should be a light jersey, cycling undershorts, and socks in a high-tech fabric such as polypropylene that wicks moisture away from the skin and retains body heat. The top layer should be a weatherproof shell in a breathable fabric such as Gore-Tex or Thintech, which keeps out wind and rain, yet allows perspiration to evaporate. In very cold conditions, insulate with a middle layer of wool, fleece, or down-filled garments. Protecting your hands, feet, and head is absolutely necessary. Use full-length gloves, winter shoes or insulated shoe covers, and a Gore-Tex helmet cover.

Mass Rides

Organize 20,000 cyclists for a mass bike ride, and 40,000 will turn up. Since they began in the mid-1970s, mass rides such as the UK's London to Brighton, New York's Five-Boro, Canada's Tour de Montreal, and Mexico's Rosarito to Ensenada have all become cycling phenomena. Each started with just a few hundred riders, and now attract 50,000 cyclists or more, who have to book to be assured of a place. Mass rides are appealing, because being out in the open with a crowd all riding to the same place on a chosen route, often in aid of a charity, generates instant camaraderie. The sense of occasion of a mass ride turns it into a natural jamboree, celebrating the delight of being on the open road, riding at your own pace. All aspects of cycling life surface for such events; some riders arrive in costumes, or on vintage bikes, racers, tourers, mountain bikes, tandems, and **HPV**s. You can create impromptu **pelotons** with the people around you, experiencing the fun of **drafting** and the sensation of moving at high speed in a group. Although mass rides are terrific fun, if you are riding, prepare yourself by obtaining any literature about the route, maps, club notes, potential refreshment points, and where the medical facilities will be based. Make sure your bike is in good working order, and take along a puncture repair kit and basic tools. Carry some food and drink, even if you plan on a refueling stop with some friends.

THE VARIETY OF POLAND
A group of cyclists enter a Polish town during a 2-week tour of Eastern Europe (above). With its absence of cars, Poland has become increasingly popular for bicycle touring.

SOLITUDE OF EASTERN EUROPE
Cycling along quiet roads (right) is just one of the ways of seeing Poland. You can choose between a self-contained tour or a deluxe tour, with prebooked hotels.

LONDON TO BRIGHTON
One of the best ways to start long-distance cycle touring is by entering a mass ride. Well-organized rides like the 56-mile (90.3-km) London-to-Brighton route (left) provide support that is hard to equal. The route along country lanes has already been tried and tested by experienced cyclists. Everything is well-signposted so there is no need to read a map, and traffic hassels are minimal since car access is restricted. There is little to carry; food and mechanical support are provided along the route. There are even special trains to take you home once you get there, so all you have to do is ride.

Sports/Credit-Card Touring

The modern trend in cycle touring is to go fast and light. Popular organized tours now have vans to carry cyclists' baggage or provide extra transport if necessary between stops. Some tours are guided, others give you a map and let you ride at your own pace. The bikes have also adapted to these new riding trends. Traditional touring bikes were designed to remain stable when laden with bags. Sports touring bikes now emphasize performance rather than load-carrying capacity. Credit-card cyclists prefer sophisticated, light bikes and take the minimum of accessories. These new lines all encourage a much more dynamic approach to cycling vacations and tours.

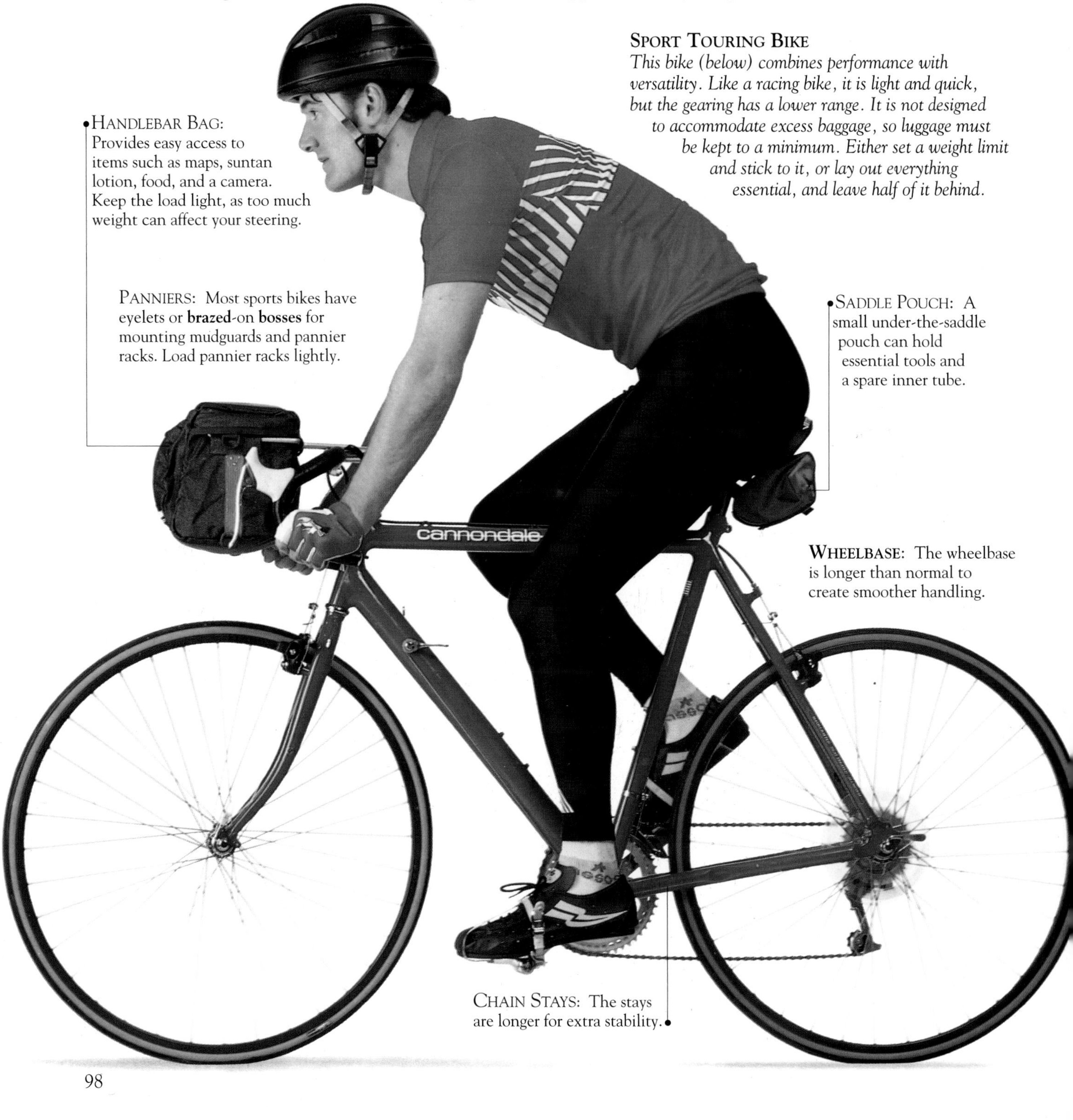

HANDLEBAR BAG: Provides easy access to items such as maps, suntan lotion, food, and a camera. Keep the load light, as too much weight can affect your steering.

PANNIERS: Most sports bikes have eyelets or **brazed**-on **bosses** for mounting mudguards and pannier racks. Load pannier racks lightly.

SPORT TOURING BIKE
This bike (below) combines performance with versatility. Like a racing bike, it is light and quick, but the gearing has a lower range. It is not designed to accommodate excess baggage, so luggage must be kept to a minimum. Either set a weight limit and stick to it, or lay out everything essential, and leave half of it behind.

SADDLE POUCH: A small under-the-saddle pouch can hold essential tools and a spare inner tube.

WHEELBASE: The wheelbase is longer than normal to create smoother handling.

CHAIN STAYS: The stays are longer for extra stability.

LIGHTEN YOUR LOAD

Credit-card touring is pure and simple (right). All you take are the clothes you wear, a small tool kit, and credit cards. You ride hard, fast, and as far as you can get. When you stop, you eat in fine restaurants and stay in comfortable hotels. Touring such long distances, you must become aware of your body's needs. Food is your fuel, so eat often but lightly: fruits, salads, and carbohydrates all transform quickly into usable energy. Fatty foods take too long to digest, and too much sugar can cause the body's metabolic rate to go down, leaving you worse off. You must also drink steadily, and although you may not feel thirsty until you've lost up to half a gallon of fluid, that replenishment is hard to achieve at once. In hot weather you can sweat more than 5 pints an hour.

STAMINA: Build your strength gradually. Limit daily distances to 20 – 30 miles (30 – 50 km). Runs of 50 – 60 miles (80 – 97 km) are the practical limits for regular day-after-day touring.

CREDIT-CARD TOURER

This is the sort of bike (left) that working pro riders, who spend 20,000-odd miles (32,250 km) a year in the saddle, often choose for themselves. These bicycles tend to be sleek, well-finished, and made of ultra-lightweight materials like titanium, carbon-fiber, and aluminum. They are elegant, supple, and comfortable, and extremely fast for traveling long distances.

Major Expeditions

Ever since three Britons pedaled around the world in 1896, the bicycle has proved the perfect means for achieving extraordinary ends. Modern expeditions now tend to be difficult, dangerous, and even exotic, to attract media attention for the charities that back them. With this in mind, cousins Nick and Dick Crane decided to ride to the Center of the Earth. The place most distant from open sea in any direction turned out to be a desert in northwest China. Estimates showed they had just 50 days after the snows melted on the Himalayan passes and before the desert heat crept to 105°F (41°C) in mid-June. They made it in 58 days.

NICK CRANE'S BIKE
The bike was built in lightweight Reynolds 753 tubing by Gerald O'Donovan. Nick has also crossed North Africa's Atlas Mountains and the 14 peaks of Snowdonia, Wales, in 24 hours.

THE FRAME: The light tube frame has a geometry of 74 degrees seat tube and a head tube of 73 degrees.

HAZARDS
A cave (below) provides some nighttime shelter during a blizzard. The Cranes – mountain bike conquerers of Kilimanjaro (see p.38) – also experienced monsoons, snow, ice, dust, temperatures of up to 115°F (46°C), altitudes of 17,500 ft (5,000 m) above sea level and 1,000 ft (300 m) below. They carried no food, no tents, no extra clothes, and just one bottle of water each. Their only breakdowns were two punctures each, and a broken cable caused by Tibetan children playing with a gear lever.

ACTIVE IN THE TRAFFIC
Coping with rickshaw traffic on day two of the journey (below) was far easier than a meeting with the Bangladeshi police, who accused the Cranes of political activism in their country.

GEAR CHANGE: There is no derailleur or front lever, so the inner chainring was shifted by kicking the chain down, or by lifting it up with fingers to change up.

TRAVELING LIGHT

The Cranes' trip was an epic in self-sufficiency (below). All they carried with them were their bikes and minimal spares. Weight saving was critical to avoid extra bulk and subsequent delay on the expedition. Their bikes weighed only 22 lb (10 kg), while their combined luggage and clothes weighed 18 lb (8 kg). Every piece of equipment was pared down to the minimum. The labels were snipped off their underwear, the edges taken off their maps. The wrench was drilled with holes and the spoke key was sawn in half. The chopsticks were partly hollowed out and the lens caps for their cameras were of a special lightweight rubber.

Thick balaclava

Sailor's thermal undershirt

Spare tires

Map of region

Chopsticks

Down sleeping bag

Water bottle

Spare spokes

Pump

Spoke tool

Chain tool

Tire lever

Allen keys

Swiss army knife

Puncture repair kit

Wrench

Lenses

Sunglasses with nose protection

Passport & friend's photo

Pen

Sand mask

Digital watch

Waterproof Gore-Tex trousers

Gore-Tex jacket

Camera & film

Lens hoods

Wind-proof mittens

Leg/arm warmers

Sand from the Gobi Desert

Map labels

500 MILES

N

USSR

CENTER OF THE EARTH

URAMQI GOBI DESERT

Day 58

Day 50

Day 42 DUNHUANG

TIBET

Qaidam Pendi

Day 38 GOLMUND

HIMALAYAS

Day 28

LHASA

WORLD LOCATION: TIBET

Day 21 KATHMANDU

Day 12

DHAKA

Day 1

16409
13124
9843
6562
3281
1640
656
0
HEIGHT IN FEET

JOURNEY TO THE CENTER OF THE EARTH

The 286-mile (460-km) trip began on a Bangladeshi beach, passed along through the Ganges Delta, up to the Tibetan plateau, and across the Gobi and Taklamakan Deserts. They flew home.

Have Bike, Will Travel

When you travel, take a bike with you. Bikes travel well and are easy to manage if you plan ahead. A bike on vacation is great for exploring and opens up possibilities, such as traveling extra distance to a secluded beach. For trains, label the bike with your name and the destination station. Load the bike into the baggage car yourself, secure it with elastic straps, and remove panniers and other gear. For airlines, check details before booking and take out insurance. Some airlines will refuse bikes; others provide a box for free, or charge a small fee. Prepare the bike by removing the pedals and rear derailleur. Loosen the **stem** so that the bars can be turned parallel with the frame. Deflate tires to half-pressure. If the bike is just going roll-on, tape cardboard to the frame to protect it. If the bike is in a box, or better still a soft fabric bike bag, remove the front wheel and insert a block of wood between the fork dropouts to brace the blades, then line the box with clothes or bubble plastic.

CARRIERS

A bike with the wheels removed will fit easily into the trunk of many small cars, but if you carry passengers or any more bikes, then a bike car carrier is a better solution. There are two types of carrier: top-mounted (right) and rear-mounted (facing page, bottom), and each type has different advantages. Single-rail models bolt to a mounted roof rack. Multirail models have their own mounting hardware, and while the installation is usually straightforward, the carrier can become more of a semipermanent fixture, left in place until it is needed. When you use the bike carrier, you should check the mounting bolts and the bike fastenings as frequently as you possibly can. It is also wise to protect vulnerable parts, such as leather saddles, and cover them with plastic, or even remove them. If you leave the vehicle, be sure the bikes are securely locked.

TOP-MOUNTED CARRIERS

The top-mounted carrier (left) can hold four or five bikes. The frames are held upright and are separate and unlikely to be grimed with road grit. Each bike must be firmly anchored in place; at 60 to 70 mph (96-112 km/h) the wind force on a top-mounted bike is extremely strong, and the additional aerodynamic resistance will significantly increase fuel consumption. The performance of small-engined cars will also be affected by this additional wind resistance.

REAR-END CARRIERS

Rear-end models (right) are usually mounted with fastenings, which hook onto the edges of a trunk lid and can be installed whenever you need them. Most models hold two bikes, some carriers accommodate three. The bicycles are easy to lift and place on the carrier, but care must be taken so that they do not rub against each other and cause damage to paint finishes. Bikes on rear carriers tend to accumulate grit.

BICYCLE CASES

Hard-shell bike cases are usually made from fiberglass and lined inside with foam. They are extremely strong, and although fairly lightweight, most models have castor wheels for ease of handling.

*The bike should be snug and compact inside the case. With most cases the seat, pedals, front wheel, and **stem** have to be removed and carefully arranged with extra foam. If the bike and case are to travel by air, drop the tire pressures by half.*

PORTABLE BIKES

Clothes and valuables can fit into a small carry-on bag (right), leaving an arm free to carry your bicycle case onto an airplane or train. At the end of your journey, you will usually be able to check the case in a baggage claim at a train station, or if you plan a point-to-point ride, you may be able to send the case ahead to the next airport en route.

The
EVERYDAY BIKE

The bicycle is the world's favorite form of personal transport. There are some 800 million bikes on the planet; most of them are everyday machines used for all reasons and all seasons. The course of most human activity tends to be local, with everyday life involving short journeys that can be walked within an hour, but are up to four times faster by bike. In the Third World the majority of these journeys are made on a sturdy black roadster, whose design has hardly changed since the end of World War I.

Lamp

No-nonsense Bikes

This machine is responsible for nearly two thirds of all bicycles sold worldwide; it is a tough, no-non-sense, all-steel bicycle with relaxed angles, roller-lever brakes, sen-sible tires, and a wide, comfortable, well-sprung saddle. It is a simple form of individual local transport for doctors, teachers, and even government officials. Hooked to a trailer it provides haulage for farmers and craft workers taking their goods to market. Hitched to a rickshaw it becomes a taxi, converted to a trike it becomes a small wagon. Harnessed to a water pump it can become a human-powered motor. In the West, the bike is now making a comeback. It is seen as a friendly and local

U-Lock

Brake arms

means of transport, used by the environmentally aware and wise whenever possible: to carry us to work or school, deliver groceries and mail, and provide the police with community-friendly transport.

Helmet

Fitness and Freedom

It is the bike that makes everyday activities more fun, reduces slavery to the car, introduces kinetic activity, physical fitness, and freedom into our lives. It is the bike that is celebrated for its relative lack of weight, bright packaging, performance, and its use of most modern materials. Increasingly, the bike favoured for everyday tasks is the moun-tain bicycle: millions are sold each year, not to go off-road, but because their wide tires cope better with the potholed streets and their cantilever brakes provide more certain stopping power in city traffic. Special in design, they are everyday in usage – and the better the bicycle is, the more enjoyable cycling becomes.

Derailleur

Commuter

The City Cyclist

At rush hour in any big city, there are two groups of cyclists threading their way through the knot of traffic: commuters riding to work and bicycle messengers whose work is riding. For the messengers, time is money. The more drops and pick-ups they make, the more they earn. They need to be fit, fast, skillful on a bike, possess a natural sense of direction, a memory like an address book, nerves of steel, and a sixth sense for trouble in traffic. Cycle commuters may not really need the same physical attributes, but they do need to be able to acquire the same sort of confidence and sense of vigilance that is only really achieved with improved bike handling skills.

SHOULDER BAG:
This is preferred by messengers as it saves time and weight and holds more than pannier bags.

SADDLE HEIGHT:
A high saddle, together with low handlebars, offers the ultimate riding position for a messenger, mixing power riding with good all around visibility.

THE BIKE MESSENGER
Being a cycle messenger isn't just a job, it's a lifestyle and a subculture. Clothes are as much about identity as function. A bag, two-way radio, cycling shorts, clip-on cycle shoes, and goggles to keep out grit are the essentials. The bikes should be fast, agile, reliable, and too ugly to steal, so messengers will often opt for deliberately unattractive road bikes. In flat urban areas, being a messenger is like riding intermittent sprints, 10 hours a day, and elite riders pare down to light, fixed-gear bikes.

LEVERS:
Mounted on top of the handlebars, they save time when changing gear.

TOP TUBE: Black tape wound around the tube protects paintwork and conceals the real value of the bike from thieves.

THE COMMUTER

*Cycling to work can make a pleasure out of a necessity, but skills have to be acquired to deal with the busy city traffic. Learn how to remain on your bike while stationary, with your feet in the clips, by rocking on your **cranks**. By doing this you can stay at the front of the line, ready to move off ahead or abreast of the first vehicle. Riding to work in a business suit is feasible for short, nonstrenuous journeys in dry weather. For anything more vigorous, it is advisable to wear cycling clothes as they are far more comfortable.*

HELMETS: Helmets are essential for safety in traffic.

HAZARDS OF THE CITY

Whether cycling for business or pleasure, the city traffic requires extra care. The art is to combine a defensive attitude with an assertive presence; make motorists aware of your existence, yet always be ready to take evasive action – on the assumption that drivers and pedestrians alike may not have seen you. Whistles, bells, and even air horns are legitimate methods for signaling your presence to motorists cocooned in their cars. Whenever possible, use hand signals, and force drivers to recognize your presence by making eye contact with them at intersections or by placing yourself where they would expect to find another vehicle.

THE BIKE: Potholes, bumps, uneven surfaces, broken glass, and other trash quickly take their toll on a city bike. This *Trek 790*, a **hybrid** of a road and mountain bike, combines the best aspects of both – powerful cantilever brakes, an upright riding position, large wheels, mudguards, and medium-size tires.

REFLECTOR BELT: This can help you to stay conspicuous and stand out in traffic.

U-LOCK: Always carry a lock on your bike and also keep one at your workplace for any emergency.

LIGHTS: These are a defensive tool and an aid to survival in the dark.

Cycle Activism

Cycle activism is about campaigning to get cycling into the mainstream. Transportation in the West is politically dominated by the car, with paid lobbyists and contributions to the coffers of political parties. At the behest of the road lobby, roads are built, traffic rules legislated, and road taxes are set at low, below-inflation rates. The result is a massive subsidy for car transportation at the public expense. It need not be so. In those countries and communities where bike campaigners have

actively lobbied, bicyclists have gained amenities that make cycling more convenient and safer. Gains include the provision of bikeways, canalside and riverside trails, access to main bridges, special bridges for cyclists, and bike parking facilities. Forward-thinking corporations have been persuaded to provide bike lockers, showers, and changing rooms, and to pay mileage allowances to encourage employees to use bikes instead of cars on company business. Today, as people and

CAR FREE
To relieve traffic congestion and discourage car use, the city of London, England, has a comprehensive network of special lanes restricted to buses, taxis, and bikes at peak travel times.

DIRECT ACTION
This campaigner (above) is painting white lines to create cycle lanes on the Montreal North-South Axis, an event organized by the pioneering Le Monde à Bicyclette of Montreal, Canada. Campaigns like this concentrated on

specific goals, using imaginative and bold tactics. Today, the tradition of direct, nonviolent action is buttressed by increasing sophistication in gaining popular public support and also manipulating political power.

CYCLISTS ONLY
Kingston-upon-Thames, England (above), due to the high student population, is a bicycle-oriented town, and to reduce accidents, the one-way traffic system includes contraflow cycle lanes with their own traffic signals.

communities become aware that cars pose an ever-increasing threat of pollution, congestion, and energy consumption, the climate has never been better for campaigning for bikes as clean, nonpolluting, energy-efficient transport. Still it is not an easy battle. Support a campaign group, even if only with a contribution or membership – every little bit of help is vital. If you can and will, become a cycle activist yourself. Campaigning is in your interest and more; a better deal for cyclists is a better deal for society. The end result is a greatly improved quality of life for everyone.

PARKING
The common problem for cycle commuters is where to park. Lamp posts become adorned with bikes that are vulnerable to theft and can obstruct pedestrians. The problem is especially acute at train stations, but the solution is to provide cycle racks on the platforms, as shown here at an English station.

MIXED-MODE TRANSPORTATION
In Montreal certain bridges can only be used by motor vehicles, hence the provision for carrying bikes (above). In Japan, a cyclist can ride from home, take a bus, and then ride the rest of the way.

GET ACTIVE!
- Join a bicycle campaign group, or start your own.
- Talk to local cyclists and find out what changes are needed, like bike lanes, pothole repairs, parking, or access on trains.
- Make friends with the local government group that makes the transport rules and each time a cycling-related issue comes up, present the group with documented facts.
- The master plan for the development of your town is reviewed every few years. If you can get cycling issues addressed in this document, it will spare many smaller battles at the individual road and building level.
- Form an advisory committee to brief government bodies and agencies on bike-related issues.
- Use the media. Write press releases and talk to reporters.

PROTECTION AGAINST AIR POLLUTION
In practice your first line of defense in polluted air is your nose. Breathe through it instead of your mouth, because it's lined with tiny hairs and mucus that trap particles. The second strategy is to avoid riding in heavy slow-moving traffic when pollutant levels are greatest. Studies show that these drop by 50 percent if you ride on side streets. If your journey involves main streets, get to the front at traffic lights. Don't sit behind a vehicle's tailpipe; emissions are at their most toxic when engines are idling. In cities where smog exceeds safe levels, consider using a carbon-filter mask. Unlike other pollutants, ozone, smog's main constituent, is not trapped by the hairlike filters in the nose.

FACE MASKS
An air-filter mask is a city cyclist's last line of defense in the battle against breathing in polluted air. The effectiveness of masks in combatting each of the noxious gases caused by vehicle emissions is not conclusive. Nor are masks comfortable or feasible when riding energetically. However, carbon-filter masks have proved effective in removing 96 percent of ozone, a pollutant which can cause breathing problems.

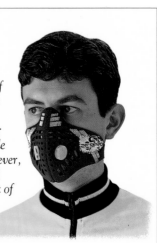

Locks and Lights

Bike thieves should be locked up, using those ultra-invincible locks that the pestilence of bike theft has forced upon us – and the keys thrown away. Few things are so dismaying as having a bike stolen – and thousands of bikes are stolen every year. The friendliness and social virtue of cycling might mislead you into thinking that theft will pass you by. Not so. It's up to you to become security-conscious and protect your bike from theft, possibly using two locks of different kinds as an additional deterrent. It is also your responsibility to guard against nighttime hazards, since after dark, motorists will have sharply reduced vision. Reflectors and lights are a legal requirement because without them you would be invisible to motorists. Not using lights is playing Russian roulette with your life. Bikes are about freedom and enjoyment. Locks and lights may seem to be cumbersome and awkward, but for everyday cycling they are a fact of life.

ARMORED CABLE LOCK
Also known as a link lock, this type of lock is made of links connected together by ball joints. It is flexible and easier to fit around awkward shapes than a U-lock. Because it has different weak points than a U-lock, the combination of the two should deter most thieves. Strong locks such as this are quite heavy for regular journeys such as commuting, so it is worth keeping a lock at the place where you regularly secure your bike.

STEEL LOCK
The U-lock is made with hardened steel and has a pick-proof lock. An extra accessory for the higher crime areas is a T-shaped pipe joint over the cross bar and shackle.

CASING: The steel rollers are surrounded by a vinyl casing.

LOCK MECHANISM: The lock has 100,000 different combinations.

BRACKET: A U-lock is heavy and awkward to carry. A frame-mounted bracket to hold it is convenient.

BIKE ALARM
The SSB bike alarm (right) emits a powerful 95-decibel noise if the bike is disturbed. Like car alarms, it has a time-delay mechanism for locking and unlocking, and has an automatic reset button in case of a false alarm.

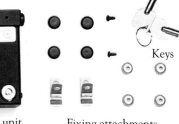

Nine-volt battery   Alarm unit   Fixing attachments   Keys

BATTERY LIGHTS

The lenses on most battery lights produce a diffuse, widely dispersed beam that is more easily seen by other road users, but is too dim to see by when riding on a dark road or track. Halogen bulbs give more light, but reduce battery life. Battery lights are convenient as they can be fitted in seconds, but they are expensive to run unless used with rechargeable batteries. However, rechargeable batteries only suit predictable patterns of use, as they can, and do, die without warning. Battery lights are convenient when locking up on the street because they can be quickly detached and slipped into a pocket. They are also useful as a general light for map-reading and roadside repairs.

Front bracket attachment

Rear attachments

Front light   Rear light   Battery housing & batteries

Front light

Rear light   Dynamo bottle

Dynamo bracket bolts

Front & rear bracket attachments

DYNAMO LIGHTS

*These have just enough power for seeing where you are going, and are cheap to run. Bottle dynamos press against the tire sidewall and are reliable. Bottom-bracket dynamos press against the center of the tire tread, and are unreliable in the rain. Permanently mounted, dynamo lamps are an invitation to theft when locking on the street. Unless fitted with a back-up, they dim as you ride slowly, and go out when you stop. At high speeds, dynamo bulbs can burn out unless the system is fitted with a **zener diode** to regulate power. Not everyone likes the way a dynamo partially diverts pedaling energy.*

RECHARGEABLE UNITS

The route to serious lighting power is 6- and 12-volt rechargeable battery systems, using bulbs from 6 to 50 watts. Batteries are either lead-acid, also called gel cell, or nickel-cadium, usually called ni-cad, with a life from 1 to 6 hours, depending on the power of the lights. These systems are expensive, but high-quality. Options include dual headlights for dipped/high beams, bike- or helmet-mounted headlights. Most systems can also be fitted with flasher units.

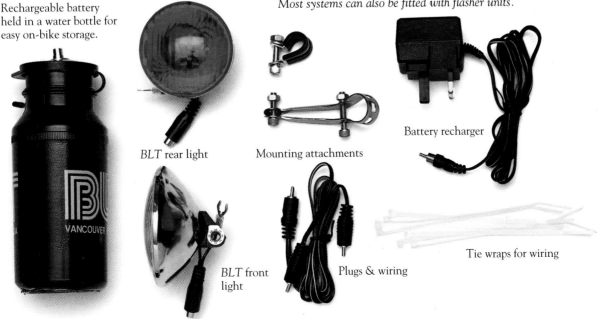

Rechargeable battery held in a water bottle for easy on-bike storage.

BLT rear light   Mounting attachments   Battery recharger

BLT front light   Plugs & wiring   Tie wraps for wiring

The Working Bike

Working bikes are tools first and bikes second. They are designed to do a job, whether used for delivering groceries; as a mobile ice-cream stand; carrying a window cleaner's ladders; or to transport policemen. With cops on the beat, the concept has turned full circle: nearly a hundred years ago, the London bobby on a bike was a common sight. But with the arrival of the motor car, police gave up two wheels for the squad car. Nowhere was this takeover more complete than in the USA. Yet the bicycle is making a comeback as part of standard-issue police equipment, thanks to the versatile mountain bicycle, and increasing automobile traffic .

Street Patrol

This bike resurgence originally started in Seattle, when two car-bound cops, Paul Grady and Mike Miller, managed to convince their bosses that they would be far more effective working a congested city center on bikes. It paid off. Within the first two months they made 500 arrests – five times as many as officers in cars or on foot. The bikes allow the police to ride through alleyways, across rough ground, or curb hop to swoop down on criminals quietly. The glamour of the mountain bike also gives policemen instant street credibility, which the squad car never can.

UNIVERSAL TRANSPORT
The bicycle still provides the most efficient and obvious means of transporting people and their goods. The low costs involved in buying and maintaining a bicycle have given this machine worldwide accessibility.

RUGGED VERSATILITY
The bobby on a bicycle never disappeared from some parts of Britain and Europe. But the equipment is changing. The original three-speed, sit-up-and-beg machines are now being replaced, and officers have begun to appreciate patrolling by mountain bike.

METAMORPHOSIS

A bike can be transformed into almost any form and use. At one point flower sellers used adapted bikes as mobile flower stands.

THE NEW ELITE

Seattle's squad (below) uses basic mid-price Raleigh bikes with added components, such as upgraded pedals, to cope with the high wear and tear. The front chainwheel is a 50-tooth instead of a standard 46, to provide higher speeds on the flat. Seattle retires its bikes after 18 months or 7,500 miles (12,750 km), before repair costs outstrip the price of a new bike. Standard equipment carried on the bike includes a first-aid kit and traffic penalty tickets. Uniforms have also been redesigned for cycling.

BICYCLE HARDWARE

Messengers' bikes are as tough and resilient as the police bikes used to survive high speed traffic, interweaving, or curb-hopping.

Learning to Ride

A child's work is play. Learning to ride a bike should be a natural extension of that play. It is one of the great moments of childhood, the sudden discovery that you can ride a bike, the sense of triumph at being able to propel yourself along. It should be easy, yet so often we get it wrong by trying to *teach* a child to ride instead of letting the child *discover* how to ride. A common mistake is to add a set of stabilizers to the two-wheeler of a child who cannot ride. They prevent the child from experiencing the balance the bike requires. The process outlined here works because it is built around letting the child learn at his or her own speed. It works for countless children and it has never failed. Make every step fun, don't hurry it, and move on only when the child is ready and wants to try something new.

THE RIGHT BIKE
To aid confidence, a child should learn on the bike that he or she is going to ride regularly. It should be set up so that the child's hands can reach the brake levers easily.

WRONG WAY TO LEARN
Running behind, holding the back of the saddle and waiting to let go, is the hit-and-miss method. If you're lucky, the child starts pedaling and will forget that your hand is no longer there. Invariably, when you take your hand off, your child's confidence and sense of balance disappear with it. All you've done is create unnecessary anxiety in your child.

SEAT HEIGHT: The height of the seat is what gives a child confidence, and should always be at a lower than ideal height for riding (see pp.20-21 for correct sizes). Once the child can ride, raise the saddle bit by bit until it is at the optimal height.

SEAT: Lower the seat until your child can comfortably touch the ground.

1 SIMPLE BALANCE AND CONTROL

Remove the pedals from the **crank** *arms. Starting off on flat, open ground, explain how to use the hand-brakes, and encourage your child to just push along using alternate feet. Once he's rolling, encourage him to experiment with the brakes so that he may get the feel of slowing and stopping the bike.*

2 THAT FREEWHEELING FEELING

As soon as your child is ready, suggest propelling the bike forward with both feet together. In those first few short seconds when both feet are off the ground and the bike is rolling forward, he's experiencing that exhilarating sensation of simply freewheeling. Find a short and shallow slope, and let him build up speed. Suggest starting near the bottom. As he builds up speed he will decide when he's ready for a longer, steeper start.

PEDALS: Removing the pedals from the **cranks** allows a child to discover how to steer the bike, and not to worry about what his feet are doing.

PEDALS: Carry a wrench so you can replace the pedals quickly. Some children learn fast.

3 ADDING PEDAL POWER

As the child gets the hang of freewheeling, suggest he rests his feet up on the **cranks***. If he feels happy with his feet in that position, offer to put the pedals back on. Using a slope to freewheel down, suggest that he tries to turn the pedals once or twice as the downward momentum runs out. This is the magical moment when a child first experiences the freedom of cycling.*

Bikes for Children

Children need and deserve good quality bikes. On a bicycle, a child can develop physical coordination and experience freedom and motion. To a child, a light, easy-to-ride bicycle is just like a car to an adult: it's a set of wheels, personal transport, and the key to independent travel. Lightness and quality are the really important things to look for. Give a child a bike that is too heavy or too stiff to ride, and like all bad toys it will be too quickly discarded, because it is no fun to play with.

False Economy

Stores are full of cheap children's bicycles that are sold on the premise that there is little point in spending more because a child will soon outgrow it. Buying cheap is unlikely to pay off and could even put a child off cycling for life. By contrast, investing in a good quality bike

HAND-BUILT BIKE

The Condor Junior Roadracer has been tailored precisely to fit this young rider. Custom-built bikes for children might seem an indulgence. Paradoxically, the cost over time is less than buying a cheap bike, and this Condor, with its hand-crafted Reynolds 531 frame, will bring a good secondhand price.

BRAKES: Powerful cantilever brakes provide safe and assured stopping power.

JUNIOR MOUNTAIN BIKE

The Offroad MT10 is designed specifically for small cyclists aged 8 to 12, and measuring 4 ft 6 in to 5 ft (1.37 to 1.52 m) tall. The MT10 has only a 10-in frame and uses 24-in-diameter wheels compared to the 20-in wheels found on many children's mountain bikes.

GEARING: The simplified gearing uses only a single chainring at the front, instead of three, reducing possible gear choices from 18 to 6.

COMPONENTS: All the lightweight equipment of this *Condor* – the hand-built wheels, its *Shimano 600 Utegra* group set, *Cinelli* bars and **stem** and *Turbo* saddle – are high quality. Hence they are worth stripping off and fitting to a larger size frame as the child grows up.

QUALITY BIKE

The Cannondale SM's *lightweight aluminum frame and high-grade components create a bike that is easy and fun for young legs to ride. The 15-in frame is 1 in smaller than the smallest size usually available in adult mountain bikes. The wide-range gears make it easy to pedal on the steepest hills and powerful cantilever brakes provide safe and assured stopping power.*

• SEAT POST: In the early years this 15-in frame bike is ridden with the seat post down. The 6 in of extension can be raised gradually as the rider grows.

• GEARS: The wide-range gears make it easy to pedal on the steepest hills.

• WHEELS: The frame is about as small as it is feasible to build to accommodate full-size 700C wheels, which have less rolling resistance than the smaller wheels normally fitted to children's bikes.

may seem extravagant in the short term, but it is sure to give a child many hours of enjoyable play, and a grasp of traffic and road sense.

Sizing for Children

Bikes for children are classified by wheel size. The common sizes are: 12-in for tricycles and bikes for 2- to 3-year-olds (inside leg of 14 to 16 in/35 to 40 cm); 16-in for small BMX-style bikes for 4- to 6-year-olds (inside leg 17 to 22 in/ 43 to 55 cm); and 20-in for 7- to 11-year-olds (inside leg 23 in/58 cm). After the age of about 11 a child should be ready for a small-framed adult bike using full-size 26-in or 700C wheels.

THE HOBBY-HORSE

Hobby-Horses, propelled by pushing feet against the ground, are now only nursery toys. Before the bicycle was invented the Hobby-Horse was the fastest road vehicle of its day, capable of outrunning a four-horse coach.

Family Cycling

Whether as passengers or participants, young children take a special delight in cycling. Being out in the world, moving along, opens up a new sense of freedom and wonder for a child. There's nothing quite like the happy sounds and remarks of a child enjoying a first bike trip to spice up an outing. Between the ages of one and six, a child can travel long distances only as a passenger. This requires some additional planning. You need to make sure your child is protected against the weather, because he can't move around. A helmet is essential. Plan extra stops to give your child time to get down and run around. Take extra food, drink, and small toys, attached with a short piece of string to keep them from being dropped.

TRAILER BIKE
Ideal for 6- to 10-year-olds who have grown out of rear seats, a trailer bike like this Covaci (right) is attached to a special carrier fitted on the rear of any standard bicycle or tandem. The child pedals at his own speed but the adult controls braking and steering. For a child just becoming accustomed to cycling, it provides an accompanied introduction to traffic, while minimizing most of the risks. Riding with an attached trailer bike can be as speedy as riding a tandem. The combination of trailer and bike has the same aerodynamic frontal area as a single bike, but 1½ to 2 times the amount of rider power.

CHILD TRAILER
*With a wide **wheelbase**, thick tires, cushioned seats, and a small friend alongside, a trailer makes an enjoyable way to ride (above). A snap-on hood with windows can be added for changes in the weather.*

OLDER CHILDREN:
A bicycle train requires a greater co-ordinated effort and suits older children who are ready to contribute more pedaling output.

THE BICYCLE TRAIN
Cycling historian Jim McGurn solved his family-outing problems by developing this alternative to the station wagon. It runs on goodwill and free energy and delivers plenty of smiles per hour. The driver rides a tricycle and each carriage – a trailer mounted with a tricycle rear end – is linked to the one before, making the train system, in theory, infinitely extendable.

THE CARRIAGES: Each section of the train is linked by a simple click-on ball and socket joint. Each section is independent and each rider creates as much power as he can.

CHILD SEATS

From the moment a child sits up properly and holds his head steady, at about 10 months, he's ready for a child seat. Most seats will take a 4-year-old, but the upper limit is set by weight, 40 lb (18 kg) being the point when the seat becomes unstable. Go for a robust, all-in-one shell with mounting hardware, built-in footrests, a safety harness, grab bar, and head restraint.

SAFETY: An unattended child should never be left in a child seat. •

• MOUNTAIN BIKE: An ideal machine for towing or carrying a child. With its strong-frame, wide-range gears, and powerful cantilever brakes, it delivers stability with reliability.

SIDE BY SIDE: Very young children enjoy riding side by side on the back of a trike. By having the seats face backward, they can also see and talk to the parent sitting behind. •

SMALL-WHEELED TRIKE: With a low center of gravity, the 20-in wheel trike is very stable and perfect for carrying small children or shopping. •

Tandems

Tandems add an extra dimension of pleasure and performance to cycling. With double the human power of a solo bike, but the same frontal area and a higher power-to-weight ratio, tandems can go like blazes. Two well-matched riders on a tandem can travel farther and faster than a lone rider. Above all, tandems are sociable, and two riders of unequal strength can ride together without having to compromise on the effort each one puts in.

THE TECHNIQUE FOR RIDING IN TANDEM

*Riding in tandem, as on this Santana mountain bike tandem, demands cooperation, co-ordination and good communication between the **captain** (front) and the **stoker** (rear). Starting to ride illustrates the challenge. Start with both pedals level, right pedal forward and the stoker seated with his feet on the pedals, while the captain steadies the bike. The captain calls to say that he's ready, the stoker confirms, and the captain pushes forward to start cycling. With the captain controlling brakes and gears, and able to see the road ahead, every change of gear, every use of the brakes, every single turn has got to be communicated to the stoker.*

THE STOKER: The **stoker** should have complete trust in the **captain** and must avoid leaning into corners.

THE CAPTAIN: Steering control can sometimes be easier if the front rider is heavier.

CHAIN DRIVE: Known as a **crossover drive**, the left-side chain connects the two riders, which then synchronizes their output.

TIRE PRESSURE: Tires must be inflated harder than on a solo bike to carry two riders. For the off-road tandem, 70 **psi** is advised.

TANDEM FRAMES

OPEN
This unbraced frame is cheap to build and will often produce a heavy and lifeless ride.

DOUBLE DIAMOND
This traditional design is poor at coping with the pedaling forces from the front bottom bracket.

UPTUBE
A modern American design with good rigidity, this is more suitable for riders of matched power.

LADYBACK
The drop top tube at the rear is for those who dislike a crossbar frame. It is too flexible for serious riding.

SINGLE MARATHON
This vintage design overcomes any side-to-side flex. It is most suitable for riders of equal power output.

DOUBLE MARATHON
The expedition-grade flex-proof tandem with ultralight tubes is best for riders of matched power.

DIRECT LATERAL
This is a modern design, popular with US framebuilders. It is best for riders of unequal power.

TWIN LATERAL
This lightweight and inexpensive frame is very popular. It is only suitable for light riding.

TOURING TANDEM
This Cannondale touring tandem is light and fast. The record for crossing America was by a racing tandem, in 7 days, 14 hours, and 55 minutes. The solo bike record is 18 hours, 40 minutes longer.

REAR HANDLEBARS: These are fixed and provide hand support only. As there are no brake hoods to rest hands on, dummy hood covers are attached instead.

FRONT FORKS: The bike's weight distribution exerts a strong force on the front forks, so thicker gauge tubing and bigger section fork blades are used.

WHEELS: The extra weight requires wheels with 40 to 48 spokes.

GEARING: Climbing is slow and lower gears are needed. Faster descents mean using higher gears.

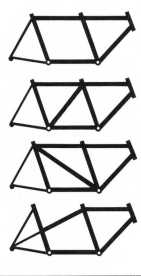

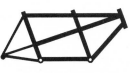

Classic Bicycles

To enthusiasts, the bicycle is aesthetically beautiful. Its technical perfection, innate efficiency, and convivial nature as a human-scale machine engenders affection, admiration, and appreciation. At this level the bicycle is more than mere machinery, more an art form in its own right, with the most beautiful examples deserving to be preserved in collections that exist to be both viewed and ridden. Pride of place in these go to the exquisitely restored bikes from a previous golden age of cycling – a classic era when the framebuilder's skill was paramount, bicycle companies were still small-scale, and customers traveled a long way for the best in custom frames. Those framebuilders may be gone, but their work still survives, painstakingly restored by enthusiasts who dedicate their lives to these glorious bikes.

STAYS: *Hetchins* builder Jack Denny tried curly stays as an experiment to soften road shock, copying the curve of front forks. The design was patented, but enthusiasts continue to debate its efficiency.

LUGWORK: The ornate **lugs** that join the tubes were the result of experiments, in which strips were stiffened to strengthen straight lugs that fractured under stress. Jack Denny found the extra strips ugly, and began to ornament the stiffeners and cut away the lugs. Later lugs like this *Magnum Bonum* set were cast from scratch and the design patented.

FORK CROWN: The embellished, patented fork crown consists of two plates. Almost 3 in (8 cm) long, the whorled design adds strength in the guise of decoration.

TUBING: *Hetchins* frames need no identifying sticker for their *Reynolds 531* **double-butted** tubing – customers already knew that *Hetchins* would use nothing else.

CRANKSET: Inscribed 177 mm **crank**set and pedals are made by the now defunct, but once top-rated, *Chater-Lea*.

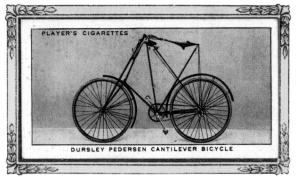

PLAYER'S CIGARETTES

DURSLEY PEDERSEN CANTILEVER BICYCLE

COLLECTORS ITEM
The Dursley-Pedersen was immortalized in one of a series of cigarette cards (above) produced in the 1940s entitled "Cycling – 1839-1939."

TUBING: By using small tubes triangulated in pairs, Pedersen built a bike weighing under 23 lb (10.5 kg). Its rigidity, lightness, and relative lack of vibration earned it an enthusiastic following then and nearly a century on.

A DISTINCTIVE BIKE
The unique shape of its curly seat stays, combined with some ornate lugwork and very high-quality frame construction, has given Hetchins (left) a world-wide following. Curled tubes on the rear triangle were added as a design experiment and then adopted to circumvent pre-1945 racing rules, which forbade amateurs to ride bicycles advertising the builder's name on the frame. This 1957 Curly Hetchins, built originally for Six-Day racing, was discovered in a loft 30 years later by its current owner, British aero-engineer Reg Turner. Typical of a Hetchins enthusiast, he took 18 months to restore the bike to its original state, tracking down parts all over the world.

A CLASSIC BIKE
One of the classic veteran bicycles, the Dursley-Pedersen design continues to attract new fans, who ride variations of the original like this one (below) by Kempler. The first model was patented in 1893 by Mikael Pedersen, a Dane living in England. He had invented a new hammock bicycle seat, but finding it would not fit a conventional bicycle, decided to redesign the bike, resulting in the geometrically perfect Pedersen frame.

SADDLE: This is attached by seven spiral springs to the seat pillar and by an adjustable strap to the front.

AN ELEGANT BIKE
Thanet was a British cycle firm created after World War II, but only 400 Thanet Silverlights (below) were sold. Made of undersized tubing, it claimed to be the lightest steel frame at 3 lb 12 oz (1.7 kg).

CRADLE: The distinctive V-shaped bottom-bracket cradle was probably copied from aircraft design.

Carnival Bikes

Ever since the invention of the bicycle, back-yard builders have taken its basic elements and remixed them to try to improve on the original. How far the formula can be stretched is shown in the Kinetic Sculpture Race, held each May in California. The challenge is to create a human-powered vehicle that can cross sand, mud, and water, and provide spectators with pedal-powered entertainment.

SAND MOBILE
This futuristic entry (above) for the three-day event is fully prepared for the 38-mile (61-km) course that runs along sand dunes near Ferndale, California. Each wheel is built from five bicycle rims laced on one hub to give sand traction. The external paddles allow it to travel through the water.

WAGON ROLL
This human-powered brewery vehicle (left) is taking full advantage of the "no limit on length" race rule to bring its own supplies along and comply with the spirit of the event that holds that "cheating is a right, not a privilege." The five-man team powers a 10-wheel drive system that rolls on 59 bike tires. However, entries can be no more than 15 ft (4.5 m) high and 8 ft (2.4 m) wide. Sculptures are awarded points for speed, art, and engineering. Vehicles that have passenger space are given bonus points.

INGENIOUS CHAIN AWARD
This triple chainring setup (right) is typical of how the principles of the humble chain drive are stretched to new limits by the designers of kinetic sculptures. It manages to drive several sets of wheels, with the freewheel delivering pedal power to the front axle, and two crossover chains transmitting it to the rear wheels – an arrangement that, in theory, allows as many sets of wheels as riders to be added. Function, however, isn't everything, and one of the many prizes dreamed up is the "Ingenious Chain Award," given to the competitor whose chain setup also manages to drive parts that have amusement value only.

INGENIOUS VERSATILITY

This vehicle (right) cunningly uses ultra-wide tires to provide buoyancy. The spare tires are topped with thin bike tires to reduce rolling resistance on land. All vehicles must cross water and meet the design requirement of "something to go camping in that doesn't use gasoline."

SCRAP METAL REVITALIZED

The universal joint below has been lovingly crafted and chromed onto a steering arm. Competitors will spend months sculpting machines with parts cannibalized from bikes, old motor bikes, and even lawn mowers. The race dates back to 1969 when Hobart Brown decided to make his son's tricycle more interesting, and turned it into a tall, wobbly five-wheeler. Other Ferndale artists thought they could better, and so the race was born. Since then it has inspired six similar events in the US.

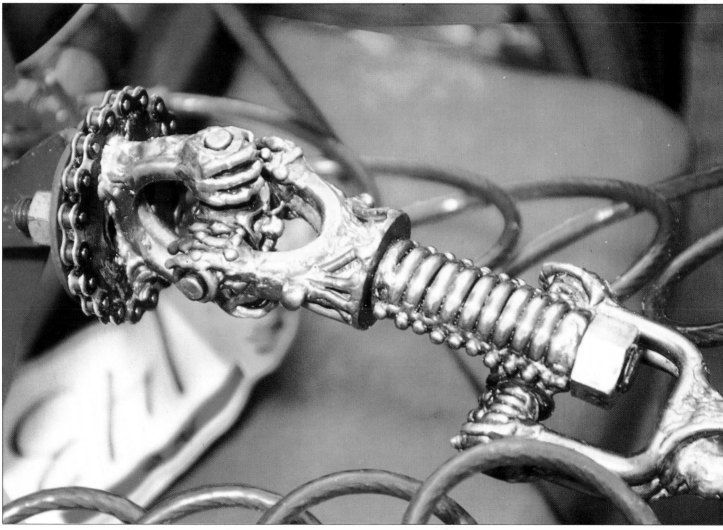

The FUTURE BIKE

"Speedy"

Friends of the bike hail it as the great modern invention: the ultimate means of energy-efficient, nonpolluting, inexpensive transportation. Such praise could suggest that the bike has been perfected. But has it? Traditionalist diehards prevented any experimenting by restricting the design of the bike to a chain-driven machine with two wheels to be ridden upright. In the 1930s, a Frenchman, Francois Feure, rode a recumbent bicycle, the Velocar, and smashed the speed records for both the mile and kilometer. The UCI's response was to rule that the Velocar wasn't actually a bicycle, instantly stunting an interesting branch of cycle evolution.

The Progress of HPVs

Fortunately, good ideas never die. In the 1970s, as bike sales in the US boomed following the 1973 oil crisis, two academics, Chester Kyle and Jack Lambie, promoted the idea of a better bike, faster and safer than a conventional bicycle. The only rule of their International Human Powered Vehicle Association (IHPVA) was that machines must use only human power. Most of the designs inspired by the IHPVA start where conventional bikes leave off. Improve a bike's

Drum brake

Plastic wheel

aerodynamic profile by halving its height and streamlining it, and the gains are considerable. All significant speed records for human-powered propulsion are held by human-powered vehicles (**HPV**s). These are not what the UCI considers to be bikes, but they still retain the virtues of pedal power, chain drives, and gears.

Kingcycle

Winning Design

The land speed record of 65 mph (105 km/h) is held by an HPV; the world record for human-powered speed on water is held by a pedal-driven hydrofoil. And the dream of human-powered flight has now become a reality, due to a remarkable fusion of nineteenth-century pedal power and late-twentieth-century aerospace engineering. Developments continue and, with no rules to limit them, pioneers are reaping the harvest of advances in materials technology. For these designers, the ultimate bicycle is still in the making.

KINGCYCLE **BEAN**

The Bean

HPV Anatomy

Human-powered vehicle (**HPV**) designs vary according to function and purpose. The *Windcheetah SL "Speedy"* is a street racer that can also be ridden in everyday traffic. A front-steering tricycle, it has a cruciform frame and a low center of gravity. This gives quick, agile handling and strong cornering grip, and permits full use of the powerful twin drum brakes on the front wheels. In addition, a streamlined **fairing** can be fitted (see p.139), to provide some weather protection, aerodynamic efficiency, and a greater speed. In a short sprint a *Speedy* can achieve over 40 mph (65 km/h). A cyclist who averages 18 mph (30 km/h) on a conventional racing bike will increase to around 22 mph (35 km/h) in a *Speedy*.

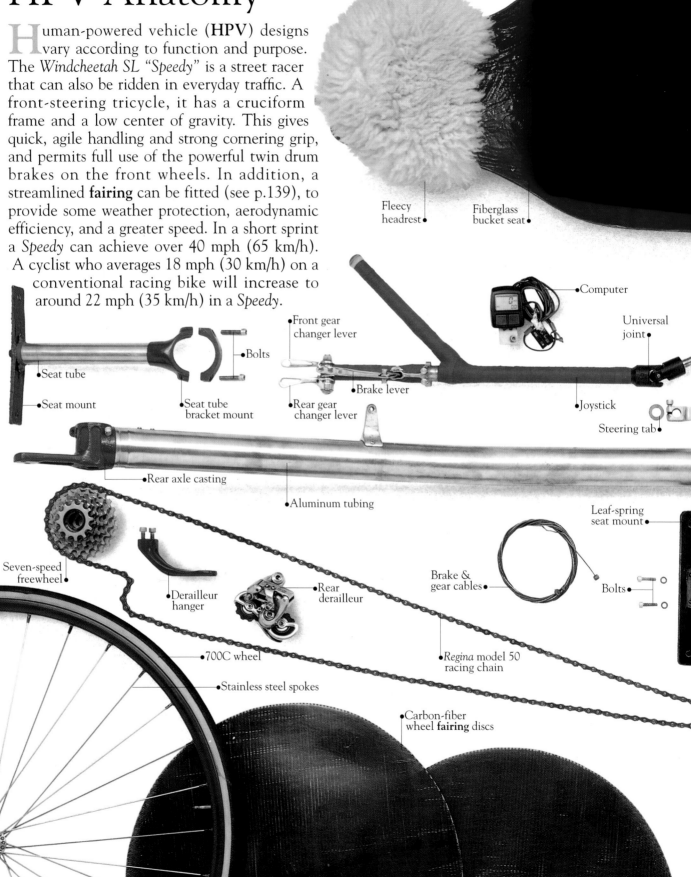

Fleecy headrest

Fiberglass bucket seat

Computer

Universal joint

Front gear changer lever

Bolts

Seat tube

Brake lever

Seat mount

Seat tube bracket mount

Rear gear changer lever

Joystick

Steering tab

Rear axle casting

Aluminum tubing

Leaf-spring seat mount

Seven-speed freewheel

Derailleur hanger

Rear derailleur

Brake & gear cables

Bolts

700C wheel

Regina model 50 racing chain

Stainless steel spokes

Carbon-fiber wheel **fairing** discs

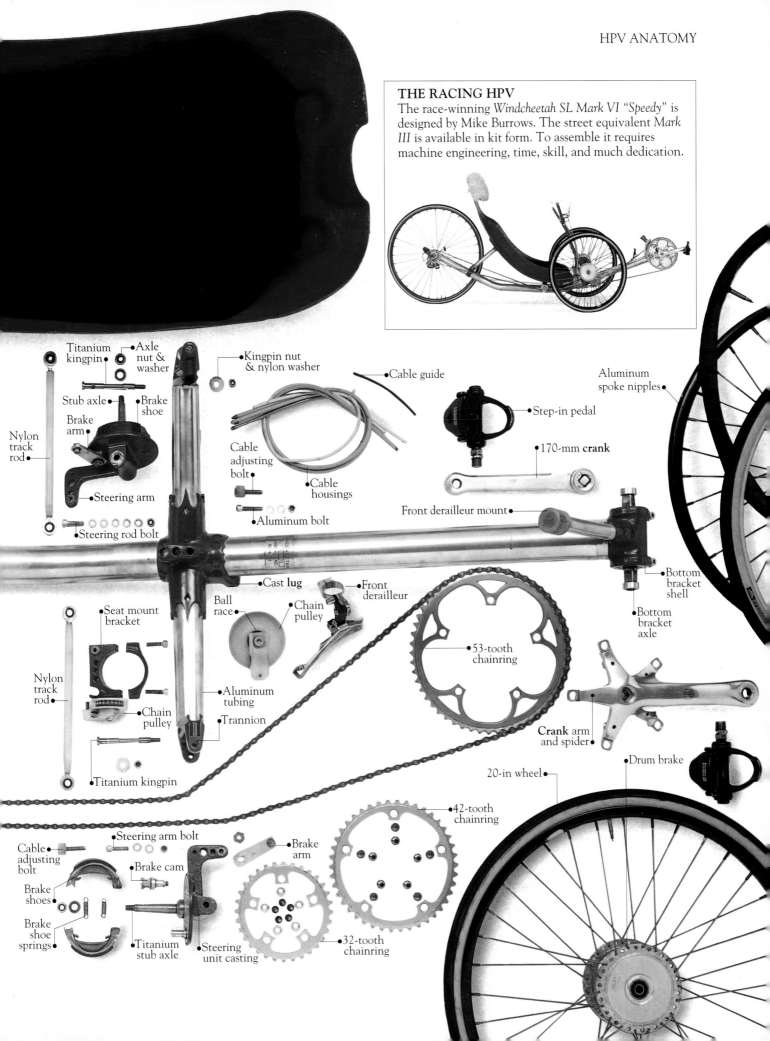

THE RACING HPV

The race-winning *Windcheetah SL Mark VI "Speedy"* is designed by Mike Burrows. The street equivalent *Mark III* is available in kit form. To assemble it requires machine engineering, time, skill, and much dedication.

Titanium kingpin

Axle nut & washer

Kingpin nut & nylon washer

Cable guide

Aluminum spoke nipples

Stub axle

Brake shoe

Brake arm

Nylon track rod

Cable adjusting bolt

Cable housings

Step-in pedal

170-mm **crank**

Steering arm

Aluminum bolt

Front derailleur mount

Steering rod bolt

Cast **lug**

Front derailleur

Bottom bracket shell

Ball race

Chain pulley

Bottom bracket axle

Seat mount bracket

53-tooth chainring

Nylon track rod

Chain pulley

Aluminum tubing

Trannion

Crank arm and spider

Drum brake

Titanium kingpin

20-in wheel

42-tooth chainring

Steering arm bolt

Brake arm

Cable adjusting bolt

Brake cam

Brake shoes

Brake shoe springs

32-tooth chainring

Titanium stub axle

Steering unit casting

Man and Machine

Human Powered Vehicle designs embrace a range of objectives: greater speed, better handling, more powerful braking, larger cargo space, greater comfort and safety, and weather protection. The design varies, but improving the performance by reducing aerodynamic **drag** is usually paramount. At 20 mph (32 km/h), a conventional bicycle and rider displace some 1,000 lb of air a minute, work which accounts for about 85 percent of a rider's energy output. Most **HPV**s are recumbents, for their smaller frontal area reduces drag by about 25 percent.

A recumbent is easier to fit with a full-length **fairing** that smooths air flow and can cut drag by up to 80 percent. Maintaining 20 mph (32 km/h) on a conventional bike requires a strong rider capable of a steady ¼ hp output; on a street HPV with a body shell, half the effort, ⅛ hp, is needed. Recumbents also score on cornering power, agility, stability, and safety. Most have more powerful braking because of better weight distribution and/or a lower center of gravity. The net effect is confidence inspiring, and results in better, more skilled riding.

FAST TRIKE

The Windcheetah SL (street legal), *or* "Speedy", *was originally designed as a training machine for* **HPV** *speed-record attempts. It turned out to be practical, fast, and exceptionally agile, and has won many road races and practical vehicle competitions. A tricycle, with a low center of gravity, the "Speedy" is stable, and can be drifted through corners. "Speedy" riders revel in slippery and icy conditions.*

LEGS: "Rubber" legs are a common first-ride experience. The muscles used for cycling perform in different ways, and new muscles are called into play. Consequently, progressive conditioning is essential.

CRANKS: Spinning the cranks smoothly is vital; high thrust forces can be generated, with care taken not to damage the knees.

PEDALING: This is continuous, with no risk of grounding. Toe clips and **cleats** that lock feet to the pedals, or clipless step-in pedals, are essential.

RIDER POSITION: With the rider leaning back, the chest cavity is open and free to breathe easily.

SPEED AND TECHNOLOGY

The Moulton AM *is one of the most advanced bicycles ever made. A 1983 redesign of the original Moulton, the AM has independent front and rear suspension, allowing the use of small wheels with hard, fast tires. Fitted with a windscreen and a complete* **fairing***, the Aero Moulton factory racer has exceeded 50 mph (80 km/h) in speed trials.*

HEAD: The head is well supported, yet vision to the side and rear is unobstructed.

SUSPENSION: The front shock absorbing mechanism is adjustable to suit rider weight and conditions.

BLOCK: A rubber block is engineered to provide shock absorption and **damping** of the rear swing-arm.

BACK: The back has full support, but the rider can move freely.

PROFILE: The most frequent objection to recumbents is that the profile is too low for safe riding in traffic. Actually, the height of a recumbent is the same as low-slung sports cars – highly visible and attracts a lot of attention.

SEAT: Buttocks are fully supported. Anyone who has had chronic problems with normal saddles should try a recumbent.

WHEEL: The rear wheel is loaded lightly, and can be spun with hard pedaling. It is sometimes possible to drift on slippery surfaces, controlling attitude and direction with wheelspin.

The Ecocar

The *Ecocar 2000* **HPV** is a practical, everyday commuting vehicle that is fast and comfortable, gives protection from the weather, carries luggage easily, requires minimal maintenance, and is simple to build. Created by Wim Van Wijnen, a Dutch opthalmic surgeon, the *Ecocar 2000* is typical of the home-made green machines now appearing with increasing frequency throughout Europe, where, compared to the US and Australia, average journey distances are shorter, cars are more expensive, and conditions for cycling are better.

Environmentally Sound

The idea of using pedal power for all-weather, personal transport vehicles for travel over short distances, has a compelling logic in terms of economy, efficiency, and environmental soundness. But because motor vehicles now dominate private transportation in Western society, no major firm has yet dared to attempt the large-scale mass production of HPVs. Development in this area has been done primarily by a few forward-thinking university engineering departments, and by those single, iconoclastic, highly self-motivated individuals who, in order to satisfy their own personal transport needs, have designed and built their own vehicles.

BODY SHELL: The folding rain cover drops down instantly and provides adequate protection so long as the vehicle is moving.

DUAL HALOGEN LAMPS: A rechargeable battery powers the full/dipped beam lights and radio for 4 hours per charge.

GEARS: Front wheel drive with a *Sturmey-Archer* 5-speed hub transmission. Front wheel drive is simple, allowing the use of a short chain and standard wheels.

CONSTRUCTION
The Ecocar 2000 is made using box-shape frame construction and riveted sheet aluminum, in an arched configuration which gives a simple and stiff frame. The front wheel does not turn in a headset. Instead, the frame itself is articulated via two headsets, each one angled at 40°, one below the rider, the other in the arch above the rider's head. The handlebars are attached to the forward half of the frame, while the seat rests on the rear half of the frame. This arrangement – known as center steering – may sound strange, but it works well, and a low center of gravity makes the Ecocar 2000 handle quickly.

RAIN COVER: The rear half of the *Ecocar 2000* articulates and has pneumatic suspension, augmented by two tennis balls underneath the seat.

ECOCAR 2000

DESIGN PRINCIPAL

Designer Van Wijnen chose a bicycle configuration because it is faster and more nimble in traffic than the 3- and 4-wheel **HPVs** which in shape and size are more akin to cars than bicycles. He also wished to avoid an all-enclosing body shell, which can be hot and noisy, instead opting for a narrow roof with a drop-down rain cover. The open sides were designed to reduce vulnerability to lateral crosswinds, and on the next model, the surface area on the front part of the frame will be even smaller, thus further improving steering stability.

ROOF HOUSING

The arched roof houses the cables and switches for lights and carries the gear and brake cables. Instrumentation includes a key switch for the battery, horn, speedometer, clock, and radio. There is a sunroof hatch for extra ventilation in good weather. The next model will have a larger front window, and will include a windshield wiper.

DID YOU KNOW?

Wim Van Wijnen built his first recumbent bicycle in 1963. This unusual machine constantly aroused interest from the police, who eventually arrested him, claiming the bike was unsafe. Undaunted, he went on to make a series of such bikes that were used for making a 15-mile (25-km) journey to work each day. The latest model, the *Ecocar 2000*, is thus a practical vehicle in every respect, designed and developed through pragmatic trial and error in everyday use.

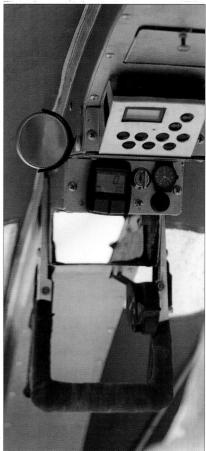

• **DRUM-SHOE HUB BRAKES:** Weather-resistant brakes designed to maintain performance in wet conditions.

The Aerodynamic Bean

Aerodynamic efficiency increases speed potential: the more smoothly an object cuts through air, the faster it can go. On a bike, as speed increases, a proportionately greater amount of the rider's pedal power is used to overcome air resistance. With a rider putting in ¼ horsepower of effort, a conventional bicycle does about 21 mph (34 km/h). Doubling the effort to ½ horsepower increases the speed to just around 26 mph (42 km/h). To attain 60 mph (97 km/h) the effort needed is an impossible 6 horsepower. Because of this, the way to reach higher speeds is not greater power, but greater aerodynamic efficiency. This can be achieved with a low-slung **HPV** like the *Bean* (below), with its streamlined body shell that minimizes

FRONTAL AREA: The *Bean's* small Cd means the aerodynamic resistance is 10 times lower than a racing bike.

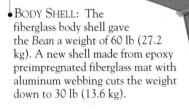

KINGCY

BODY SHELL: The fiberglass body shell gave the *Bean* a weight of 60 lb (27.2 kg). A new shell made from epoxy preimpregnated fiberglass mat with aluminum webbing cuts the weight down to 30 lb (13.6 kg).

RECORD BREAKER
Pat Kinch rode the Kingcycle Bean to a sea-level hour distance record of 47 miles (75.6 km) in September 1990 at Milbrook, England. In contrast, the sea-level hour distance record for a UCI-legal bike is 31 miles (50 km), set by Francesco Moser.

WHEELS: These are 17-inch *Moultons* with high-pressure *Wolber* slick tires.

resistance as it eases the flow of air around it when traveling at high-speed. A well-designed HPV can cut aerodynamic **drag** by 80 percent, reducing rider effort by a massive 70 percent. Fast Freddy Markham, riding the *Easy Racer Gold Rush*, has achieved 65.49 mph (105.37 km/h) in a sprint, on human power alone.

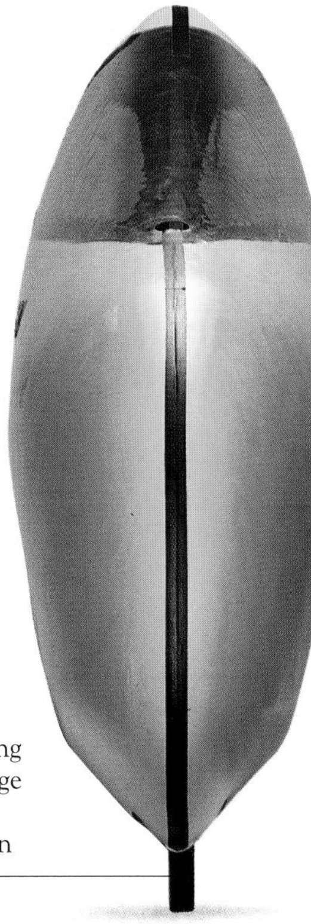

FRONT-WHEEL DRIVE: When setting the hour record Pat Kinch used a huge 186-inch gear, more than 1½ times as great as the largest that is found on a conventional bicycle.

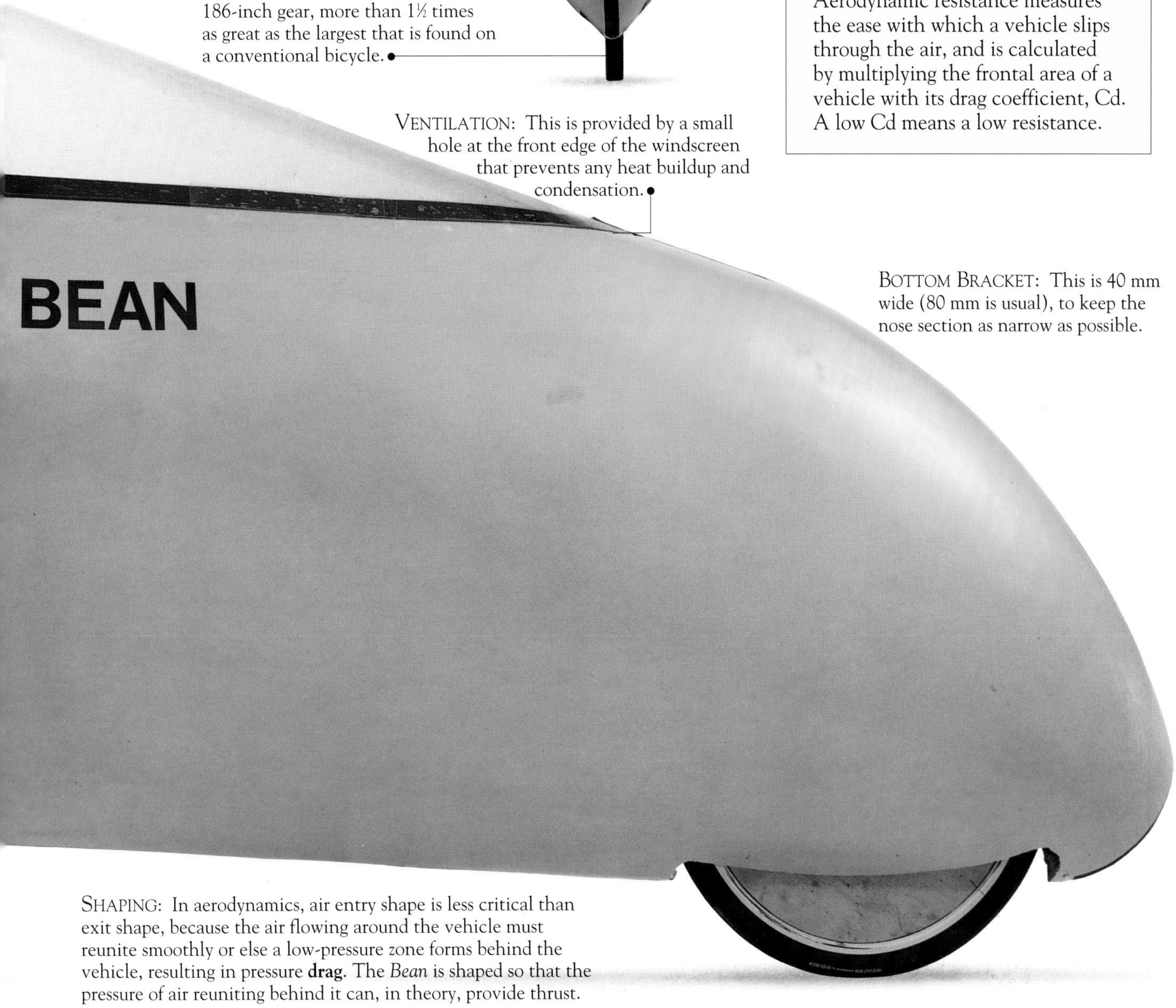

VENTILATION: This is provided by a small hole at the front edge of the windscreen that prevents any heat buildup and condensation.

DRAG – A BEGINNER'S GUIDE

Aerodynamic **drag** is a combination of air pressure drag and direct friction. A blunt, unevenly shaped vehicle disturbs the air flowing around it, making it separate from the surface of the vehicle. Low-pressure regions form behind the vehicle, resulting in a pressure drag that can have considerable force. Streamlined designs help the air close smoothly around a shape and reduce pressure drag. Friction drag occurs when the layer of air immediately next to the surface of the vehicle separates from it. It is reduced by smooth surfaces, and by minimizing the surface area. Aerodynamic resistance measures the ease with which a vehicle slips through the air, and is calculated by multiplying the frontal area of a vehicle with its drag coefficient, Cd. A low Cd means a low resistance.

BEAN

BOTTOM BRACKET: This is 40 mm wide (80 mm is usual), to keep the nose section as narrow as possible.

SHAPING: In aerodynamics, air entry shape is less critical than exit shape, because the air flowing around the vehicle must reunite smoothly or else a low-pressure zone forms behind the vehicle, resulting in pressure **drag**. The *Bean* is shaped so that the pressure of air reuniting behind it can, in theory, provide thrust.

Street Recumbents

The first **HPV**s were experimental machines for exploring the limits of aerodynamics and speed. But from the start, developers dreamed of building vehicles practical for use in everyday traffic: able to carry baggage and provide weather protection, and capable of averaging 30 mph (48 km/h) on human power alone. Today, street HPVs routinely average speeds of more than 25 mph (40 km/h) over considerable distances, and ultra-lightweight custom racing models are achieving close to 30 mph (48 km/h). For HPV specialists, the future has arrived; for the mass market, it isn't far away.

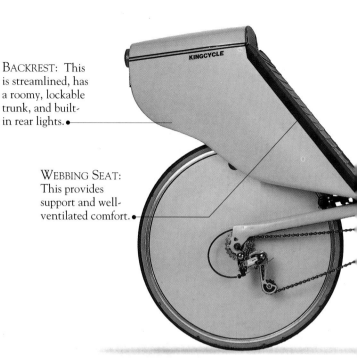

BACKREST: This is streamlined, has a roomy, lockable trunk, and built-in rear lights.

WEBBING SEAT: This provides support and well-ventilated comfort.

HEIGHT: The low center of gravity gives good handling and cornering. Control is enhanced by being able to pedal through corners without fear of grounding a pedal.

SEAT: The tensioned webbing seat provides good support with ample ventilation.

SUSPENSION: The rear wheel suspension is via swing-arm stays and a rubber **bushing**. The rear will accommodate a standard pannier rack and heavy, bulky baggage.

LONG WHEELBASE RECUMBENT
*Long **wheelbase** (LWB) recumbents, such as this Peer Gynt II from Germany, are very stable, particularly at high speeds. Its upright riding position and a low bottom bracket requires the leg muscles you use on a conventional bike to make little adaptation, because pedaling is still in a downward motion and the feet do not have to be lifted far to reach the pedals.*

LIGHTS: The lighting system is 6-volt, with a pop-up headlight and a brake light.

HANDLEBARS: These are beneath the seat, allowing the arms to fall to a natural position and keep the chest open.

HYDRAULIC BRAKES: With its inherently stable design, these give the *Peer Gynt* superb braking.

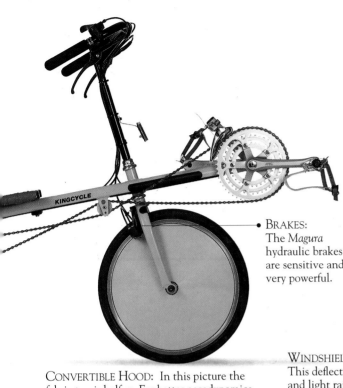

SHORT WHEELBASE RECUMBENT
Short **wheelbase** *(SWB) recumbents, such as this Kingcycle, are quicker and more nimble than LWB models. A higher bottom bracket raises the pedals and reduces the frontal area to give a significant aerodynamic advantage over conventional bikes. This creates a thoroughbred racing bike that climbs well and is good for touring and commuting.*

RECUMBENT TRICYCLE
The Windcheetah SL "Speedy" is a recumbent tricycle (for chassis details, see p.128). The Mark IV is a one-of-a-kind model with full suspension. With three wheels, the machine is extremely stable, even in strong crosswinds. "Speedys" have won both races and practical vehicle competitions. They are excellent for long-distance touring and for commuting in everyday city traffic.

BRAKES:
The *Magura*
hydraulic brakes
are sensitive and
very powerful.

LUGGAGE
SPACE:
This is behind
the rider, with
access via a panel
on the right side
of the vehicle.
There is additional
storage under the
seat, and in elastic
pouches which line
the cockpit.

CONVERTIBLE HOOD: In this picture the
fabric top is halfup. For better aerodynamics
or weather protection, it can be zipped up
so that it extends around the rider's neck.
In very hot weather it can be removed.

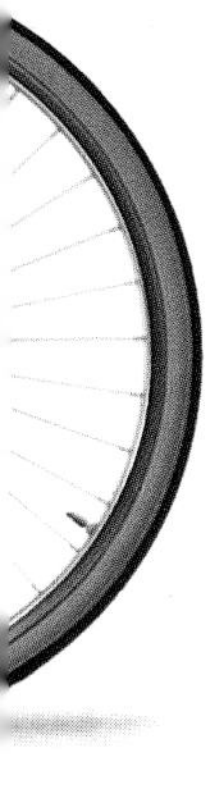

WINDSHIELD:
This deflects wind
and light rain.

BRAKES: Twin
Atom drum brakes
have superb
stopping power.

FAIRING: A
small hard-shell
top can be fitted
for racing or
bad weather.

RECORDS
This 36 lb (16.3 kg) *Mark VI* has achieved an
average speed of 31 mph (50 km/h)
over 37 miles (60 km) in
everyday traffic. The
latest *Mark VII* has a
carbon-fiber chassis
and, with a slimmer
fairing, weighs 30 lb
(13.6 kg).

Material Advances

Frames made of composite materials such as carbon-fiber are set to revolutionize bicycle manufacture. Carbon-fiber has surpassed other conventional materials such as steel and aluminum in the production of ultra-lightweight frames. A 2 lb, 4 oz (1.02 kg) frame has been built and one weighing less than 2 lb (0.9 kg) is now a practical possibility. With the weight barrier shattered, these frames are about to break price barriers, as messy and expensive labor-intensive production methods give way to cleaner, faster, and cheaper thermoplastic binding. Instead of using epoxy resins, carbon-fiber is woven with strands of thermoplastic to produce a dry fabric, which is easy to cut, shape, and set. With such a great reduction in material costs, this new process now promises an abundance of lightweight, high-quality cheap frames.

QUEST FOR AERODYNAMICS
The cantilever design is much easier to build, sacrifices little if anything in strength, and is considered more aerodynamic. Plus it makes changing tires a smoother operation!

FUTURISTIC DESIGN
The Windcheetah Carbon Cantilever (UK) is a superbly aerodynamic bike that demonstrates how bicycle design can be transformed by new materials. The streamlined frame is a carbon-fiber/fiberglass/epoxy composite with bonded alloy inserts for the head set, bottom bracket, and rear axle bearings.

•WHEELS: As part of the exercise of making as aerodynamic a bike as possible, the cantilever wheels are attached to stub axles – there is no matching **dropout** or fork blade on the other side of the bike.

THE RECYCLABLE BICYCLE

The prototype frame of this UK-designed *Kirk Precision* is pressure die-cast from 91 percent pure magnesium, which promises mass-produced lightweight frames at very low cost. Magnesium is the lightest structural metal on Earth, and its supply is theoretically almost infinite because it is extracted from sea water. It can also be recycled easily. Racing prototypes have survived races such as the Tour de France, but questions still hang over the concept itself. Magnesium is actually weaker than aluminum and is best used structurally for frames in chunky pieces. If it is used in the long, thin pieces characteristic of a bicycle, the strength and weight advantage fades away. Magnesium is also very vulnerable to corrosion, especially from electrolysis, a form of corrosion occurring when dissimilar metals come into contact. *Kirk Precision*'s manufacturers claim that its frame is strong, durable, and corrosion-free. Time will tell.

COMPOSITE PROTOTYPE

*Using a carbon-fiber and Kevlar mix, this 26½ lb (12 kg) prototype Radical ATB dispenses with traditional off-road frame design, and instead uses a modified cruciform shape. Advantages of this are that the rear of the frame acts like an elevated chain stay, reducing the length between rear axle and bottom bracket to a tight 15½ in (39.5 cm) The composite materials permit a bend in the chainside stay, so that the rear wheel does not need **dishing**.*

SEAT POST: Made of an unusual carbon/ *Kevlar*-covered alloy.

FRAME: Constructed from a mixture of carbon-fiber and *Kevlar* over a foam core, the frame is finished by curing it in a special mold.

Practical Vehicles

Concern for the environment has added fresh impetus to the quest for the ultimate personal vehicle, a practical machine that can compete with the car for convenience without polluting, consuming nonrenewable energy resources, or absorbing unnecessary amounts of road space. Basic criteria for such a vehicle is that it is weatherproof, can carry small loads, is safe, can be secured, and achieves all these without unduly sacrificing maneuverability or speed. The challenge is considerable, and many of the principles of **HPV**s are being used by designers as the basis for prototypes that experiment with different options, including solar-generated electric power assistance, new transmission systems, and innovative materials.

WEATHER PROTECTION
In damp weather both riders (left) can be fully enclosed by adding a polycarbonate zipper **fairing**.

SOCIABLE TANDEM
The Swiss-designed Twike is an optionally electronically assisted, three-wheel recumbent. Under pedal power alone, it can achieve 19 mph (30 km/h), but can reach 44 mph (70 km/h) with the aid of the motor.

LIGHTS: Headlights, brake lights, indicators, and a windshield wiper are all fitted to meet Swiss traffic laws.

HOT AIR VENT: To meet rules demanding a windscreen defroster, inventor Ralph Schnyder added a hair dryer, powered by the electric motor.

EASY TREADLER

The UK-designed four-wheel *Kingsbury Fortuna* overcomes the usual design problems of bullet-nosed, **faired HPV**s by changing the rider position to produce a more aerodynamically wedged shape. Instead of a rider rotating **cranks**, which requires room for foot clearance, the rider sits and pushes two treadles back and forth. Treadles require less space, making for a shorter, lower vehicle. The *Fortuna* also has all-wheel steering.

CONTROL COLUMN

The control column (right) controls steering, electric acceleration, and braking. The joystick element moves on a near-vertical axis, driving a rod that steers the front wheel. The **torque** *lever on top of the column controls the electric motor output. The driver turns on the motor when climbing to keep up with commuter traffic. The unit's 2.5-kw ni-cad batteries run for 62 miles (100 km) before being solar recharged in 5 to 6 hours.*

BODY SHELL: The award-winning *Twike* has a fiberglass body mounted on an aluminum chassis and has sufficient luggage space behind the riders to carry loads up to 65½ lb (30 kg). •

DRIVE AND BRAKE

Pedal power (below) is transmitted via a five-speed hub gear on the left rear wheel, while the motor drives both rear wheels. Braking is both electronic and mechanical by automatically retarding the motor just before drum brakes on both rear wheels cut in. A parking brake is included to meet Swiss laws.

WHEELS: The 20-in tires range from BMX to motorcycle grade, depending on conditions.

Sunlight Racers

The car's internal combustion engine has at least two terminal defects: pollution and inefficiency. Carbon dioxide accounts for half the warming effect of greenhouse gases, and automobiles are responsible for releasing 17 percent of this gas into the atmosphere. The practical efficiency of the internal combustion engine is normally less than 25 percent. By comparison, electric motors are 60 percent efficient and are pollution-free when operating. They also help to decrease CO_2 emissions if their electricity is from an energy source that is renewable, such as sunlight.

Solar Energy

Since their introduction in the first space exploration programs, photovoltaic cells, which turn sunlight to electricity, have become both practical and cost-competitive, achieving efficiency rates of up to 30 percent. With new technology, today's solarmobiles are capable of speeds in excess of 85 mph (137 km/h), and 0 to 60 mph (96 km/h) acceleration in under 9 seconds – using only 5 percent of the energy consumed by gas-driven automobiles. However, the technology is still at a relatively early stage of development: the long-distance, sunlight-power-only solarmobiles are impractical and expensive, requiring large surface areas for solar cells, complex control mechanisms, while remaining ultralightweight and efficient. For short journeys there are two more practical types of solar vehicles: a battery-powered electric car with rechargeable solar panels, and a hybrid: a bicycle or **HPV** with a small, sun-powered, backup electric motor.

FORMULA 1 RACER
*A solarmobile (above) racing in the 1989
Tour. These high-tech vehicles have solar
cells mounted on the vehicle and are not
allowed to charge from outside sources.
They consume little energy – equivalent
to 10 oz of gasoline per 62 miles.*

COMBINATION BIKE
*Sunpower (left) is a hybrid pedal/solar
electric bicycle with a top speed of about
28 mph (45 km/h). Based on a Peer
Gynt recumbent bicycle, and fitted with
a partial **fairing** made from Kevlar, it is
equipped with a motor-gearbox powered
by twin 12V lead-acid batteries and solar
cells. Electric and pedal power combine
for starting, accelerating, and climbing.*

ADAPTED ROADSTER
*Neufeld (right) is a standard road bike
fitted with electric power assist and a
solar cell roof. It weighs 160 lb (73 kg)
and is capable of 22 mph (35 km/h). It
is not a racing vehicle, but Neufeld did
cover the entire six-day course of the
Swiss Tour de Sol, including climbing
the rugged Gotthard Pass.*

The Future

The development of the bicycle in its first 100 years has been slow and inconsistent. Now, thanks to the explosive popularity of mountain bikes and the pressing ecological need for satisfactory alternatives to the car, bicycle technology is becoming increasingly sophisticated. Each component and every mechanical notion is coming under a refreshing new scrutiny. The enormous strides taken in materials technology, micro-electronics, computing, and manufacturing processes mean that the only common features state-of-the-art bikes in the year 2000 will share with their predecessors are human power, pedals, and wheels. At the forefront of developments, microchips and sensors are already being used to regulate gear-changing, braking and suspension systems. More than ever the bicycle is becoming a highly-refined mechanical extension of the body, giving a human being even more potential than any other creature to be the fastest self-propelled mechanism on Earth. This potential is also being harnessed to power prototype machines in the air and on water. All run on the premise

RECLINING VEHICLES
*One of the first recumbents to be built, this six-speed 1933 French Velocar has front and rear **hub brakes**, with balloon tires for safety and comfort.*

TRANSMISSION CHANGES

Electric Transmission
The computer-controlled *Chilcote* transmission automatically changes **gear ratio** in response to changes in pressure on the pedals and **cadence**, both of which are monitored by sensors in the hub. When a preset range is exceeded an electronic mechanism slides the 24 freewheel sprocket teeth to a new position and a new gear ratio.

Belt Drives
The quest for a lighter, cleaner, quieter, lubrication-free alternative to the greasy bicycle chain is likely to mean many more experiments with notched rubber belt drives, as on this *Twike*. Belt drives are already used on some folding bicycles, but the inherent problems of stretch and tension are only slowly being overcome.

Treadle Drives
Treadle drives should become popular with **HPV**s, since the driving motion is downward, and not circular as with pedaling. Less space is required and the bodyshell nose can be wedge-shaped. Pushing down from a seated position also makes better overall use of body muscles, without any loss of mechanical efficiency.

that a fit rider can generate one-third of a horsepower and for short bursts, up to one horsepower, pedaling devices that, like the bike, are basically chain-driven lever-operated machines that convert human energy into power. Provided a vehicle is light enough, pedal power, in theory, should be able to drive it.

Pedal-Powered Aircraft

Reducing a machine's weight to improve its power-to-weight ratio is a key concern of human-power pioneers. With new ultra-light, strong carbon-fiber-based materials, these weight problems are being solved and pedal power is now driving experimental airplanes, helicopters, boats, and submarines with varying success. Operating these machines requires real skill, especially while pedaling at top speed, and advances will come as computerized sensors are developed that automate control functions.

THE EAGLE
A prototype pedal-powered aircraft with the wingspan of a DC-9 jet flies across a California desert in proving trials for the Daedalus Project. A similar human-powered aircraft flew 75 miles (120 km) from Crete to Greece to re-create the myth of Icarus.

FLYING FISH
The pedal-powered hydrofoil Flying Fish *is the world's fastest human-powered watercraft over 328 ft (100 m), capable of 16 knots (18.5 mph) – 4 knots (4 mph), faster than a rowing eight. As its chain-driven 2-blade propeller spins, it rises up on inflated pontoons and flies on a 6-ft (2-m) wing.*

What's Next?

The mountain bike changed the cycle business in less than a decade. Yet it was pioneered by outsiders who ignored convention because they knew their invention was exciting and easy to ride. Similarly, **HPVs** that can outrun bikes on a flat and offer seated comfort also come from outside the cycle industry. Could HPVs that offer the bonus of wet weather protection catch on? Will a market develop in the flatlands of Northern Europe, with its ample bike paths and affluent customers? (HPVs cost twice as much as a normal bike.) Or will the HPV pioneers in traffic-free Eastern Europe create a market for HPVs as car substitutes? The future will tell.

CYCLE MAINTENANCE

6-in-1 tool

One of the great beauties of the bicycle is that you can look at it, study how it works, and service and maintain it yourself. Some jobs require more specialized tools and skills of course, but if you are at all unfamiliar with bikes, or machines in general, then just begin by checking the tyre pressures and adjusting control cables and brake blocks.

Complex Maintenance

Gradually you can work your way up to more complex tasks such as replacing bearings and transmission maintenance. You will soon learn how to keep your bike in good shape, and appreciate that some aspects of bike mechanics are quite sophisticated. Unless you are a professional, you should not expect to be able to true a wheel on any more than a rough-and-ready basis. This type of work is best left to a skilled specialist. Some jobs such as frame alignment are infrequent, but they require expensive equipment and considerable experience. So part of looking after your bike is finding a shop or mechanic that you trust to do good work: this is not always easy. During the summer, most shops will always have more repair work than they can cope with and quite naturally, bikes purchased from that particular shop will always

Multitool

3-in-1 tool

have the first priority – an important point to bear in mind when buying a bike.

Reputation

How do you discover a good shop? By reputation. The better shops will always look after their customers, because they know that the customers are their business. Ask other cyclists who they recommend, then give them a try. You'll easily be able to judge the results for yourself, because an awareness of a bike's mechanical condition is a natural part of riding. The more often you ride, the more aware of your bike you become, and the better you will be at looking after it. Maintaining the optimum performance of the bike is part of the fun.

Chain tool

Headset spanner

Wire cutter

Making repairs

Tools and Equipment

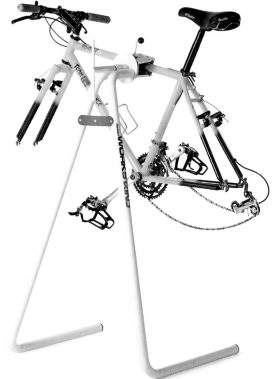

T he key to effective bike maintenance is organization: a space to work in, with a workbench or table; a means to hold the bike with the wheels off the ground; and the right tools, parts, and lubricants required for the job. Use good-quality, purpose-specific tools. Cheap tools are frustrating and can damage a bike.

Mechanically, bikes are quite diverse, and there is only enough space in this section to cover the basics and a few useful tricks. For more information, refer to repair manuals, attend a class, or use instructional videos. Your bicycle should have, or once had, an owner's manual with servicing instructions. Alternatively, try to obtain the manufacturer's leaflets for your bike components. A bicycle shop would probably have some extras, or allow you to photocopy a set.

BLACKBURN WORKSTAND
A freestanding, adjustable Workstand with a vinyl-coated grip that rotates so that the bike can be clamped by any of the main frame tubes and worked on from most angles.

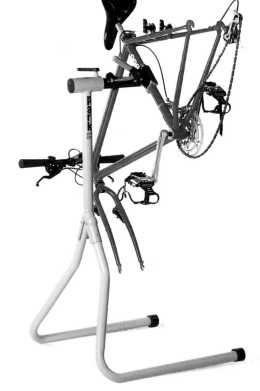

FREESTANDING CYCLE STAND
The Park PCS-1 freestanding floor stand gives access to the bike from every side and can be folded flat and easily stored in a closet. Better models also allow the bike to rotate.

TRIPOD STAND
The Kestrel Trio is a simple, inexpensive stand which holds the bike by the stays, permitting gear adjustments and removal of the rear wheel. Light and portable, it also serves as a convenient parking stand.

WORKBENCH STAND
Most manufacturers include a model such as the Kestrel that can be clamped into a vise-grip type workbench. The stand lifts the bike to a comfortable height for working on while standing.

CONTINGENCY TOOLKIT

Always carry a basic toolkit for roadside repairs and a pump with the right valve fitting for your tires. The kit should be small and light so that it can be slipped into a pocket or saddle pouch. Good quality multipurpose tools are very effective.

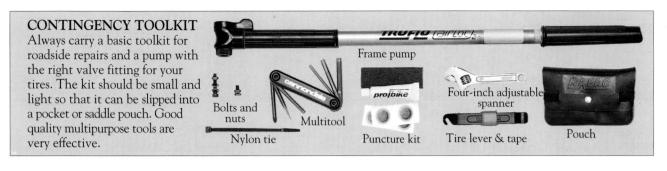

Frame pump

Bolts and nuts

Multitool

Nylon tie

Puncture kit

Four-inch adjustable spanner

Tire lever & tape

Pouch

HOME WORKSHOP

With the exception of the six-inch adjustable spanner, each tool in this selection has a specialized function. Some of the tools are quite lightweight and can be carried on a long ride. If you are riding with friends, be smart and carry one set for the whole group.

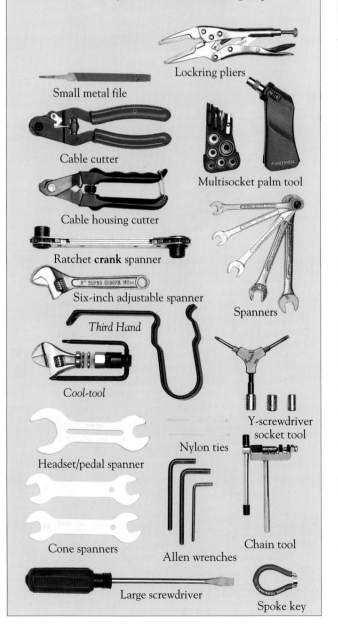

Lockring pliers

Small metal file

Cable cutter

Multisocket palm tool

Cable housing cutter

Ratchet **crank** spanner

Six-inch adjustable spanner

Spanners

Third Hand

Cool-tool

Y-screwdriver socket tool

Nylon ties

Headset/pedal spanner

Cone spanners

Allen wrenches

Chain tool

Large screwdriver

Spoke key

PROFESSIONAL

Tools in this category are specialized and well made for repeated use. Workshop-quality tools are expensive, but extremely effective. The better bike shops will always stock them.

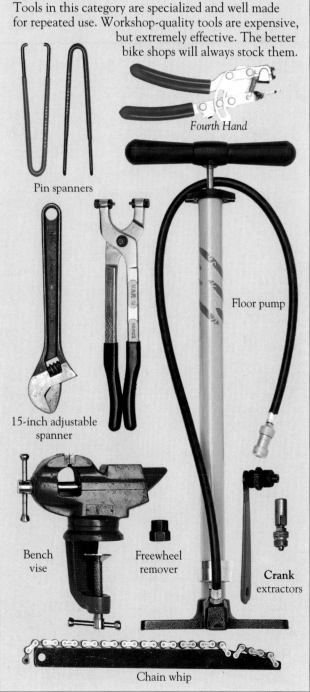

Fourth Hand

Pin spanners

Floor pump

15-inch adjustable spanner

Bench vise

Freewheel remover

Crank extractors

Chain whip

Thirty-Minute Service I

The 30-minute service is a good, systematic check of your entire bike. If the machine is sound, the job can be done quite quickly. If there are problems, the work will naturally take longer. The following pages provide you with details of the techniques you need to know in order to give your bike the thorough service it requires. Personally handling a bike is the key to understanding it and keeping an effective check on its mechanical health. This is best achieved as part of your regular cleaning routine (see p.186). In time, you will develop a kind of sixth sense for any problem areas. Something will look, feel, or sound wrong, and you will instinctively know where to start looking for the cause of the problem.

SADDLE CLAMP: Tighten (S). These bolts sometimes feel tight when in fact they are still loose; check by trying to move saddle.

SEAT POST BOLT: Tighten (F).

CABLES: Check that the housings are sound, the wires have no kinks or fraying, and that cables move easily. Tighten the cable anchor bolts just enough to start denting the wire (D/F), but not enough to strip the bolts. Most importantly, check that the wires do not slip.

BOTTOM BRACKET: Check bearings for play by pushing the crankset in and out; clicking indicates loose bearings. Disengage the chain from the chainring. Spin the **cranks**; grinding indicates tightor rough bearings. Then tighten the steel lockrings (S) and alloy lockrings (F).

BRAKE BLOCK BOLTS: Tighten (F). Check that brake blocks accurately meet the rim, with the correct toe-in (p.168).

FREEWHEEL: You should hear a healthy, even, and rapid clicking sound when freewheeling. Sprocket teeth must not be chipped or bent. Test for skipping by pedaling hard for a while in each gear.

FRONT DERAILLEUR: Check high/low travel (see p 176). Tighten the mounting bolt (F) and the cable anchor bolt (D/F).

REAR DERAILLEUR BOLT: Tighten (F).

CABLE ANCHOR BOLT: Tighten (D/F).

REAR DERAILLEUR: Operate gears to check high/low travel and, if included, the indexing operation. (See p.176 for adjustments.)

PULLEY BOLTS: Tighten (F).

SPOKES: Test for bends or breaks, and ensure each spoke is evenly tight. On the back wheel, the spokes near the freewheel will be less tight than those on the opposite side.

CHAIN: Pedal backwards, watching the derailleur rollers for any frozen links. Check wear (see p.152).

PEDALS: Check bearings (p.152). Tighten (S).

MOUNTING BOLTS: Tighten (F).

CRANK BOLTS: Test for tightness (see p.152). Tighten steel bolts (F). For alloy bolts, first use a steel bolt (F) then replace the alloy bolt (D).

CHAINRINGS: Check rings are true and teeth are not chipped or bent.

• STEM BOLT: Tighten (F). The bolt should be tight enough to remain in place when riding, but move if the bike takes a fall. To test the front wheel, hold it with your knees and twist the handlebars.

• BINDER BOLT: Tighten (F). Make absolutely sure that the handlebars cannot move unexpectedly.

• BRAKE LEVER MOUNTS: Tighten (F). The brake levers should be tight enough to stay in place when riding, but move in a crash. •

• HEADSET: Check bearings (see p.181). Tighten steel headsets (S) and alloy headsets (D/F).

• BRAKE PIVOT BOLTS: Tighten (D). Tighten side-pull brakes (F) also.

• CABLE ANCHOR BOLTS: Tighten (D/F).

• HUBS: Check bearings (see p.152). Tighten the axle nuts (S) and quick-release levers (F).

• RIMS: Check for trueness by holding a tool near the rim and spinning the wheel. More than 3 mm (⅛ in) of side-to-side or up-and-down movement calls for trueing (see p.158). Check that the rims are clean and not dented, splayed, or dimpled.

FORCE
Alloy bike parts can be damaged by over-tightening. Always use small tools on the small nuts and bolts. Three gradings of tightness are marked on the illustration: **S-Solid** *– tighten as hard as possible;* **F-Firm** *– tighten until resistance is felt; and* **D-Delicate** *– tighten with caution.*

• BRAKE LEVERS: Check travel, adjust via the cable adjusting bolt and/or cable anchor bolt (see p.166).

• FRAME AND FORK: Check frame alignment and tubes for dents and scratches. Pay close attention to the forks, checking the underside of the down tube where it meets the head tube. Any fractured paint on a steel frame may well be due to structural failure. A discolored ring on either bonded aluminum or carbon-fiber frames could be due to glue failure.

• TIRES: Check the pressure, the thread for wear, and the casings for cuts, embedded gravel, or glass.

WORKING IN ROTATION
Check that every bolt and nut is secure. Work by tool, checking all the 4-mm hex bolts, then all the 5-mm hex bolts, and so on. Ensure the tool fits the part; a wrong fit may cause damage. If you have used thread adhesive, do not disturb the bolt or nut, but do check that it is secure.

POINTER THREADS
Most components have right-hand threads which tighten when turned clockwise and will undo when turned counterclockwise. The left side pedal and locknut usually have left-handed threads which tighten counterclockwise and undo clockwise. Avoid cross-threading parts. When inserting a bolt, turn it backward until a small click is felt, and then inward. If resistance is felt, remove the bolt and closely examine the threads on it and in the bolt hole. Carefully smooth any nicks or cuts with a sharp file and try again. If you find a bolt or nut frozen in place, soak it in penetrating oil while tapping it lightly to help the oil work in. Wait for a few minutes and try again. Use a tool which fits the part exactly. If it still won't move, hacksaw or file the bolt off, and drill out the bolt hole. Be organized while you work. Lay out all your tools, parts, and materials beforehand and keep small parts in jars or egg cartons.

Thirty-Minute Service II

A bicycle is a dynamic extension of your body. Learn to tune in to your bicycle, so that you automatically listen to it and watch it as you cycle along. The better you ride, the more aware you will become of the bicycle's mechanical condition, and the more you will tune and maintain it as a matter of course.

Hearing

Any bicycle produces a constant melody of sounds, whirs, clicks, and soft hisses that form a rhythmic pattern when all is working well. Listen for any unusual noises, and when they occur, try to track down the source immediately. If you hear a rapid clicking, then pause in your pedaling for a moment. If the noise persists, it is most likely in the wheels. Stop and spin each wheel individually to locate the cause.

Touch

Your sense of touch is always vital. If the bike feels strange as you bank through a corner or swoop down a hill, then trust your senses. Stop and check the tire pressures. If they are okay, check that the wheels are firmly mounted and

properly aligned. Or you might be climbing up a hill or short incline, standing out of the saddle, and suddenly you feel a click and an odd bump on the downstroke. The click might be a chainring bending under the pressure and rubbing against a derailleur cage. The bump is a clue that the crank or the pedal might be coming loose.

Vision

Your eyes, like your ears, will develop a natural sense of order for the bicycle as you become accustomed to the way it works. If you happen to watch the chain and rear derailleur working, you might notice if the derailleur arm suddenly moves to and fro as the chain passes over the pulleys. The cause of this is probably a stiff link in the chain. Or if the chain rises slightly as it feeds onto part of the chainring, a chaintooth may be chipped or bent. You won't consciously look for the things which are wrong, but if you keep a constant eye, ear, and hand on the bike, you will notice right away when something is incorrect and not functioning properly.

CHAIN WEAR
Test the chain for wear by lifting it onto the large chainring. If one of the chainwheel teeth is fully exposed, it is worn out. Alternatively, measure, pin-to-pin, a 12-in (30.5 cm) length of chain. If it measures 2 ⅛ in (30.8 cm) or more, *the chain is worn. Replace the chain, chainrings, and the sprockets all at the same time; a new chain will perform badly on worn sprockets. If your bike has specific chainring/sprocket combinations, then you can retain those that are not worn.*

CHAINTEETH
Check that the chainrings are true, without any side-to-side wobble. Check also that none of the teeth are chipped or bent. Very worn chainteeth look like a shark's fin or a series of little waves — and their replacement is long overdue.

THE HEADSET
Check the headset bearings by firmly engaging the front brake, and push the bike back and forth. A click-clunk sound indicates loose headset bearings or a loose brake mounting bolt. Lift the front wheel and lightly rotate the handlebars. Any roughness indicates the bearings are too tight and/or need regreasing.

LOOSE CRANKS
*Creaking noises are often caused by loose **cranks**. To test them, place the cranks horizontally, and press down hard on both pedals at once. Rotate the cranks 180° and then press the pedals again. If the crank moves, the crank mounting bolts need tightening. Check the cranks frequently on new bikes.*

BEARINGS
The hubs, bottom bracket, pedals, and freewheel of a bike all use ball bearings to reduce friction between the moving parts – for example, between a wheel hub and an axle. Some bearing mechanisms are fixed, so they can't be adjusted. Adjustable bearings have a ball race or cup that is fixed in place, and a movable cone or cup held in place with a locknut or lockring. A basic technique for adjusting the bearing is to slacken the locknut or lockring and hand-turn the adjustable cone or cup flush against the bearings. Reverse it ⅛ to ¼ turn. Hold it in place, lightly retightening the locknut or lockring. Test the adjustment, which should be slightly loose and should give a very light click when pushed back and forth. Firmly tightening up the locknut or lockring will draw the bearing into perfect adjustment – but always check: hub bearings will tighten slightly when the wheel is fastened to the frame.

PEDALS AND CRANK
*Grasp the pedal and **crank** firmly, and push the pedal back and forth. Clicking sounds indicate that the bearings are loose and need some adjustment. Then spin the pedals. Grinding and sticking indicates the bearings may be too tight. If you use toe clips, check them for splits or cracks. Make sure the straps are in good condition and do not have grooves that could allow the buckles to slip.*

Wheel First Aid

A bicycle wheel is one of the strongest engineering structures in the world. The lighter the wheels, the faster a bike handles and accelerates. Accordingly, road and track racing bikes use slim, light wheels and narrow tires, while mountain bikes, used for pounding over rocks and through potholes, use wider, heavier wheels and stouter tires. There are many shadings within this light/heavy spectrum, and by using different sets of wheels, a bike can have several different personalities. A mountain bike rider might use gnarly knobbies for off-road riding, wet-traction road tires for commuting, and treadless slicks for fast road riding.

Bearing Adjustment

Wheels should be regularly checked and tuned, adjusting the spokes so they are evenly tensioned, and the rim is true – when the wheel spins, the rim does not wobble from side-to-side, or move up and down. Hub bearings with adjustable cones should be checked for binding (too tight) or excess play (too loose). Some hub bearings cannot be adjusted.

TRACKING
An important first step when looking at the wheels on your bike is to check the tracking – the alignment of the wheels. With the bike resting upside down on its saddle, sit behind one of the wheels so that, at eye level, you can see whether the wheels are in line.

CLEANING AND LUBRICATING HUBS
When dismantling hubs in order to clean and/or lubricate them, always ensure that you count the bearings as they are removed. Clean all parts in a biodegradable solvent and dry thoroughly. Pack cups with grease and press the ball bearings into the grease.

HUB BEARINGS
*Check with the wheel in the **dropouts**, as tightening axle nuts or a quick-release slightly tightens bearings. Grasp the wheel and pull it back and forth. If you can feel a definite clicking, the bearings are loose. Next, hold the wheel off the ground with the valve at 3 o'clock. When it is released, the valve's weight should pull it down to 6 o'clock. If not, the bearings may be too tight. If so, remove the wheel for cone adjustment.*

ADJUSTING CONES
On wheels with freehubs, first ensure that the right side locknut and cone are firmly locked. Undo the left side locknut and cone, taking care not to dislodge bearings. Screw the cone finger-tight against the bearings, reverse it ⅛ to ¼ turn and lock it in place with the locknut. Test with axle nuts or the quick-release clamp in place. (Note: Remove Hyperglide or thread-on freewheels before adjusting cones – see p.182).

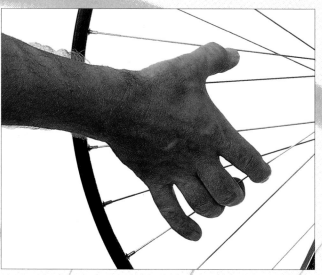

TRUEING A WHEEL

Wheel trueing is an art, and beginners should not expect first-time perfection. Spokes should be checked for bends and breaks. Check for even tension by plucking the spokes. Front wheel spokes should all sound the same. On the rear wheel, the spokes on the freewheel side of the hub have less tension than the spokes opposite. If any are loose, tighten them until they feel and sound the same as the others.

1 *Mark lateral high spots by holding chalk or a marker against one of the stays while the wheel is spinning. Slowly bring the chalk in until it comes in contact with the high points on the rim. The longest mark made by the chalk indicates the area where the rim is most out of true and where the spokes need adjusting.*

2 *Even tension is vital, so if a spoke within the marked area is out of step, bring it back into line, even if this means adjusting it more than the others. Regularly spin the wheel to check progress. With the first mark correct, move to the next longest mark.*

4 *Mark vertical high spots by holding a marker over the top of the rim and spinning the wheel. Where there are high spots, tighten the spokes in groups of four; with flat spots, loosen the spokes. After these adjustments, check side-to-side play, and correct if necessary.*

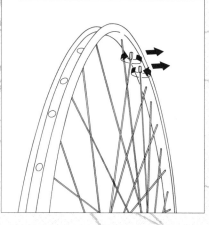

3 *Loosen the spokes that lead to the hub flange on the same side as the mark and tighten the spokes to the opposite flange. Work a half turn at a time, balancing each side. If you loosen two spokes a half turn each, tighten two opposing spokes a half turn each.*

5 *Examine the inside of the rim and file any protruding spokes or sharp edges that might puncture the inner tube. Handling a spoke key makes you appreciate the craft of trueing a wheel, and with time you should be able to work confidently on a wheel.*

TIRE PRESSURES

To make a bike go faster, inflate the tires to the correct pressure. Under-inflated tires increase rolling resistance and puncture risk. The pressure listed on the sidewall is only a reference point calculated by inflating the tire to twice that pressure without blowing it off the rim. Optimum pressures vary according to weight and conditions, so experiment, as 5-10 psi can affect performance.

Fixing a Flat Tire

There are few things more frustrating than riding your bike and suddenly discovering that a tire has a puncture. Although a flat tire is a nuisance, if you carry a pump, and a spare inner tube or a puncture repair kit, you can be mobile again within minutes. Make sure that the pump you carry is for the type of valve on your tire, and that the spare tube is the same size and valve type as the tube you are replacing. Valve widths vary, and a car-type *Schrader* valve might not fit through a rim hole designed for a narrow gauge *Presta* valve. Try to reduce the possibility of getting a puncture by regularly inflating your tires to their correct pressure, inspecting them for wear, and removing any sharp objects that are embedded in the tire tread.

1 *Remove the valve cap and locknut. On the Presta valve, undo the valve and push it in to deflate the tire completely. On a Schraeder valve, use a pen, screwdriver, or other small implement to push in the valve. Press the valve stem through the hole in the rim.*

TWO-MINUTE TUBE CHANGE

2 *Pinch the tire walls firmly together all the way round the tire, pressing back and forth to work the bead of the casing away from the rim. The tire and rim will then separate easily. Make sure both beads are down in the rim well. If necessary raise the tube valve clear of the bead.*

3 *If the tire is a loose fit, lift one side over the rim with your hands. If the tire is tight, carefully insert a tire lever, making sure not to pinch the tube, and lever the tire bead over the rim. Work all around the rim until one wall of the tire is completely off the rim.*

4 *Lift the valve out through the valve hole and remove the tube. Mark the location of the puncture hole in the tube with chalk. Inspect the tire for the cause of the puncture and remove any particles from the casing before inserting a new or repaired tube.*

5 *Partially inflate the replacement tube so that it has sufficient shape to avoid becoming creased, wrinkled or pinched. Place the tube inside the tire and insert the valve stem through the rim hole, making sure it is straight. Then fit the valve stem locknut loosely.*

6 *Tuck the rest of the tube into the tire, ensure it is even all the way around, then deflate it completely. Push the valve stem up into the tire. Slip the tire bead over the rim. Keep the valve stem clear of the rim or the bead may catch on it, creating a bulge in the tire.*

7 *Use your thumbs to press the side of the tire back over the rim. Work back and forth to prevent the tire popping off at either side. Knead with a steady pressure. If the last few inches are tight, reach across the tire and yank it into place. Then reinflate the tire.*

Two-Minute Tube Change

Fast tire changing involves a couple of essential tricks, which with practice make it possible to change a tube in two minutes. (It has been done in one minute!) The key to a really quick tire change is to make sure that the sides of the tire are pushed away from the edge of the wheel and down into the rim well. This will loosen the tire (which tends to stick to the rim after months of use) so that one side of the tire can be easily maneuvered over the rim edge. Your hands are always the best tools for the job, although you might need to use a tire lever. Take care, though, not to pinch the tube with the lever.

Puncture Repair

To mend a puncture you need a repair kit with tire levers, patches, and a tube of glue. Sandpaper and a piece of chalk are useful. Work methodically. The key to a successful repair is thorough preparation and cleanliness. If your hands become dirty removing the wheel, clean them so that no oil gets on the inner tube. If there is no sign of a puncture, it may be a leaky valve. Punctures on the under side of the often result from protruding spokes. These should ideally be smoothed out with a file. As a temporary measure, cover the end with tape.

PUNCTURE REPAIR

1 Locate the puncture by inflating the tube and holding it next to your face, rotating it. If you cannot feel or hear any air escaping, test the valve with a drop of saliva. If you still cannot trace the hole, fully inflate the tube, immerse it in water and watch for air bubbles.

2 Once you locate the puncture, dry the tube and roughen the area around the puncture with sandpaper. Make the sanded area larger than the repair patch. If you do not have any sandpaper, a cement surface will do. Give the tube one last thorough cleaning.

3 Clean your hands. Spread an even layer of rubber cement over the sanded area. Let the cement dry until it is tacky, so that the solvent in the cement evaporates completely. Do not allow anything to touch the cement during this time. Put the tube aside in a safe place.

4 While you are waiting for the cement to dry, feel inside the tyre for the cause of the puncture and remove it. If the puncture is on the inside of the tube, the cause may be a protruding spoke. If you cannot smooth the spoke, cover it with several layers of tape.

5 Peel off the foil on the patch, being careful not to touch the adhesive area that you expose. Press the patch firmly down onto the puncture hole, rubbing from the center to the edges. Use some sandpaper and chalk to powder the cement around the patch.

6 Leave the patch to set for a couple of minutes, then pinch the tube and patch it together so that the cellophane back of the patch splits. Peel the cellophane away from the centre, taking care not to peel off the patch. Inflate the tube, and then check the patch.

Roadside Repairs

It's the moment any cyclist dreads: you're out on a ride and one vital piece of equipment breaks without warning. You are not carrying any spares or tool kit and the nearest telephone is a long way away. If you're out in the wild on a mountain bike, you could be in a real mess. Try a little ingenuity – the solution may be closer than you realize. Your tire blows, the inner tube is beyond repair and you don't have a spare? Fill it with grass so that it's sufficiently packed to ride home on. A screw on a pannier rack works loose and you haven't got a screwdriver? Use a small coin instead. A fork **dropout** gets bent out of true: try using the hollow end of a seat post to lever it straight again. A cable breaks? Try to reroute it, or replace it with string. The list of quick fixes for bike emergencies is endless. All they require is a little imagination and a view that most things can be fixed with objects on hand.

SPLIT SADDLE: When a saddle splits down to its frame the choice is between riding standing up or fixing it. If there is any padding left, bind the saddle back together.

BANDAGED SADDLE: If the saddle padding is shot, wrap a shirt or sweater around the seat and secure with a piece of string.

PATCHED PEDALS: If a pedal cage shatters but the spindle survives, rebuild it with bound wire, or make a substitute wood pedal. If the spindle breaks, lash a piece of wood to the side of the **crank**.

LOST GEAR: For a broken derailleur, leave the chain on a middle cog and strap the derailleur with a cord to keep the jockey arm extended and the chain taut.

BROKEN CHAIN: If a link pin disappears, insert a twig or wire through the link holes and bind it with tape or cloth. Expect to rebind it every half-hour or so, but it will keep you going.

CABLES: If you damage the small cable housing channel on a gear lever and the cable flops out when you use the lever, then wrap a cable tie around the housing to keep the cable in the channel. Cable ties are useful as they hold components in position without any hindrance.

HEADSET BEARINGS: If conditions are muddy or you ride through a stream, protect the bearings by sliding a section of split tube around the headtube base.

BRAKE LEVER: Force a short, hollow tube over the remaining stump if the lever snaps.

SNAPPED STRADDLE WIRE: Frayed or broken brake cables that do not run through a cable housing can be replaced with string.

FRONT DERAILLEUR: If it breaks, remove the cable and the mechanism, and move the chain to the middle chainwheel.

THE ART OF MENDING

While the motor car is now a necessary fact of life, bicycles outnumbered cars by 3 to 1 during the inter-war years in Europe. Roadside scenes like this were commonplace.

REPAIR AND REPAIR AGAIN

Don't despair if your first attempt to fix a broken part falls apart after a few miles. If it can be repaired once, it can be repaired again, and although a journey might be slower than originally planned, you'll still go faster than pushing the bike home. It is worth carrying a few essential items, such as a piece of wire, a bungee cord, some string, a penknife, and tape. With these items you are sure to be able to mend most breakdowns temporarily.

TEMPORARY PATCHES: Modern skinwall tires are thin, and a badly gashed sidewall can leave a hole big enough to let an inflated tube bulge through. The trick is to line the hole in the tire casing with some thin material: bits of cardboard, old inner tube, tree bark, even gum wrappers. Then insert the tube and reinflate.

STUFF IT: Every cyclist should carry a pump, but the odds are that you will be without one when you need it most. Artificially reinflate the tire by filling it with grass or leaves, thin branches like hazel switches,or even old newspapers.

TIRES: For a slow puncture, take out the inner tube carefully and wrap tape around the leak.

Roadside Repairs II

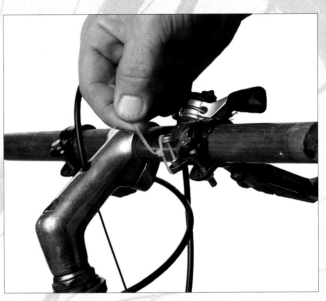

STICK AND STRING

One way to improvise a spanner is to tie a length of string or wire to a small, preferably flat-sided, stick. Wrap the string or wire around the nut, or part you want to move; wind the string clockwise to tighten it, counter-clockwise to undo it. Brace the short end of the stick against the nut and use the longer end as a spanner handle. This technique may be somewhat desperate, but it is surprisingly effective if you ensure that you wind the string or wire sufficiently tightly.

ZIP TIES

You should always maintain a good supply of zip ties. They are made from a flexible, and yet incredibly strong plastic, and they are very handy. They can be used to mount parts to the bike – especially useful where bolts have snapped, or bind a freewheel with frozen pawls to the spokes: their uses are literally endless. Zip ties can be stored in numerous places on a bike: taped to the saddle rails or to a rack strut, or hidden in the seat post. They can be stored almost anywhere.

WOODEN BOLT

*If you have a pocket knife – a piece of equipment no off-road rider should be without – a temporary replacement for a missing bolt or part can be carved out of wood. Look around you for an old tool handle, bits of fence post, or any other piece of dry wood, ensuring that it is as hard as possible. This **crank** bolt (above) was carved just slightly too large, so that the threads in*

the crank would cut matching grooves in the wooden bolt when it was inserted. Naturally, a wooden bolt has limited strength, but all it has to do is hold the crank in place. The get-you-home technique is to use the metal bolt from the crank on the opposite side to tighten the loose crank, and then to hold it in place with the wooden bolt.

CABLE MENDS

A broken cable can be rejoined by tying the ends to another object: a stick, an old tin can, a length of rag, or a portion of shoelace. If it isn't possible to rejoin the cable because it has broken off close to the control lever, you can improvise another means of operating the part. For example, a front derailleur cable can be tied to a frame tube or rack strut in such a way that, to allow you to shift gear, the cable could be pulled and hooked over a water bottle bolt or some other handy item.

WIRE PIN CHAIN

If you snap a chain and lose the rivet, a piece of wire can hold the links in place. The kind of wire used to make coat hangers is ideal for this function. Try to run the chain on a rear cog that is large enough to keep the chain clear of the other cogs, or else the wire may get caught in the space between the cogs. It may help to insert the wire, bend the ends back along the chain, away from the direction of travel of the chain, and bind it in place with tape. The cog teeth will then punch holes in the tape as they rotate.

POTATO CHIP STOMP

Anyone can become a victim of a badly buckled wheel. You may have twisted and braked too hard on the front wheel or slid sideways with the back wheel into a rock. Whatever the cause, you've got a major problem: the wheel is now bent into a shape that resembles a potato chip. First, remove the wheel and hold it so that the sections curving away from you are at the top and the bottom. Place the wheel at an angle against a tree, post, wall, or any other solid object. Brace the bottom of the wheel with your foot, grasp each of the sides that are curving toward you (at 3 and 6 o'clock) with your hands, and push against them firmly. Continue pushing as necessary until the rim is straight enough to fit back on the bike. Use a spoke key to tighten the spokes and true up the wheel as best you can. If you don't have a spoke key, a small adjustable spanner, or vise-grips, all is not lost. Remove the tire and use a screwdriver to adjust the spoke nipples. Ride home extremely slowly.

Adjustments for Comfort I

Setting up the most efficient and comfortable riding position can involve a whole series of interrelated measurements and adjustments. If one setting changes, so must all the others. For example, when you increase your saddle height, then the distance between the saddle and the handlebars will increase. To maintain a comfortable position, it may be necessary to move the saddle forward – or, if your saddle is already as far forward as it can go, to use a **stem** with a shorter reach. The system given here is methodical, and if at some point you make a change in the bike, such as installing longer or shorter **cranks**, or raising or lowering the height of your handlebars, start the adjustment process anew from step one. The changed set-up may feel awkward at first, but give it a fair trial, 50 miles (80 kilometers) or so, to allow your body time to adjust to a new position.

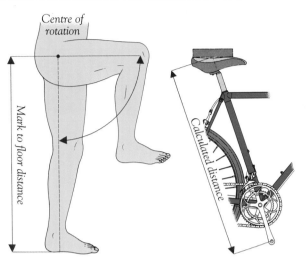

Centre of rotation

Mark to floor distance

Calculated distance

SADDLE HEIGHT

To work out your correct saddle height, multiply your inseam length (stand against a wall with bare feet, and measure from the floor to your crotch) by 0.885, and add on the thickness of your shoe soles and **cleats**. If your feet are large for your height, add an extra 0.1 in (3 mm). The result is the distance you need between the top of the saddle and the center of the bottom bracket axle. A more precise method is to stand barefoot against a wall and mark the center of rotation of your upper femur (the most outward bump on the hip above the hip socket). As you lift your thigh up parallel with the floor, it should stay in line with the mark. Measure each leg from the mark to the floor three times (in mm), average each measurement, and multiply by 0.95. Add on your shoe sole and cleat thickness, and the height of the pedal cage above the pedal axle. The result is the distance needed between the pedal hole and a halfway point between the top of the saddle and a straight edge.

CHECKING FRAME SIZE

A rough guide for the correct frame size is: With the correct saddle height, 3½ to 5 in (8.9-12.7 cm) of seat post should be exposed for racing bikes, 3 to 4 in (7.6-10.2 cm) for touring bikes, and 6 to 8 in (15.2-20.3 cm) or more for mountain bikes. The clearance between your crotch and the top tube should be 1 to 2 in (2.5-5.1 cm) for racing bikes, 1 in (2.5 cm) for touring bikes, and 3 in (7.6 cm) or more for mountain bikes and other **hybrid** bicycles.

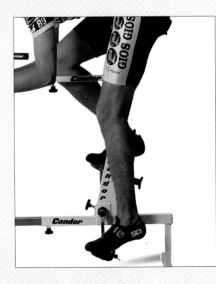

QUICK CHECKS

In addition to the more precise methods of adjustment detailed above, there are several standard checks that reveal at a glance whether your saddle is at the right height. Seated on the saddle with the ball of your foot on the pedal and the pedal down, your knee should be slightly bent (left). If your hips rock from side to side when pedaling, your saddle is too high (right). Another check: With one pedal straight down, your heel should not quite reach the other pedal. A clearance of 0.1 in (3 mm) should be fine. For conventional **cleats**, *give a 0.1 to 0.2 in (3-5 mm) clearance. Lock-type clipless pedals should have a 0.2 to 0.3 in (5-8 mm) clearance.*

SADDLE ADJUSTMENTS

Saddle Fore and Aft
Sit with **cranks** level, and drop a line from the knee protrusion to the pedal axle in front. Set the saddle 0.4 in (1 cm) forward for a high **cadence** rate, 0.4 to 0.8 in (1-2 cm) back for power.

Saddle Tilt
To alter the tilt of the saddle, adjust the angle of the seat bolt clamp. Conventional saddles (above left) are adjusted using spanners, while micro-adjust seat clamps (above right) use a

6 mm hex key. Starting with the saddle completely level (above), lower the nose slightly if you feel uncomfortable. Too far down will strain your arms and back. Too high up will hurt in time.

PEDALS
Always pedal with the widest part of your foot over the pedal axle for the most comfortable and powerful riding. The pedal is essentially a platform for your foot as it pushes against the **crank**. *If you use toe clips, make sure there is a gap of at least 0.2 in (5 mm) between the tips of the shoes and the clips.*

SLOTTED CLEATS
Align the slotted **cleats** *with the natural rotation of your foot. Slightly loosen the mounting bolt so that the cleat moves as your foot twists on the pedal. Ride in various positions, spinning fast. When you feel comfortable, stop and undo the strap. Lift the cleat off without altering its position and tighten the bolt.*

PEDAL TENSION

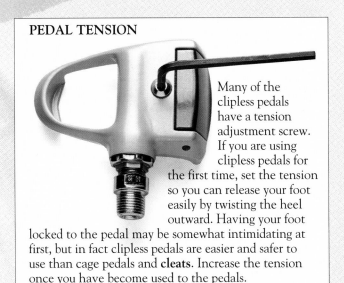

Many of the clipless pedals have a tension adjustment screw. If you are using clipless pedals for the first time, set the tension so you can release your foot easily by twisting the heel outward. Having your foot locked to the pedal may be somewhat intimidating at first, but in fact clipless pedals are easier and safer to use than cage pedals and **cleats**. Increase the tension once you have become used to the pedals.

CLIPLESS STEP-IN PEDALS
Most clipless step-in pedals allow up to 10 degrees of rotational play or twist for the foot, but should still be aligned using the loosen-ride-tighten method for slotted **cleats** *(above). You'll need a friend to tighten the mounting bolts, because you won't be able to free your foot from the pedal without disturbing the cleat.*

Adjustments for Comfort II

After correctly positioning the saddle, the next step is to adjust the reach to the handlebars so that the rider's back inclines forward at an angle of 45 degrees to the hips, with the arms slightly bent to absorb road shock. Reach is determined by the extension length of the **stem**. Road bike (drop handlebar) stems extend straight forward, so finding the correct size is simple. Mountain bike stems, however, extend forward and rise, and the handlebars can be straight, or swept rearward up to about 12 degrees. With this number of variables, finding the right combination often requires experimentation. One way to do this is to temporarily fit an adjustable stem. Another method is to use a frame fitting machine.

HANDLEBAR POSITION
*The **stem** should be at such a height that it positions the handlebars 1 to 3 in (2.5 – 7.6 cm) below the saddle. A lower handlebar position is suitable for long arms and torso, and fierce riding; a higher position suits short arms and torso, and more relaxed riding.*

HEIGHT ADJUSTMENT
*Loosen the **stem** bolt and tap it with a hammer and wooden block to remove it. Grease the stem and replace it, tightening the stem bolt firmly. The handlebars should be secure, but able to move if the bike falls. Test by holding the front wheel between your knees and twisting the handlebars.*

MAXIMUM EXTENSION
*There should be at least 2½ in (6.3 cm) inside the steerer tube. Most **stems** have a mark of the maximum safe extension. Stem extensions range from 2 to 5½ in (5-14 cm), measured from the center of the bolt to the center of the handlebars. The safe limit is 12 cm (4½in)*

DROP HANDLEBAR EXTENSIONS

Short Extension
Too short an extension causes the back to arch, compressing the diaphragm and impairing aerobic cycling performance. Note: with hands on drops and forearms parallel to the road, knees should overlap elbows at the top of the pedal stroke.

Long Extension
Too long an extension results in locked elbows, and back strain. You may want an additional ½ – 1 in (1 – 2 cm) of extension later. Your handlebars should obscure the front hub if you ride with your hands on the brake lever hoods.

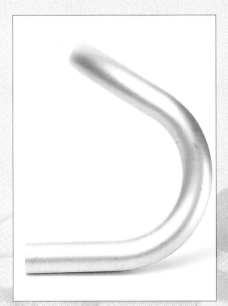

HANDLEBAR DROP
The depth of the drop (left) is very much dependent on your hand size. A depth of 5½ in (14 cm) is shallow, 5½ to 6 in (14-15 cm) is medium, and over 6 in (15 cm) is large. Position the handlebar ends parallel with the ground or raked to a maximum of 10 degrees.

HAND MEASUREMENT
To measure your hands (right), grasp a tubular object with the same diameter as the handlebars in your fist. Put your fist on a table with the tube horizontal. Measure the fist height. Under 2¾ in (7 cm) is shallow, 2¾ to 3½ in (7-8.9 cm) is medium, over 3½ in (8.9 cm) is large.

BRAKE LEVERS
On drop handlebars, the brake lever (left) should be mounted so that the tip of the lever just touches a straightedge laid along the handlebar end.

BRAKE LEVER ADJUSTMENT
The mounting bolt, (right) is inside the brake hood. Depress the brake lever to gain access with a hex key.

HANDLEBAR ADJUSTMENTS

Handlebar Width
Handlebar widths range from 21 to 24 in and should be at least as wide as your shoulders. Wider bars give better slow-speed control: narrower bars suit racing, and squeezing through tight gaps in urban traffic.

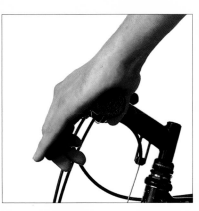

Handlebar Position
A straight wrist is the key to both the correct handlebar and brake lever position. Keep your thumb, pinkie, and ring fingers around the handlebar grip, and middle and index fingers on the brake lever.

Lever Adjustment
Most brake levers have an adjusting screw to set their distance from the handlebar. Tighten the mounting bolt firmly enough so that the levers stay in place, but can move in case of a fall.

Brakes

Before you service your brakes, you should always undertake three basic checks. First, ensure that the rims on both wheels are true (see pp.154-55) and in a decent condition without any dents, dimples, or splaying, which could affect the braking performance of the bicycle. If they are streaked and dirty, then clean them with steel wool. Then check the brake blocks for wear and tear, and clean out any embedded grit. Inspect for kinks and frayed cable wires, and the cable housings, for damage. Last, replace all the old parts and any suspect components you find.

BRAKE LEVER
Adjust the levers so the brakes engage when your grip is comfortable, but your hands don't hit the bars under pressure. The cable adjusting screw (left) is on the brake lever mount of cantilever brakes, and on the brake mechanism of side-pull brakes.

CABLE ADJUSTING BOLT
Undo the lockring (right) and move the screw in or out. Reduce tension when moving it out by holding the cable housing as you apply and release the brake lever.

SIDE-PULL BRAKES

1 *If there is too much play in the brake levers of side-pull brakes, and the cable adjusting screw cannot be turned out any farther, you should reset the cable anchor bolt. Turn the adjusting screw clockwise until it is all the way back in. To prevent the brake springs from forcing the cable wire out of the bolt while you are loosening it, you should compress the brake arm so that the shoes are held against the rim. A useful tool for this is a Third Hand tool, which holds the brake shoes in place, leaving your hands free to do the work.*

2 *Once you have compressed the brake arm, slacken slightly, but do not completely remove the anchor bolt. Use either a pair of pliers or a Fourth Hand tool to draw the cable through the cable anchor bolt, and then retighten the bolt. Just before tightening the anchor bolt, remember to check the quick-release tab, which is used to open out the brake arms so the wheel can be removed quickly, is closed. If it is open, then the cable anchor bolt setting is likely to be too tight and you will have to reset the bolt once again.*

CANTILEVER BRAKES

1 *Cantilever brakes have strong springs, so use a Third Hand tool as an aid if the cable anchor bolt must be reset when the brake lever cannot be adjusted via the cable adjusting screw. Turn the adjusting screw until it is all the way in, and compress the brake arms to ensure that the shoes are flush against the rim. A Third Hand tool will prevent the cable wire from pulling out of the anchor bolt. Some brakes have the anchor bolt on the brake arm and can be easily adjusted with just one spanner. Other brakes have both a bolt and nut, so you will need to use two spanners for the work.*

2 *Be sure to turn the nut and not the anchor bolt, since the cable wire passes through a small hole in the anchor bolt. If you do turn the wire, it will probably twist. (If your bicycle has anchor bolts with drilled holes, it is prudent to carry a spare wire in your permanent tool kit.) The angle formed by the straddle wire and the brake arm affects both the leverage and stopping power of the brakes. This angle varies, so refer to the manufacturer's pamphlet for the correct angle. There is usually no need to re-set the length of the straddle wire, but make sure it stays clear of the tires.*

POTENTIAL DANGERS
A danger of using cantilever brakes for front wheels without mudguards is that in the event of a cable anchor bolt failure or a snapped cable wire, the straddle wire will snag the front wheel. This can throw the rider right off the bike and cause some serious damage. One way to avoid this potential danger is to mount a front reflector through the fork hole and pass the straddle wire over the reflector bracket. Another method is to use a bolt long enough so that it can catch the straddle wire. If you want additional security, try taping the cable wire back on itself, so that if the anchor bolt slips, the straddle wire may still be held clear of the tire.

HYDRAULIC BRAKES

Hydraulic brakes use fluid rather than wire cables. Replacing or fixing hydraulic lines can be tricky unless you are experienced, so take this kind of work to a bike specialist in hydraulic systems. The method described here for fixing a popular model, the *Magura Hydro-Stop*, should be used as a rough guideline only: hydraulic brake designs are evolving rapidly, so work from your manufacturer's leaflet. To fill and vent, position the master cylinder so that the end with the line and vent screw is tilted up. Unscrew the filler plug from the brake caliper. Fill the syringe with a low-viscosity mineral oil such as *Castrol LHM 1756, Pentosin LHM, Hanseline H-LP 10,* or *Citroen Hydraulic Oils.* (Do not use glycol-based brake fluids.) Expel air from the syringe and put it in the filler hole of the brake caliper. Remove the vent screw and fill it until the air is gone. Replace the vent screw using a new seal ring, remove the syringe, and replace the filler plug with a new seal ring. To test the brakes, apply the brake lever and maintain pressure. No oil should leak from the line connections or screw plugs. Release the lever and the brake pads should return to the park position.

BRAKE SHOE ADJUSTMENT

Your bike brake shoes must press accurately against the wheel rim. The shoes compress slightly under hard braking pressure, and if they are too high on the rim, they may dig into the tire when compressed. If they are too low on the rim, they could slip off and foul the spokes. Side-pull brakes are upward toward the tire, while cantilever shoes are downward, toward the spokes, so to allow for the compression, position side-pull shoes closer to the inside of the rim, and cantilever shoes nearer to the tire.

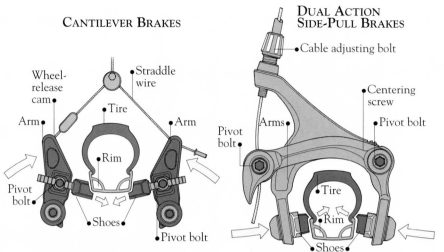

CANTILEVER BRAKES

Wheel-release cam — Arm — Tire — Straddle wire — Arm — Rim — Pivot bolt — Shoes — Pivot bolt

DUAL ACTION SIDE-PULL BRAKES

Cable adjusting bolt — Centering screw — Pivot bolt — Arms — Pivot bolt — Tire — Rim — Shoes

CANTILEVER POSITION

One type of cantilever arm has a brake shoe mounting bolt with a locknut. First slack the nut, and use a hex key on the mounting bolt to move the brake shoe into position. Tighten the nut and use the brake to check the shoe position.

CANTILEVER POSITION II

Another type of cantilever arm has a single mounting bolt. Undo the nut and move the shoe into position. If tightening the nut twists the shoe out of line, set the shoe slightly askew, so that it moves to the right position when tightened.

CANTILEVER TOE-IN

The leading or front end of a shoe must strike the rim before the rear end of the shoe. A toe-in is adjusted by loosening the brake shoe mounting bolt, and then rotating the beveled washer underneath it or repositioning the bolt on the arm.

SIDE-PULL POSITION

Side-pull brake shoes always have a single mounting bolt. Undo the nut to position the brake shoe. If tightening the nut twists the shoe out of line, undo the nut and set the shoe slightly askew, so that it moves to the correct position when tightened.

SIDE-PULL TOE-IN

Toe-in is not normally adjustable on side-pull brakes. It can be done, however, by snugging an adjustable spanner over the brake arm and bending it – a technique to use with caution. Another method is to shape the arm with a file.

SIDE-PULL CALIPER ACTION

Both brake shoes should strike the rim at the same time. Shimano dual-pivot side-pull brakes can usually be centered via an adjusting screw. Single-pivot bolt brakes must be centered by undoing the pivot bolt nut behind the forks.

CANTILEVER – PIVOT BOLTS

*The brake arms rotate on **bosses** that will need to be kept clean and lubricated. Disengage the straddle wire to relieve the spring tension on the brake arm, and undo the pivot mounting bolt. Lift off the brake arm, and clean and lightly grease the boss. If the boss is at all scratched or scarred, smooth it with some emery paper and steel wool. Take away as little of the boss as possible – if you make it smaller, the brake arm will fit loosely, and braking performance will deteriorate.*

CANTILEVER – SPRING TENSION

*If the **boss** has a series of holes for the brake arm spring, then the choice of hole will determine the strength of the spring tension. Use more spring tension for muddy conditions and in winter. After you have replaced the brake arm, tighten the pivot bolt firmly, but not too hard, as this could splay the end of the boss and cause binding of the arm. If this happens, smooth the boss with a file, pausing frequently to check the fit of the arm. Then polish the boss with steel wool.*

SIDE-PULL – DUAL-PIVOT BOLT

Shimano dual-pivot brakes are adjusted by undoing the locknut, turning the bolt home (clockwise), and reversing the bolt slightly. Then resecure the locknut back in place. Tighten the locknut firmly and check the adjustment. This is important, for when the locknut is tightened up, the adjustment will also tighten. Periodically disassemble the pivot bolts and clean and lubricate them. Check each component very carefully, and if any bolt becomes corroded or pitted, polish it up with steel wool or rubbing compound.

SIDE-PULL – SINGLE-PIVOT BOLT

Single-pivot bolt brakes are adjusted by first undoing the locknut, turning the adjusting nut home (clockwise), and reversing it slightly. Then resecure the locknut. To remove the brake mechanism from the bicycle, undo the mounting nut located behind the fork crown. To clean and lubricate the pivot bolt, undo and release the brake arm spring, then undo the locknut and adjusting nut, and finally remove the brake arms. Keep a careful track of washers and all other parts – each bit is very important.

CARING FOR BRAKES

Brakes that make squealing noises may need an adjustment of the brake shoe toe-in. When the leading edge of the shoe is touching the rim, the gap made between the shoe's rear end and the rim should be ⅛ to ¼ in. There is a slight amount of slack in the brake mechanism, which allows the shoes to twist a little bit when the brakes are engaged. When correctly toed-in, the brake shoes should twist flush against the rim.

Wet Weather

In wet weather conditions the performance of caliper brakes is dramatically weaker – a full stop can take up to four times the distance required for dryer conditions. When riding in the rain, periodically wipe water off the rims by applying your brakes with a touch of pressure. Brake shoes made of synthetic materials are much better performers in the wetter conditions than rubber brake shoes are. Another option for improving on the wet-weather performance of brakes is rim wipers. These are small devices designed to be mounted on the brake shoes. They press very lightly against the rims and scoop away water and mud.

Emergency Braking

The technique for a maximum deceleration stop is to try to transfer most of your body weight to the pedal and shoot your stern rearward up off the saddle as you apply the brakes. Keep feathering the rear brake so that the wheel is just short of locking up and skidding, and so that the front brake is just short of causing the bicycle to cartwheel and pitch you over the handlebars. Do at least one maximum deceleration stop on every ride – to check both brakes and to keep you in form so that in an emergency your reactions are automatic.

Cable Changes

Smooth-running, well-lubricated cables are essential for sensitive bike control. You will find that regular servicing and replacement will also make breakages a rare occurrence. For brakes, you should use the thickest cables that your system will accept, particularly with hybrid and mountain bikes. Thicker cables are stronger and less likely to stretch, and have a better, more positive feel. In left-side-of-the-road Britain, most people use the left-hand lever for the rear brake. The rest of the world uses the right-hand lever for the rear brake. Gear changer cables are much the same in principle as brake cables, therefore guidance on their general maintenance can be applied to both.

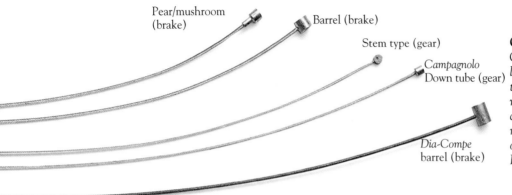

Pear/mushroom (brake)

Barrel (brake)

Stem type (gear)

Campagnolo Down tube (gear)

Dia-Compe barrel (brake)

CABLE TYPES
Cables come in different thicknesses and lengths (upper left), and with different types of nipples. Always obtain the right size and type, particularly for gear changing systems. Either order for your make and model of bike and components, or take the bike or old cables to the shop. Keep a spare set in case one breaks.

HOUSING PROBLEMS
Check the cable housings for kinks and fractures (lower left) and the cable wires for fraying. If there are problems, replace the wires and/or housings as soon as possible. It is prudent to replace wires in pairs, gear and brake. After cutting cable housing, if ends are burred and uneven, neaten them with a file.

SIDE-PULL BRAKES

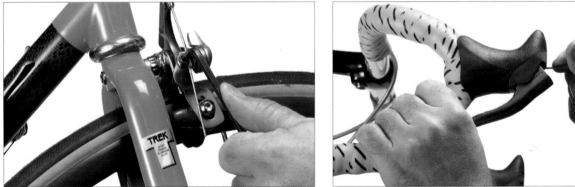

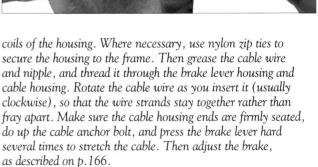

REMOVAL AND REPLACEMENT
Turn the cable adjusting screw fully home (clockwise). Fit a Third Hand to the brake mechanism and undo the cable anchor bolt (above). Depress the brake lever and extract the cable wire (above right). If you are replacing the housing, remove the old housing and install the new one, passing it through the cable guides if required, and refitting the ferrules (little caps on the ends of the cable housing) if your system uses these. When cutting cable housing, use cutters with large-enough jaws, and avoid squashing the housing flat by nesting the jaws between the coils of the housing. Where necessary, use nylon zip ties to secure the housing to the frame. Then grease the cable wire and nipple, and thread it through the brake lever housing and cable housing. Rotate the cable wire as you insert it (usually clockwise), so that the wire strands stay together rather than fray apart. Make sure the cable housing ends are firmly seated, do up the cable anchor bolt, and press the brake lever hard several times to stretch the cable. Then adjust the brake, as described on p.166.

CANTILEVER BRAKES

REMOVAL AND REPLACEMENT

Turn the cable adjusting bolt fully home clockwise. Fit a Third Hand to the brake mechanism and disconnect the straddle wire and cable anchor bolt, above. Align the slots in the adjusting screw and lockring with the slot on the brake lever,

and slide out the cable wire through the slots, and the nipple out of the brake lever. Replace the cable housing if required, and grease and install the new wire. Insert the nipple into the brake lever, and nest the cable housing securely in the adjusting bolt.

Pass the wire through the cable anchor bolt, make sure the cable housing ends are fully nested in their stops, tighten the bolt, and connect the straddle wire. Press the brake lever hard several times to stretch the cable, and then adjust as described on p.166.

GEAR CABLES

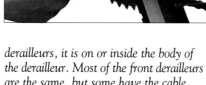

REMOVAL AND REPLACEMENT

Put the chain on the smallest chainring and sprocket. Screw the cable adjusting bolt(s) fully home clockwise. Reverse the bolt on the rear derailleur two turns, to give leeway for future adjustments. Undo the cable anchor bolt. (On rear

derailleurs, it is on or inside the body of the derailleur. Most of the front derailleurs are the same, but some have the cable housing stop on the derailleur body and the cable bolt on the bicycle frame.) Dismount levers (not always necessary

on down-tube levers) to withdraw the cables. As for the brakes, above, grease and insert new cables, and tighten all mounts and bolts. Stretch the wires where they are exposed by pulling them outward. Adjust the gears if necessary.

CABLE CUTTING TIPS

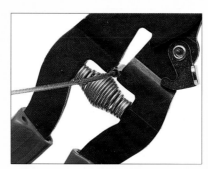

If possible, wait until you have installed the new cable wire before cutting off any excess wire. Cutting will sometimes cause the end of the wire to fray, making it difficult to

thread the wire through the housing and cable anchor bolt. Use good-quality wire cutters – ordinary pliers will fray the cable. When the cable wire has been installed and trimmed, crimp

a cap to the end to prevent it from unraveling. When cutting cable housing, first use a knife to cut the vinyl sheath and expose the metal housing. See "Fine Tuning" (p.186).

Removing and Fitting Chains

A bicycle chain can be up to 98 percent efficient – so long as it is clean and lubricated (see p.184). Each of its 116 or so links is a set of simple but precise roller bearings. Dirt in the chain grinds away the bearing surfaces and increases wear. As the link pins enlarge the holes in the side plates, the chain stretches and ceases to mesh smoothly with the teeth on the chainrings and freewheel sprockets. Derailleur shifting deteriorates and, under pressure, the chain starts to jump sprockets. When replacing a chain, renew the chainrings and sprockets: a new chain will kick on worn sprockets. This is the time to change **gear ratios** if you want. Ensure that a new chain is the correct type for your transmission, and seek advice before buying since the quality of chain/freewheel combinations can vary.

1 Breaking and joining a chain is easy once you have the knack: begin by practicing on an old length of chain. First nest the chain in the chain tool with the outer link plate braced and the pin exactly centered on the rivet.

2 Rotate the chain tool handle 6 to 6½ turns until the rivet is clear of the inner link plate, but still held by the outer link plate.

3 Flex the chain to separate the link. If the rivet has not been driven out far enough, you may have to use the chain tool again to drive the rivet a little farther.

Work with care, turning the handle slowly. Only rotate by one third of a turn at a time, so that the rivet does not go too far.

4 To rejoin the links, place the chain in the tool as before. Drive the rivet in firmly but if it sticks, back off, wiggle the link to line up the rivet with the holes, and try again.

• Hyper-Glide chain

• Sedis 2.38 mm gold chain

• Sedis 2.38 mm standard chain

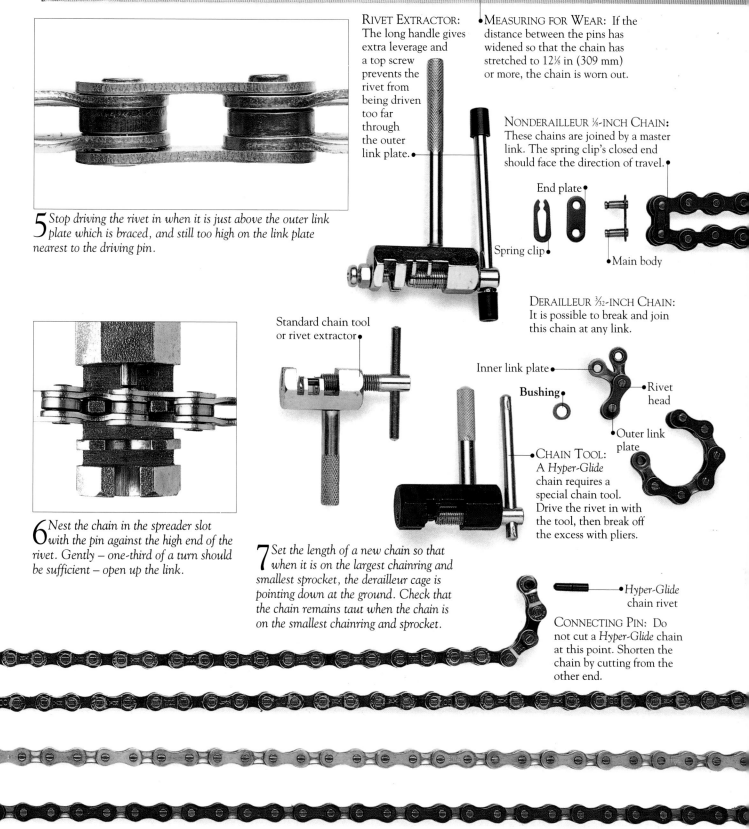

RIVET EXTRACTOR: The long handle gives extra leverage and a top screw prevents the rivet from being driven too far through the outer link plate.

MEASURING FOR WEAR: If the distance between the pins has widened so that the chain has stretched to 12⅛ in (309 mm) or more, the chain is worn out.

NONDERAILLEUR ⅛-INCH CHAIN: These chains are joined by a master link. The spring clip's closed end should face the direction of travel.

End plate

Spring clip

Main body

5 *Stop driving the rivet in when it is just above the outer link plate which is braced, and still too high on the link plate nearest to the driving pin.*

DERAILLEUR 3/32-INCH CHAIN: It is possible to break and join this chain at any link.

Inner link plate

Bushing

Rivet head

Outer link plate

Standard chain tool or rivet extractor

CHAIN TOOL: A *Hyper-Glide* chain requires a special chain tool. Drive the rivet in with the tool, then break off the excess with pliers.

6 *Nest the chain in the spreader slot with the pin against the high end of the rivet. Gently – one-third of a turn should be sufficient – open up the link.*

7 *Set the length of a new chain so that when it is on the largest chainring and smallest sprocket, the derailleur cage is pointing down at the ground. Check that the chain remains taut when the chain is on the smallest chainring and sprocket.*

Hyper-Glide chain rivet

CONNECTING PIN: Do not cut a *Hyper-Glide* chain at this point. Shorten the chain by cutting from the other end.

Transmission Maintenance I

When shifting into gear, the derailleur moves the chain to a selected sprocket or chainring, aligning the chain so that it runs smoothly. Early derailleur gears were controlled with simple, friction-tensioned shift levers and it was up to the rider to position the lever correctly. Shifting gear was done by feel and by ear. The pedaling force had to be modulated at just the right moment, the lever overshifted to make the chain climb or drop, and then the lever reversed to center the chain.

Push-Button Gears

Although most modern derailleur systems still include the option of friction-mode shifting, indexed and push-button shifting are now the

norm. Riders need only flick a lever or button, and the rest of the operation takes care of itself. There is, however, still an art to manipulating bicycle gears correctly.

Precision Systems

Modern derailleur systems are so precise that in order to function properly, the component parts must be perfectly adjusted. One bolt just half a turn out of line can disable the whole system. So while modern derailleurs are easy to use, a sensitive awareness of their mechanical needs is necessary to keep them well-tuned. Most minor adjustments are easily made and most derailleurs follow the same principles as the ones illustrated below.

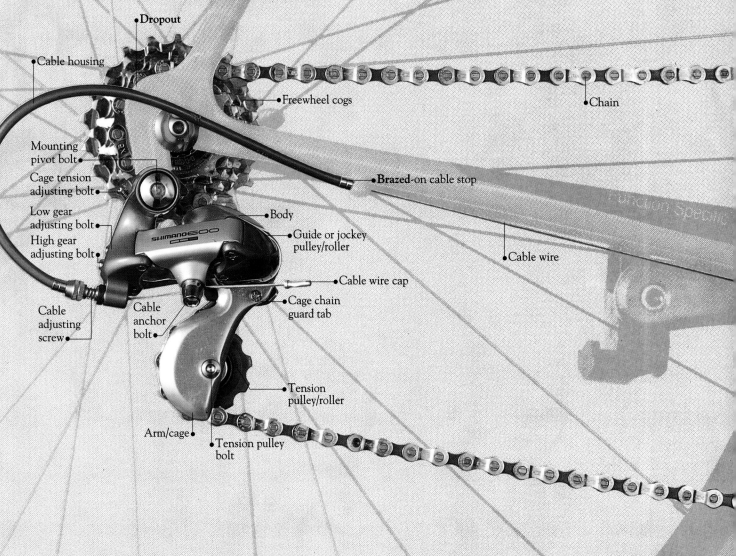

Dropout

Cable housing

Freewheel cogs

Chain

Mounting pivot bolt

Cage tension adjusting bolt

Low gear adjusting bolt

High gear adjusting bolt

Cable adjusting screw

Cable anchor bolt

Brazed-on cable stop

Body

Guide or jockey pulley/roller

Cable wire

Cable wire cap

Cage chain guard tab

Tension pulley/roller

Arm/cage

Tension pulley bolt

GEAR RATIOS

*Triple chainrings and an extra-long cage arm on the rear derailleur are common features of mountain and touring bicycles. The additional chainring, long cage, and widely spaced cogs provide a much greater range of **gear ratios** than on a racing bike. Wide ratio gears require a longer chain and do not shift as quickly and crisply as close ratio gears on a racing bike.*

GROUP SETS

Most transmissions are complete systems of components, from shift levers through to freewheel and hub, expressly designed to work together. Manufacturers usually advise that substituting one component (such as a chain or freewheel) from a different brand may result in a poorer performance. Equally, a substitution may be an improvement. Ask your bike shop for advice.

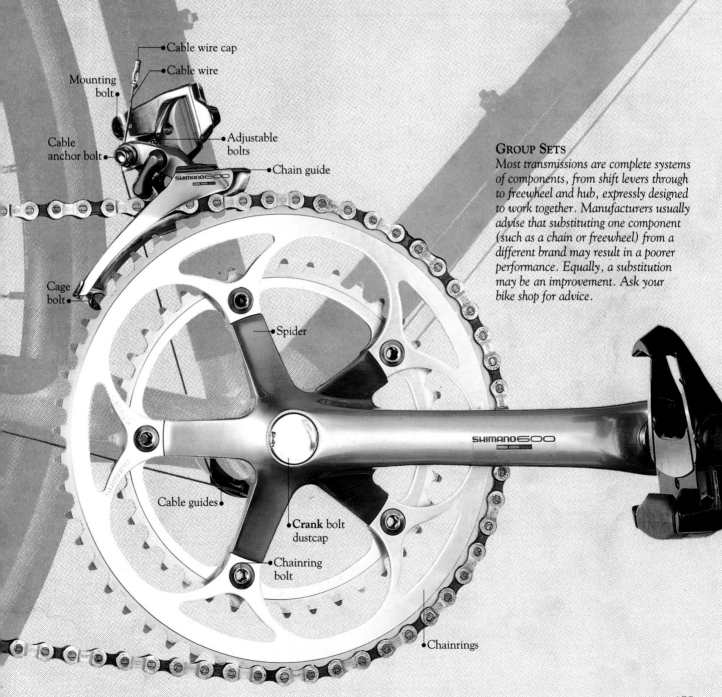

Cable wire cap
Cable wire
Mounting bolt
Cable anchor bolt
Adjustable bolts
Chain guide
Cage bolt
Spider
Cable guides
Crank bolt dustcap
Chainring bolt
Chainrings

175

THE FRONT DERAILLEUR
To position a front derailleur, correctly use the shift lever to place the outer plate of the cage above the large chainring. Use the front derailleur mounting bolt to position the outer plate parallel to the large chainring, and 1 to 3 mm above it. A tighter clearance is required for the closely spaced double chainrings, and a wider clearance for the broadly spaced triple chainrings. Note: If your bike is fitted with *Biopace* rings, make your adjustments with the **crank** pointed downward in line with the seat tube, so that the high portion of the chainring is next to the cage plates.

FRONT DERAILLEUR ADJUSTMENT

Turn **cranks** *by hand and run chain to the small chainring and large rear cog. With triple chainrings, use the low adjusting bolt to set a clearance of 1 to 1.5 mm between the inner cage plate and chain. With double chainrings, position the inner cage plate as close as possible to chain without touching it. Test cable for slack and if necessary, adjust cable anchor bolt. Run chain to large chainring and small rear cog. Use the top adjusting bolt to set the outer cage plate as close as possible to the chain without touching it. For a Shimano STI system, run the chain to the middle chainring and large rear cog, and use the cable adjusting bolt on the shift lever housing to position the inner cage plate as close as possible to the chain without touching it.*

1 *Mount the bike on a workstand or other device to raise the rear wheel off the ground. Turn the cable adjusting screw on the shift lever all the way in and then reverse it two turns. Place the shift lever in friction mode, turn the* **cranks** *by hand, and run the chain to the small front chainring and large rear cog. Turn the low adjusting bolt in or out, so that the guide pulley is in line with the large cog.*

2 *Run the chain to the large front chainring and small rear cog. Turn the top adjusting bolt in or out so that the guide pulley is in line with the small cog. Place the shift lever in SIS mode, turn* **cranks***, and shift the chain from top cog to second cog. If it won't go, turn the cable adjusting bolt counter-clockwise to increase cable tension. If it goes too far, turn the cable adjusting bolt clockwise.*

3 *With the chain on the second cog, rotate the* **cranks** *and increase cable tension by turning cable adjusting bolt counter-clockwise. Stop just before the chain makes a noise by rubbing against the third cog. Check shifting operation on all cogs. If shifts to large cogs are slow, increase cable tension by half a turn. If shifts to small cogs are slow, decrease the cable tension by half a turn.*

TENSION ADJUSTING BOLT
*Run the chain to the small chainring and the large cog. Turn the **cranks** backward and adjust the tension bolt so that the guide pulley is as close to the large cog as possible, but not touching it. Turn the cranks, run the chain to the large chainring and small cog and check that the guide pulley does not touch the cog. Adjust if necessary.*

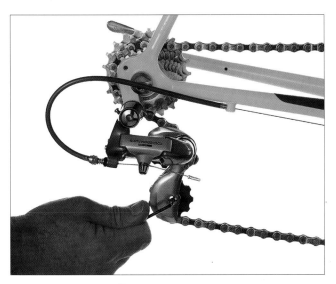

REAR DERAILLEUR REMOVAL
If the chain is on the bike, you can mount or remove a rear derailleur by undoing the tension pulley bolt with an allen wrench (above) and removing the tension pulley. It may be necessary to loosen the guide pulley so that the cage sides can be moved far enough apart for the chain to clear the chain guard tab.

REAR DERAILLEUR MOUNTING

In order for most modern rear derailleurs to work well, the rear wheel **dropouts** must be aligned with each other, and the derailleur hanger must be parallel with the center line of the bike. Frame alignment requires specific equipment and a high degree of skill, and should be done by a bike shop. Field test: stand behind the bike and visually check that a line through the guide and tension pulleys is parallel with (in same plane as) the rear wheel.

Rear Derailleur Disassembly

Derailleurs are fun to play with. They need only a few tools for disassembly, and are small enough so that you can sit down comfortably in a chair while you strip one down, learn how it works, clean and lubricate it, and then put it back together in the right order. Dismount a rear derailleur via the mounting bolt, first disconnecting the cable anchor bolt, and if the chain is on the bike, the tension and guide pulleys. From this point onward the technique for disassembly varies from model to model. The common feature is the cage stop screw, which prevents the cage from unwinding. Hold the cage and body firmly, undo the cage stop screw and unwind the cage, carefully noting how many turns it rotates. Similarly, when you separate the cage and arm, by undoing whatever obviously holds them together, make a careful note of the position of the spring. Most derailleurs are designed so that the spring tension, for example, can be easily adjusted by placing the end of the spring in one or another of a series of holes. If your transmission has wide-range gears, the spring tension should be taut. If the gearing is close-range, you may be able to use a softer spring setting for faster shifting.

Chain Length

Short-arm derailleur and double chainrings: you need a length of chain to pass over a large chainring and large cog, without going through the derailleur arm, plus two links extra. Long-arm derailleur and triple chainrings: with the chain through the derailleur arm and over the large chainring and small cog, the derailleur arm should point straight at the ground.

Lubrication

Periodically lubricate the pivot pins on the derailleur body, and clean and re-grease the guide and tension pulleys. Remove the pulleys by undoing the pulley bolts, clean in a biodegradable solvent, and re-grease with a light, fast grease (see pp.184-85).

Transmission Maintenance II

A freewheel body is formed of two main parts, one inside the other. The inner part threads or slides onto the hub. The outer body holds the cogs, or gear sprockets. The inside of a freewheel is an intricate maze of small-sized pawls, ball bearings, springs, and pins. It is important to keep it clean and lubricated (see pp.184-85), so that the pawls do not become clogged and stuck. Keep one ear tuned to your freewheel; if the steady whirring sound becomes ragged or uneven, then you will need to service or replace the freewheel as soon as possible.

Freewheel Removal and Installation

Freewheels can be divided into two main types: the threaded variety, which screws onto the hub, and cassette, which slides onto splines of a hub. There are a variety of different designs within each category, and to perform servicing, you will need to have tools that are specific to the make and model of the freewheel and hub. If you do not have access to the manufacturer's instructions, visit your local bike shop and they will be able to tell you what kind of freewheel you have and what particular tools are needed for working on it.

FITTING A FREEWHEEL REMOVER
Remove wheel and axle nuts. Fit freewheel remover (below) and replace nut, tight enough to hold the remover firmly in place.

RATCHET ACTION
One end of each pawl is pinned to the inside part. The other end is held by spring tension against a series of indentations or teeth, positioned inside the outer body. When the chain starts to drive the outer body clockwise, the pawls lock into the teeth and the inner part of the freewheel then moves, driving the wheel.

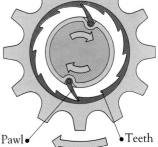

Pedal drives chain causing outer wheel to rotate

Pawl • • Teeth

COASTING
When you cease pedaling so that the wheel and inner freewheel are moving, but the chain is not – the pawls ride over the indentations or teeth in the outer body. This is the fast clicking sound you hear when coasting.

Inner wheel continues to rotate after you cease to pedal

CASSETTE ANATOMY

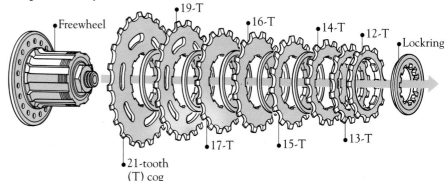

Freewheel
19-T
16-T
14-T
12-T
Lockring
17-T
15-T
13-T
21-tooth (T) cog

REPLACEMENT TECHNIQUES
Place the freewheel remover in the vise with the wheel flat down (it's sideways in the photo so you can see it), and turn the wheel counter-clockwise. Stop turning it as soon as the freewheel breaks free, and loosen the quick-release skewer or axle nut to prevent damage to the threads on the hub. Turn the freewheel remover a little more and loosen the axle nut slightly, then spin the freewheel off the hub. Grease the threads on the hub before installing a freewheel. Work carefully, because misaligning and crossing the freewheel and hub threads will damage the hub.

Headsets

The headset holds the fork steerer tube in the head tube. Test for binding by lifting the front wheel off the ground and rotating the handlebars with one finger. It should move smoothly. If there are any grinding noises or if the fork catches in certain positions, then the bearings need adjustment and/or regreasing. Test for play by grasping the handlebars, firmly applying the front brake, and rocking the bike. A clicking headset indicates loose bearings. This should be repaired immediately, because stresses in the headset area are high, and a loose headset can self-destruct rapidly. You will need to use real headset spanners; 32 mm spanners for most bicycles; 36 mm for some mountain bikes. If the headset parts are alloy, work with care to avoid bending them.

Disassembly

The headset should be cleaned and greased about once a year. Remove the **stem** (see p. 164) and anything else that is in the way. It is

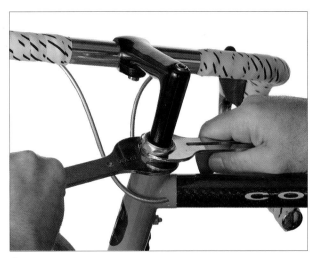

ADJUSTMENT
Undo the locknut and turn the upper cup clockwise until it is finger-tight against the bearings. Reverse it ⅛ to ¼ turn and lock it in place using a medium amount of force. Always work from a slightly loose adjustment.

easiest if you also remove the front wheel first. You can work simply with the bike flat on the ground on a layer of newspapers, or fix the bike in place on a workstand.

HEADSET ANATOMY

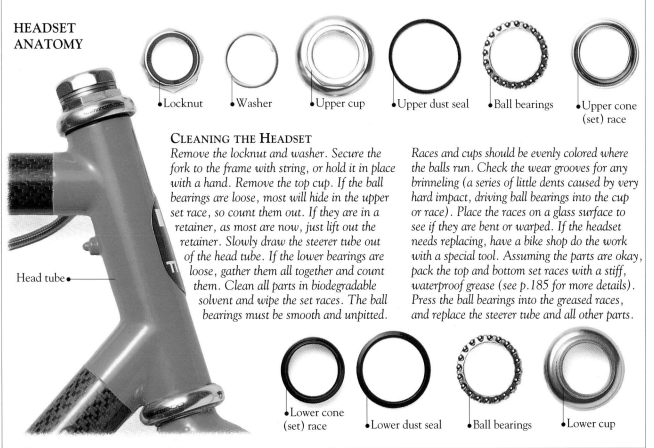

•Locknut •Washer •Upper cup •Upper dust seal •Ball bearings •Upper cone (set) race

CLEANING THE HEADSET
Remove the locknut and washer. Secure the fork to the frame with string, or hold it in place with a hand. Remove the top cup. If the ball bearings are loose, most will hide in the upper set race, so count them out. If they are in a retainer, as most are now, just lift out the retainer. Slowly draw the steerer tube out of the head tube. If the lower bearings are loose, gather them all together and count them. Clean all parts in biodegradable solvent and wipe the set races. The ball bearings must be smooth and unpitted.

Races and cups should be evenly colored where the balls run. Check the wear grooves for any brinneling (a series of little dents caused by very hard impact, driving ball bearings into the cup or race). Place the races on a glass surface to see if they are bent or warped. If the headset needs replacing, have a bike shop do the work with a special tool. Assuming the parts are okay, pack the top and bottom set races with a stiff, waterproof grease (see p.185 for more details). Press the ball bearings into the greased races, and replace the steerer tube and all other parts.

Head tube•

•Lower cone (set) race •Lower dust seal •Ball bearings •Lower cup

Transmission Maintenance III

The bottom bracket axle (or spindle) rotates on bearings inside the bottom bracket shell. There are two basic types of bottom bracket commonly found on bikes: adjustable, which uses cups and cones threaded into a bottom bracket shell; and cassette, where the axle and bearings are a complete, self-contained unit held in place within the bottom bracket shell. Some cassette units are adjustable, others are not. Bottom brackets with adjustable bearings usually have a fixed cup on the right-hand side of the bottom bracket with no lockring on it, an adjustable cup with holes, and a lockring on the left-hand side.

CRANK REMOVAL – STEP 1

*To remove a **crank**, remove the dustcap. If there is a hex key fitting or screwdriver slot in the dustcap, it is probably threaded and should be unscrewed with the appropriate tool. If the surface of the dustcap is smooth, it is probably press-fitted and should be prised off with a thin scewdriver. Once the dustcap is off, undo and remove the crank bolt. Make sure no washer is left inside.*

CHAINRINGS AND CRANKS

*Regularly check the tightness of the chainring bolts (left). Once they have been tightened a few times and have bedded-in, secure them in place with a thread adhesive. Periodically check for bent or chipped chainwheel teeth by removing the chain, placing a light behind the chainwheel, and rotating it. Chipped teeth will be visible from the side, bent teeth from above. Also check that the chainrings are true, without side-to-side wobble. If adjustment is required, they can be bent with a large spanner, but it is best to get a bike shop to do the work for you. Regularly check that the **crank** bolts are snug. Remove dust cap and tighten crank bolt with a spanner or crank tool. Tighten firmly, but not too hard, or the threads may strip. If the crank bolts are alloy, use a steel bolt to tighten the cranks, then replace the alloy bolt. Check the tightness of new cranks every 25 miles, for the first 200 miles of use.*

BOTTOM BRACKET

A bottom bracket axle should be cleaned and regreased once a year; more often if you ride in dirty, wet conditions. Remove the **cranks**, undo and remove the adjustable cup and lockring, and extract the axle. Work over a piece of newspaper to catch loose bearings. Make sure no loose bearings remain in the fixed cup. If the bearings are in clips, note which way the clips are positioned. If there is a plastic sleeve dust-guard for the axle inside the bottom bracket shell, remove it. Clean all the parts in a biodegradable solvent. Clean the fixed cup, but don't remove it unless a flashlight examination reveals that the cup is worn and pitted. Examine the parts for wear. The axle and cup should have polished wear grooves, but no pitting. If everything is okay, pack the cups with grease and press in the bearings. Insert the axle long end first, hold it in place against the fixed-cup bearings, and fit the rest of parts. Spin the cranks a few times and then adjust the bearings.

Bolt

Washer

Ball race

Dust-guard

Axle

Ball race

Adjustable cup

Lock ring

Washer

Bolt

CRANK REMOVAL – STEP 2

To remove a **crank**, fit a crank extractor (right). These have a bolt passing through a round housing, which is threaded on the outside. Reverse (counter-clockwise) the inside bolt all the way back, and then screw the housing into the crank, being careful not to cross-thread it. Snug the housing firmly into the crank, using a spanner if necessary. Turn the inside bolt of the crank extractor clockwise and do it up firmly, but not with all of your strength – the crank is made of alloy, and the threads on it may strip if you use too much force. If the crank will not come off, tap it with a wooden mallet. Slowly increase the tension of the extractor. In most cases a golden moment will occur when you can feel the crank just starting to go and the moment is right for a decisive increase in the extractor tension. If, however, there is no movement, the crank will have to be loosened with a hammer and drift punch, or with special tools at a bike shop.

ADJUSTING A BOTTOM BRACKET

Test the bottom bracket bearings for play by grasping a **crank** and firmly pushing and pulling it. A clicking sound indicates the bearing adjustment is loose. Next, lift the chain off the chainring and rest it on the bottom bracket. Spin the chainwheel and if it catches or runs roughly, then the bearings are too tight and/or need to be regreased. Check the tightness of the fixed cup on the chainwheel side. These cups have a reverse left-hand thread and tighten by being turned counter-clockwise. It is usually necessary to remove the crankarm and spider first in order to gain any access to the fixed cup. To adjust bottom bracket bearings, undo the lockring, turn the adjustable cup finger-tight against the bearings, and then reverse it a little – ⅛ turn or so. (Note: For the photograph we removed the crank so that the cup and lockring are clearly visible. However, if you use pin spanners such as the Park Tool models shown, it is not necessary to remove the crank.) Check the bearings for play. You want just a little, because the next step – tightening the lockring while holding the adjustable cup in place – will slightly tighten the bearings. If the bearings are new, set a tight adjustment to allow for bedding-in. If the bearings are already broken-in, set the adjustment as precisely as you can.

Pedals

Pedals require two main types of bearing: loose ball bearings held in place with an adjustable cone, or a cassette, which is a self-contained unit press-fitted into place within the pedal body. Some cassette bearings can be adjusted for play, others cannot. Pedals with cassette bearings can last for over two years or more without servicing, but if you do decide to service your cassette bearings you will need specialized tools. Many people do not bother; when the old pedals start creaking and grinding, they replace rather than repair them. Pedals with adjustable bearings should be cleaned and re-greased every six months. How long the pedal lasts depends on its quality. A cheap pedal may not run more than a few thousand miles; a quality pedal can turn for over 100,000 miles.

REMOVING PEDALS
*Remove both pedals with a thin-jawed pedal spanner, or if the pedal axle threads are well greased, remove them with a hex key on the **crank** end of the pedal axle. Note that the left-side pedal has a left-hand thread (above), and should always be unscrewed by being turned in a clockwise direction. The right-side pedal has a conventional right-hand thread, and it should be unscrewed by turning it counter-clockwise.*

Pedal Anatomy
A pedal needs attention if the axle clicks when pushed and pulled within the pedal body, or if the pedal runs roughly. It is especially worthwhile to check it if you can't remember when it last had any attention. Because the dust cap end of the pedal is fairly well protected, the bearings there usually have enough grease. Bearings at the **crank** end of the pedal, however, are more vulnerable to the wet and dirt, and can be dry when the outside bearings still look fine. So strip the pedal down completely and make sure everything is in good condition.

THE PEDAL
Check the axle for straightness, and if it is bent replace it at once. A bent pedal spindle can easily injure your knees.

• Axle/spindle

Check the bearings, cups, and cones for wear and pitting.

• Pedal body

• Ball bearings

• Adjustable cone

• Dust cap

• Ball bearings

• Washer

• Locknut

Disassembly and Regreasing

With the locknut and the dust cap removed (below right), you can undo the adjustable cone. It usually has two sides and should be turned with a small screwdriver. Hold the crank end of the axle and up-end the pedal over a sheet of newspaper. Then shake out the ball bearings on the dust cap side, picking out those that stick to the grease with a small screwdriver or even a matchstick. Count them all and then take out the axle on the crank side and pick out those bearings. Count these also, and clean each part in a biodegradable solvent. Repack the cups with a thick waterproof grease (see p.185) and press the ball bearings right into the grease. Slide in the axle carefully without knocking any bearings loose, screw the cone down finger tight, and replace the washer and locknut. Spin the pedal a few times to nest the bearings in place. Turn the cone flush against the bearings, and reverse it ⅛ to ¼ turn. Screw down the

STEP-IN SYSTEM PEDALS

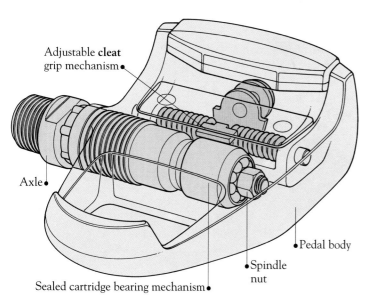

Adjustable **cleat** grip mechanism

Axle

Sealed cartridge bearing mechanism

Pedal body

Spindle nut

ADJUSTING A STEP-IN PEDAL

*The step-in pedal works together with a compatible **cleat** to operate as one unit. When the rider steps into the pedal, a mechanism will automatically grip on to the cleat. The tension on this mechanism can be adjusted by a bolt, found behind or below the pedal. Step-in system pedal axles all use sealed cartridge bearings. If a pedal is loose or rattles, either the spindle nut or the axle cartridge may have worked loose. Accessing either of these depends on the pedal's design, so check the manufacturer's instructions first. If the nylon **bushing** on the spindle nut is worn it must be replaced.*

locknut and check that the adjustment is just right, as tightening it will also slightly tighten the bearing adjustment. Finally, replace the dust cap, lightly grease the pedal axle threads and reinstall the pedal.

DISASSEMBLY: REMOVING THE DUST CAP

The first step in gaining access to the bearings is to remove the dust cap (below). Alloy dust caps are threaded, and will require a wrench or a special tool (if the dust cap is a unique design). Some plastic dust caps are not threaded, so try unscrewing it first. If this fails, pry it off gently with a small screwdriver.

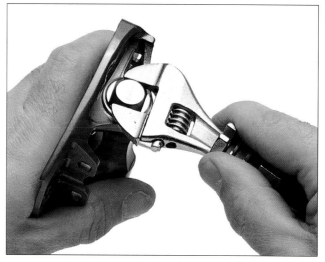

REMOVING THE LOCKNUT

*With the dust cap removed, you now have access to the locknut. Start by holding the **crank** end of the pedal with a wrench, or lock it in a vise, and then undo the locknut (below). With some pedals, the design is such that the locknut is recessed and is not easily available. If this is the case, you will need to use a pedal locknut wrench, or at least a socket slim enough to slide down into the pedal and reach the locknut.*

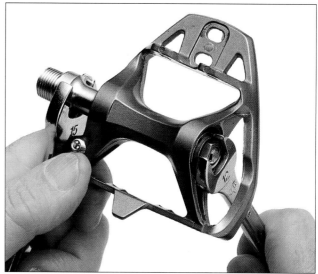

Cleaning and Lubrication

Oils and greases were not durable in the old days, and bicycle components were kept continuously awash in lubricants. Nearly all roadsters had fully enclosed chainguards, with the chain running in a bath of oil, and parts with bearings had oil-filler holes through which copious amounts of oil were frequently poured. This had to be done to try to prevent all the parts from drying out and getting ruined. Oil would leak out all over the bike, attracting dirt and making a substantial mess. Now modern lubricants are more tenacious, long-lived, and resistant to water. Many components are self-contained, with the lubricants sealed within, and will easily last for five years or more under normal conditions of use. Although modern technology has eradicated much of the messy work involved in bicycle cleaning, you should still clean and lubricate your bike on a regular basis. Always use a lubricant sparingly and with precision. A little lubricant correctly used will go a long way in preventing any friction and corrosion – but use too much, and it will attract dirt and increase wear on the parts. So always wipe away any excess lubricant, and dry the bike off thoroughly when you finish.

CHAIN

Each link in a chain is a set of precise roller bearings. Regularly exposed to wet and dirt, chains need regular cleaning and lubrication. Oil is cheap and effective, but attracts dirt, forming an abrasive mixture that increases wear. Synthetic lubricants are stronger, cleaner, and better at repelling dirt and water. New chains come ready-greased from the factory, and since oil-based greases and synthetic lubricants are incompatible, the chain must first be cleaned if you want to use a synthetic lubricant. Break the chain and let it soak in the solvent. Wipe the chainrings clean and use a freewheel brush to clean the freewheel cogs of any accumulated dirt (right). Use a wire brush on the chain to remove any last traces of grease. Dry the chain in an oven, on top of a

double boiler, or even with a heat gun. Apply a lubricant to each and every roller, flexing the links back and forth to help the lubricant penetrate. When all the rollers have been well-lubricated, wipe down the outside plates until they are nearly dry to the touch. Another way to clean and lubricate the chain is with a brush-bath such as the *Park Chain Bath* (above left). This is good for chains that are very dirty on the outside, and works best if the lubricant and solvent are from the same manufacturer. Aerosol spray lubricants such as *Superspray* are quick and convenient; simply spin the **cranks** backwards, apply spray to the moving chain, and wipe away any excess. Renew frequently. Liquid synthetic lubricants such as *Pedros Synlube* require drop-by-drop application, but are more durable.

WASHING YOUR BIKE

Wipe your bike down with a damp cloth as often as necessary to keep it clean and dust-free. Drying your bike after a wet ride automatically gives it a good cleaning. When necessary, give the bicycle a full-scale wash with a bucket of suds. A soft brush is handy for reaching into small nooks and crannies. Help to preserve both the environment and your wax finish by using either a mild, low-alkaline soap or otherwise a biodegradable cleaner such as Bike Elixir Wash & Wax. Any grease-coated alloy parts can first be wiped clean with a chain cleaner, or use a parts cleaning solvent such as Simple Green or Parts Wash Concentrate. Heavily mud-encrusted mountain bikes can be washed thoroughly with a high-pressure jet-spray hose (right), but you should be careful to avoid spraying directly at the bearings.

Greases

Grease can be either a petroleum-based oil or a synthetic lubricating oil mixed with soap or thickener to hold it in place, as well as several additives to enhance the performance. Some greases will contain a solid lubricant such as Molybdendum Disulfide or *Teflon*, which coat the bearing surfaces and further reduce the friction. Grease is used mainly for headsets, hubs, pedal bearings, bottom brackets, and occasionally for freewheels. Greases are either light or heavy: lightweight greases are much thinner and smoother, and move easily. They should only be used for cassette bearings, freewheels, and on semisealed bearings which have an O-ring seal to help keep the grease in place. Heavy greases are far thicker and tackier, and tend to suit nonsealed bearings where the grease must stay in place and provide a resistance to water.

Automobile grease is often relabeled and sold as bicycle grease. This is no problem, since the performance requirements for automobiles are much higher than for bicycles. Specifically formulated bicycle grease products, however, often give better results, particularly when the conditions of use are extreme. For example, *Phil Wood Waterproof Grease* works very well for mountain bikes that are frequently immersed in water. Road racers who think nothing of totally regreasing and lubricating their bicycles before a race, however, will want the thinnest and fastest grease they can find. Whatever grease or greases you use, take care never to mix them. The additives in the different brands available will often be incompatible, so mixing them up will result in a nonfunctional mess. So when you relubricate, start by cleaning away any old lubricants thoroughly, and make sure that the parts are all dry and free of the solvent. A tube or grease gun is a neat and efficient way to apply the grease.

SEALED BEARINGS
No sealed bearing gives perfect protection for bikes in muddy or wet conditions. So Wilderness Trail Bikes Grease Guard sealed-bearing components use a grease nipple and gun that injects new grease and flushes out old grease and dirt.

LUBRICATION POINTS
For a bike to function efficiently it should be regularly lubricated. This bike illustrates the various points where liquid (L) or grease (G) or should be applied.

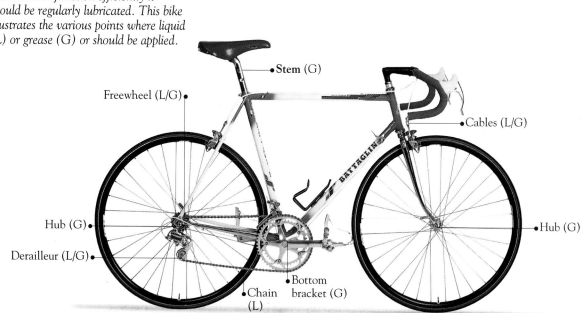

Stem (G)

Freewheel (L/G)

Cables (L/G)

Hub (G)

Hub (G)

Derailleur (L/G)

Chain (L)

Bottom bracket (G)

Fine Tuning

A clean, neat, well-tuned bicycle adds to the pleasure of riding. It is also mechanically more efficient and much easier to maintain. Several fine-tuning tricks can be used for customizing a bike to particular needs: giving extra protection against mud on off-road rides, for example, or arranging a cornucopia of locks, lights, and other equipment for urban commuting. Other tricks can hone a bike to a peak of efficiency and speed. Priorities may vary, but the process of giving personal attention to every detail and refinement can produce a feeling of real satisfaction, and the knowledge that the bike has been thoroughly prepared. This boosts your confidence when riding – whether you are sprinting for the finish line in a race or swerving to avoid a pedestrian on your way to work.

OLD TUBES
*On off-road rides, the front tire can pick up dirt and mud and throw it at the headset bearings. To provide a dust seal protector, an easy trick is to remove the **stem** and slip a short length of old inner tube over the head tube. Replace the stem and wiggle the inner tube into place over both bearings and stem.*

ELECTRIC WIRES
When you install dynamo lights, cycle computers, or any other equipment with wires, always keep the wires neat and tidy: a loose wire could snag and break. The trick is to think the job through completely before you start mounting any brackets and making connections. There will often be a way to wind the wire so that it blends in with the bike, such as along a mudguard stay or cable housing. With a headlight, you need some slack in the wire for handlebar rotation. You can make most wires curl neatly just by wrapping them tightly around the length of a pencil or a large nail.

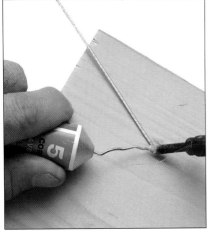

CABLE WIRES
Cable wire ends are usually capped, which is a quick and convenient way of preventing a wire end from fraying. If you remove and grease a cable wire, however, the piece of wire with the cap should be cut off. One way to prevent any fraying without using a cap is to dip the end into some glue, wiping off the excess before it dries. An elaborate method is to seal the end with solder. Remove excess soldering with a file so that the wire passes through the housing easily. If necessary, wrap the cable wire with tape and cut it through the middle of the wrap as a temporary measure.

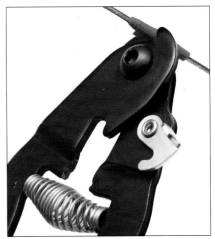

Waxing and Touching Up

Waxing a bike at least once a year keeps the paint nourished and makes cleaning much easier. If the paint finish has become dull, clean it with a color restorer such as *T-cut*, or use a hard paste wax such as *Simonize* to give a deep lustrous finish that is easily renewed. A polymer seal wax gives a diamondlike and glossy finish, but any renewal requires using a special removing solvent first. Almost any wax will do; many good bike shops use spray-on furniture polish that cleans and shines in one go. Wax will also help protect alloy components, so long as they are still in good condition. If they are oxidized and dull, bring them up with a metal polish before applying wax. If they are badly tarnished, use steel wool. For sharp-looking paintwork, use a primer as well as the outer coat. Manufacturers may give you color-matched touch-up paint when you buy a bike, or you can buy model paint and mix the colors. Remove rust with an emery cloth and steel wool, and feather any sharply defined chipped edges with the emery cloth. Apply the primer so that it overlaps the edges, and let it dry. Then apply the tinted paint with a small brush. Remove all rough spots with fine steel wool. Smooth the touch-up with rubbing compound, wash the frame, and finally, coat it with wax.

THREAD ADHESIVE
Bolts and nuts can be anchored in place using a thread adhesive such as Loctite. This is useful for those escape-prone little bolts, such as pannier rack mounting bolts, chainring bolts and bottom-bracket fixed cups. The adhesive prevents any loosening from vibration, yet can be undone with a spanner. New nuts and bolts must be bedded-in before applying thread adhesive. The wearing away of microscopic surface irregularities on a newly fitted nut or bolt creates space, so it will need tightening. Repeat twice and clean the nut and bolt. Apply the adhesive and then reinstall them.

BREAKING-IN BEARINGS

When magnified, the surfaces of the bearing cups, cones, and balls of a brand new hub look much like a lunar landscape: jagged and irregular, with sharp peaks and valleys. As the hub is used, these tiny irregularities wear away. Polished paths appear on the cup and cone surfaces, the balls become smoother, and mechanical friction is reduced. This increase in the efficiency will probably vary, but on a 100-mile (160-km) ride, the difference between a new and a broken-in hub could equal the energy needed to climb a 100-ft (30-m) hill. If you add on the other hub, a bottom bracket, and derailleur pulleys, then over 100 miles (160 km) you allow a considerable increase in efficiency. But breaking in a bike by riding requires time. To accelerate the process, bearings can be polished with rubbing compound, a fine abrasive which is used to smooth and polish paint surfaces. Practice first on an unwanted component because this process is like using a high-powered sander on furniture: it is efficient, but you can easily overdo it if you don't watch out. The components with bearings suitable for polishing are the hubs, the bottom bracket, and pedals. Disassemble each component, and clean it well with a biodegradable solvent first. Mix the rubbing compound with a thin grease, pack the mixture into the bearings and reassemble. It is crucial to be able to spin the component around without imposing a load from any one direction, or else the polishing could be lopsided. For the hub, mount the wheel in a trueing jig and over the next few days, spin it every time you pass by. A fast method is to connect the hub axle to an electric drill using a flexible hose. Position the drill and the hub carefully so the load on the axle is neutral. Then disassemble each of the components, cleaning them thoroughly so that any specks from the rubbing compound or grease mixture have been removed.

Glossary

Words in *italics* within an entry have their own entry in the glossary.

A

Aero tuck Aerodynamically streamlined body position with hands on the bar tops, elbows in, chin on hands, and back as flat as possible.

Aerofoil A structure which has a streamlined profile comparable to the cross-section of an aircraft wing.

ANSI, BSI, Snell, AS (American National Standards Institute, British Standards Institute, Snell Foundation, Australian Standards.) Organisations that have devised criteria and tests for cycle equipment safety. Standards and tests differ but frequently overlap. The privately-funded Snell Foundation standard is considered the most stringent for helmets.

Ankling Smooth and steady pedalling technique where each foot pivots on its ankle with each revolution of the *crank*.

B

Block Freewheel.

Bonk Exhaustion caused by depletion of glycogen stores in muscles.

Bosses *Brazed*-on mounting points on a bike frame for bolting on items such as cantilever brakes, down-tube gear levers and pannier racks.

Brazing Process of joining two pieces of steel tubing together using a non-ferrous alloy such as brass, that has a lower melting point than the metals being joined.

Bushing A sleeve or tube, on which a part, or parts, rotate.

C

Cadence Pedalling rate, measured in the number of *crank* rotations per minute. Tourers and commuters pedal at 55-85 rpm, racers from 95-130 rpm

depending on conditions.

Captain Cycling slang for the rider on the front of a tandem.

Chrome-moly(bdenum) High tensile steel alloy used for cycle frame tubes, especially mountain bikes. It is suitable for mass production welded frames, as the tubing is capable of withstanding welding temperatures without loss of tensile strength.

Cleat A device for locking a shoe and pedal together. A cleat is a small plastic or metal plate that is permanently attached to the sole of a shoe. The cleat is designed to engage positively with the pedal.

Crank Lever arm joining the pedal to the chainwheel and bottom bracket.

Crossover drive Most often used on tandem bicycles. The front and rear chainwheels are on the left (port) side of the bike, and are linked together with a chain. The rear chainwheel axle also has chainrings on the right side of the bike, with a chain leading back to the freewheel.

D

Damping The mechanical process used in the suspension systems on mountain bikes, of bringing a moving mechanism to rest, eg. a swing arm, whilst keeping rebound movement to a minimum.

Dishing The degree of asymmetry of the spoke arrangement on either side of a wheel. A front wheel is symmetrical, whereas a rear wheel is asymmetrical because of the offset (dish) necessary to accommodate a multiple hub.

Double-butted The description given to cycle frame tubing that has walls with a thinner gauge at the centre than at the ends for lightness plus greater strength at the joins.

Drafting The process where a following rider takes advantage of the slipstream created by the rider immediately ahead of him.

Drag Resistance. Aerodynamic drag refers to friction drag – the resistance of air flowing over a surface, and pressure drag – the resistance from low pressure zones behind a shape. Mechanical drag results from friction between moving parts.

Drop outs Fork tips at the front and rear against which axle bolts are tightened.

Durometer A device for measuring the hardness or softness of urethane dampers in suspension systems, mainly on mountain bikes.

E

Echelon A paceline in which the following riders select an angle off behind the lead rider to obtain maximum shelter and *drafting* effect while riding against a crosswind.

F

Fairing Streamlined windscreen and/or body shell to smooth the flow of air.

G

Gear ratio Amount of motion or work per amount of motion or work. On a bicycle, one rotation of a chainring with 48 teeth will cause a wheel with a sprocket of 12 teeth to rotate 4 times: a gear ratio of 4:1.

H

Honking Riding a bicycle standing out of the saddle, using body weight to drive down the *cranks*.

HPV Human-Powered Vehicle. Technically, a bicycle is an HPV. In practice, the term is used for any human-powered vehicle that is not a bicycle.

Hub axle The axle on which a hub rotates.

Hub brake A drum and shoe device, which brakes the wheel at the hub as opposed to the rim.

Hybrid Term given to a street bike design that fuses together key features of a mountain bike and a tourer: straight handlebars, bar mounted brake and gear levers, cantilever brakes and 700C wheels with narrow section multipurpose tires.

L

Lugs Sleeves that correctly position two tubes together for joining by soldering or gluing. Frequently decorative, lugs add strength by providing more surface area for the glue or solder to grip, and distributing the stress on the frame.

M

Monocoque Method of construction where the shell or external surface has a structural, load-bearing function and can serve as a chassis.

P

Peleton French term given to a large double or triple *echelon* of riders in a stage race, who have formed a temporary tactical pact to share the work of *drafting*.

R

Rake Distance between a centerline drawn through the fork tube and a parallel line drawn through the fork *dropouts*.

S

Sag wagon Motor vehicle which follows a group of cyclists, carrying baggage and assisting cyclists in mechanical or physical difficulty. Common on mass rides.

Seat cluster Joining of seat stays, seat tube, and (sometimes) the top tube.

Spinning Turning the *cranks* very rapidly and lightly, without strong muscular effort.

Stem Attaches handlebars to frame via the steering tube. The shape and size of the stem determine the fore-

and-aft and vertical position of the handlebars.

Stoker Cycling slang for the rider on the rear of a tandem.

T

Torque Measurement of twisting force or power.

Trail The distance between the point that a vertical line, drawn through the front wheel axle, meets the ground, and the point that a center line, drawn through the fork tube, meets the ground.

W

Wheelbase Distance between wheel axles on a bicycle. On conventional bicycles, wheelbase ranges from 38 to 44 inches.

Wire-on tire U-shaped tire where the lips of the casing are held against the rim sides by the pressure of a separate inner tube.

Z

Zener diode A voltage regulator.

MEASUREMENTS
Following cycling convention the dimensions for mountain bikes are given in inches, for sports bikes and touring bikes these are in centimeters. There are exceptions to these rules: for example cranks are always measured in millimeters, even on normally "imperial" mountain bikes. Also, for ease of comparison, certain frame dimensions, such as rake and trail, are given in inches.

AUTHORS' NOTE:
Where the word "he" appears in the text, it is used generically and intended to include "she" as well.

Index

Authors' acknowledgments
This book would not have been possible without the help of many of our friends in cycling, especially Mike Burrows, Monty and Grant Young of Condor, Debbie DeMeritte of F.W.Evans, Nick Fish of Trek, Nick Reardon and Kirsten Begg of Cannondale, and Mick Allen. In addition we are also grateful to those who lent help, advice, or equipment, including: Nick Crane, On Yer Bike, Hilary Stone, Evolution Imports, Simon Lilleystone, W.A.Bush, Ian Emmerson, Pete and JoAnne Pensayres, Mike Shermer, Bob Schmidt, Avis Cycles, Avocet International, Bell Helmets, John Potter, Bike Events, John Matthews, Campagnolo, Mark W. Hopkins of Du Pont, Wolfgang Haas, Fahrradtechnik, Bob Rubenstein and Han Goes of Fiets Magazine, Gary Fisher of Fisher Mountainbikes, Chris Payne, BMBF, Peter Ernst, Miles and John Kingsbury, King Cycles, Frank Kirk, Madison Cycles plc, Graham Bell of Neatwork, Jim McGurn of New Cyclist, Simon Doughty, David Hemmings, Rick Kiddle of Perfect Performance, Marti Daily, IHPVA, John Pritchard, Danny Rosen, Domenico Garbelli and Richard Strom of Rossin, Nico Lemmens of Shimano, Michael Cramer and Martin Higgins of Specialized, Nick Saunders, Sturmey Archer, Ralph Schnyder, Reg Turner, Wim Van Wijnen, Scott Yount, David Taylor of York Films, and Millie.

Dorling Kindersley would like to thank the following:
Special thanks to Dave Robinson, Senior Art Editor for first six months of the project, and to Melanie Miller for copy-editing. Also the Cooling-Brown Partnership for page make-up; Kevin Ryan, Alison Donovan, and Gurinder Purewall for additional design assistance; Alison Edmonds, Deborah Opoczynska, Lol Henderson, and Deborah Rhodes for their editorial assistance; Andrew Green, Steven Dew, Pete Serjeant, and Paul Dewhurst for artworks; Kate Grant for initial research; Diana Morris, Catherine O'Rourke, Suzanne Williams for picture research, and Peter Moloney for the index.

Picture credits:
KEY:
b bottom, *c* center, *l* left, *r* right, *t* top

Jim McGurn: p. 8 *tr, cr,* 9 *tr,* 113 *tr*
The Ricket Encyclopedia of Slides: p. 9 *br*
Le Monde à Bicyclette: pp. 10 *br,* 108 *l,* 109 *tr*
Hutchinson Library: p. 11 *t*
Trek UK: pp. 15 *br,* 16 *l,* 36 *tr,* 37, 46 *t, bl, br,* 47 *bl,* 58 *bl,* 59 *tr*
Nick Crane: pp. 38 *bl,* 39 *tl, tr,* 100 *bl, br*
Danny McMillin: pp. 44 *bl, br,* 45 *t, b*
Allsport: pp. 49 *tl,* 69 *b,* 76 *l,* 81 *tl,* 82 *b,* 83 *t,* 113 *tl, tr, b*
Stockfile: p. 49 *br*
York Films: pp. 52 *tr, bl,* 113 *b*
Actionsnaps: p. 53 *t, b*
Fountain Head Advertising: p. 59 *cr*
Graham Watson: p. 68 *b*
Action Pact: p. 71 *tr*
J. Pritchard: p. 75 *br*
J. Dickerson: pp. 78 *tr,* 79 *br*
P. Penseyre: p.79 *bl*
R. Simonsen: p. 79 *t*
Leicester City Council: p. 80 *l*
Tim Leighton-Boyce: pp. 83 *bl,* 113 *tr*
Precor USA: p. 87 *t*
Bike Events: pp. 96 *b*
Ben Osborne: pp. 97 *t, br,* 99 *tr*
Sally and Richard Greenhill: p. 112 *tr*
Imperial Tobacco Ltd.: p. 123 *tl*
Thomas Forsyth: pp. 124 *t, c, b,* 125 *t, b*
Bob Eshuis: p. 132, 133, 144 *r*
Matt Mullin: pp. 142 *bl,* 143 *tr, br,* 145 *l*
Discover Magazine: p. 144 *bl*
Lynn Tobias p. 145 *tr*
Hulton Picture Library: p. 159 *tr*
University of California: p. 192 *br*

Every effort has been made to trace the copyright holders. Dorling Kindersley apologizes for any unintentional omissions and would be pleased, in such cases, to add an acknowledgment in future editions.